Recovery from Alcoholism

A GUIDE FOR ALCOHOLICS AND THOSE WHO HELP THEM

DR. ERIC GAUDRY

Published by
COLLINS DOVE, 60-64 Railway Road,
Blackburn, Victoria, 3130, Australia

Reprinted 1986

Design and cover by Mary Goodburn
Typeset by Bookset Pty Ltd
Printed in Australia by Globe Press, Brunswick

Cataloguing-in-publication data

Gaudry, Eric.
Recovery from alcoholism.

Bibliography.
Includes index.
ISBN 0 85924 338 9.

1. Alcoholic – Rehabilitation. I. Title.

362.2'9286

Foreword

By Dr Peter Murray Pearce
Department of Community Medicine
St Vincent's Hospital, Melbourne

In the last 150 years there has been a dramatic advance in the diagnosis and treatment of illness. The most obvious advances relate to communicable diseases. However, by the mid-twentieth century preventive and community medicine and rehabilitation began to demand the attention of doctors and medical researchers. Thus alcoholism, long recognised as a major social problem but regarded as the province of prohibitionists and temperance groups, came under scientific observation. Our present understanding of alcoholism owes much to the work of Professor E. M. Jellinek, at Harvard, between 1940 and 1960. By the 1960s there was a flood of publications on the subject, mostly coming from America, but some also from England.

The Australian experience of alcohol has much in common with that of America, the two countries sharing what Geoffrey Gorer calls the frontier-pioneer mystique, where alcohol is an integral part of social intercourse. The tragic effects of alcoholism are now widely known in our community. Less well known are the causes of alcoholism and the facilities for treatment now available in Australia. In the last twenty years there has been a tremendous growth in the public and private services, and these are innovative, creative and comprehensive. For example, all alcoholics are entitled to free in-patient and out-patient treatment and medication.

In the spate of books on alcoholism there is a marked lack of discussion of the recovery process. The freshness and originality of Dr Eric Gaudry's contribution lies in his choosing the recovery process for step-by-step analysis. This is a work book for the recovering alcoholic, a source of hope and optimistic support for the patient and his family.

Dr Gaudry is a clinical psychologist who is working with recovering alcoholics. The quintessence of his approach is that he sees rehabilitation 'steadily and he sees it whole'. Once alcoholics have accepted treatment they begin to recover, and they remain at the recovery stage for the remainder of their lives. To maintain recovery, certain behaviour patterns must be understood so that effective social interaction is substituted for alcohol dependence.

Dr Gaudry rightly puts Alcoholics Anonymous as the central and essential aid to recovery. It is a sort of 'open university' of alcoholism. It provides understanding and support so that alcoholics know they are not isolated.

Dr Gaudry writes in such a way as to compel attention. His clarity means that this book may be used with benefit by the medical profession and paramedicals, by alcoholics and by their families, by employers and colleagues. Behind everything that is said in this book lies the belief in the ability of a person to change: 'to have become perfect is to have changed often' — a psychology of reality and hope. For all of the practitioners who put Christian teaching into practice when helping the recovery from alcoholism, there is the inspiration of St Iraneaus's words: 'God's glory is man, fully alive.'

Contents

For my wife, Wilma

1

Introduction

Alcoholics can and do recover from the devastating and debilitating condition called alcoholism. They can and do resume their roles as fully functioning members of society, in family, occupational and social areas. The problem for everyone is that the percentage of those who return to uncontrolled drinking is far too high. In part, this is caused by the lack of understanding of the recovery process by alcoholics themselves and by their families and friends and by their employers and workmates.

The programme outlined in this book has been designed to help alcoholics and all those who have an interest in their welfare during the recovery period. Many techniques that have been shown to help recovery have been analysed and included in an overall programme designed to break the vicious circle of alcoholic drinking and to maintain sobriety. The main source of help is Alcoholics Anonymous (AA), which is referred to constantly throughout this book and fully described in Chapter 12.

There is nothing a recovered alcoholic cannot do within the limits of his or her natural potential and opportunities. Most alcoholics do not know just what they can do or what limits they can reach because their whole adult life has been changed and restricted by the effects of excessive drinking. The main obstacle to complete recovery after treatment and discharge from hospital is that, with the exception of AA, there is little or no guidance or systematic programme for alcoholics; nor is there any clear guide for the wives and husbands of alcoholics, for those who love them or for those who have an interest in their welfare. Employers, personnel officers and social workers have a vested interest in the recovery process, yet few of them have any profound knowledge of alcoholism or its treatment and even less of the process of and associated problems in recovery.

The small percentage of alcoholics who have no further problems with drinking after their initial treatment for alcoholism makes it quite clear that recovery is no push-over. It might be thought that an alcoholic, having been helped in his or her withdrawal from alcohol and having regained physical health, would be able to look at the consequences of years of drinking and decide against ever getting into such a condition again. However, even though most alcoholics have spent fortunes on alcohol and alcohol-related activities, which has resulted in financial chaos, and in spite of the matrimonial, family, legal, social and occupational havoc commonly associated with being an alcoholic, reports of success rates vary from 0 to about the mid-60 per cent, with the average figure lying between 30 and 40 per cent. If the success rate is defined to include reasonable levels of functioning within the occupational, family and social areas and is not based simply upon consumption of alcohol, the results are even less impressive.

Many alcoholics return to uncontrolled drinking immediately after treatment, while others remain trouble-free for months and even years before relapsing. Accounts of alcoholics who have been abstinent for twenty or thirty years suddenly going off the deep end are not uncommon. The reasons given for these returns to excessive drinking cover the whole spectrum of human activities and often there is no apparent reason for this behaviour.

Alcoholics, doctors, psychiatrists, psychologists, geneticists, biologists, ministers of religion and welfare workers have sought the reasons for the high percentage of relapses without a great deal of success. Nor is it clear why some heavy drinkers become alcoholics and some do not. There is strong evidence that alcoholism runs in families, but no one knows to what extent alcoholism is passed on through genetic inheritance or to what extent it is learned within the family environment. There is an inherited component, but many alcoholics have no family history of alcoholism. Research by psychiatrists and psychologists has not isolated personality types that are more prone to alcoholism than others, but this may simply be a reflection of the low state of personality theory. Doctors traditionally have failed in their attempts to help alcoholics, but this may be because it is not predominantly a medical problem. Priests and ministers of religion have been unable to help either, because it is not just a spiritual issue that can be dealt with in traditional religious ways. Chemists and biologists have only recently been able to isolate the factors that distinguish alcoholics from non-alcoholics, but they have not as yet been able to produce a drug that will prevent alcoholic drinking. What they have provided is the drug Antabuse, which leads to a very unpleasant, violent reaction when alcohol is swallowed. It is not, however, a 'cure' for alcoholism. Sociologists and social workers have been equally unsuccessful.

Let it be made clear at the outset that there is no known 'cure' for alcoholism in the way that there is a 'cure' for pneumonia and even for some forms of cancer. Let it be made equally clear here and now that many alcoholics sooner or later become free of their alcoholic problems and go on to lead happy and productive lives. On the other hand, a great deal has been found out about alcoholism and its treatment and management by the various groups mentioned above. Chemists have produced drugs that enable medical and nursing staff to help alcoholics through the withdrawal stage without the enormous suffering that used to accompany this phase. Psychologists and psychiatrists have analysed the stages involved in recovery from alcoholism and applied the principles of learning and motivational theory to this process. The social pressures on alcoholics are now better understood in so far as they relate to giving advice on how to withstand these pressures or how to take action to avert or change the pressures. These pressures of society are, in part, different for males and females, and these differences are being shown up by a dramatic increase in research into alcoholism in females, an area almost totally neglected until the last decade. AA has been the one organisation able to demonstrate that alcoholics can be helped, and it has the proven track-record in the field. Although Alcoholics Anonymous is not affiliated with any religious organisation, it does have a spiritual basis, which suggests the deep-down nature of the alcoholics' problems.

If there is one area of agreement about alcoholics, it is the primary reason for the drinking. Alcoholics do not drink primarily because they like the taste of liquor, nor to make the taste of food more enjoyable, nor to make them feel slightly less tense. The primary reason for alcoholic drinking is to induce a state of oblivion. Alcoholics drink to escape from the reality that has become so terrible, so awful, that it cannot be tolerated. The list of circumstances that leads to this is infinitely long: some cannot cope with their jobs; others feel failures as husbands or wives; others, from childhood, were unable to cope with their families or cannot make friends; feelings of inadequacy, loneliness, friendlessness, futility are common; bereavements, loss of friends, financial problems, gynaecological and obstetric problems are frequently blamed. In short, the search for oblivion is associated with an inability to cope with one or more significant areas of life.

Alcoholics often resent the fact that some of their acquaintances who also fail to cope with significant areas of their lives, and also drink excessively and frequently over many years, do not become alcoholics, even though they may cause themselves physical harm and create vast damage to others, particularly families, while in their drunken states. The essential difference between the alcoholic and the excessive drinker lies in two directions. Firstly, *alcoholics have no control over their drinking*, in that they cannot always guarantee, if they decide just to have a few drinks, that they will stop at that point. Sometimes they are completely out of control and, once started, continue drinking as long as possible. Sometimes they can stop, but there always comes a time when the stopping point is passed and the full-scale drinking commences. Secondly, there is *dependence* on alcohol to help the alcoholic cope with life. This dependency on alcohol has *psychological* and *physiological* components.

Early in an alcoholic's drinking history he or she may drink to alleviate anxiety before going to a party or before an important business deal. She or he may drink to relieve the frustration or anger felt when a workmate is promoted; he or she may drink out of resentment of being in or out of a job; he or she may drink to relieve the tension surrounding financial insecurity. These are examples of psychological dependency. Later the drinking is triggered because the alcoholic wakes up with a hangover, the shakes and other symptoms of withdrawal, which indicate physical dependency.

Alcoholics suffer from many other symptoms, but their resentment focuses on why other people who may drink just as heavily do not display this lack of control and this psychological and physical dependency. It seems that some people are prone to alcoholism and others are not, in a similar way to the fact that some people are more prone to the common cold than others. Resentment about either is a waste of time.

The statement that there is no cure for alcoholism brings us back to the topic of recovery. In the subsequent chapters, evidence will be presented to show that alcoholism can be *arrested* by abstinence from alcohol, and that a full and fruitful life can be led by alcoholics, provided there is no return to drinking. Further evidence will be adduced to show that the chances of any alcoholic returning to 'social drinking' for a lifetime are minimal, if not non-existent. Now we can confidently predict that if cancer victims are told that they can arrest the progress of their cancer by giving up alcohol, they would probably do so. Perhaps the alcoholic cancer victim would be less likely to do so. If so, it would probably be because of the psychological dependence on alcohol.

Psychological dependence, then, may be the real problem. Alcoholics tend to deny the fact of their alcoholism in the face of the most compelling evidence and far beyond the point where their spouses, their friends, and their employers know about it. They hide their supplies, they lie about their drinking, they continue to have blackouts and memory losses until a crisis or collapse forces them to seek help. Even after treatment many continue to deny that they have a permanent problem and try to resume controlled drinking, usually with disastrous results. The problem seems to be that these people find life so difficult that the thought of going through the rest of life without the shield of alcohol to ward off the hurts cannot be tolerated.

The shield, of course, is an illusion. It does not work. The main thrust of this book is focused upon the fact that alcohol does not do what it is supposed to do, at least for alcoholics and for heavy drinkers. People drink alcohol because they are not coping with their lives. This failure to cope will be analysed, and it will be shown that drinking alcohol as a method of coping with failure has only a temporary effect and that the drinking rarely solves problems. Instead, it creates other problems and leads to an increase in unpleasant emotions, such as anxiety and depression, which ultimately leads to less efficient coping, more failures and more drinking. A method of breaking this vicious circle and specific advice on every stage is what this book is about: recovery from alcoholism.

One of the indirect causes of the high level of relapse among alcoholics is the very low level of understanding of the nature of alcoholism in the general community. Even where an alcoholic comes to understand the actions he or she needs to take to survive and to grow after treatment, this survival is influenced by the events that occur in the family, with friends, in the work-place and in society generally. It is therefore essential that family members, those emotionally close to the alcoholic, personnel managers and employers generally should have an understanding of the nature of alcoholism and of their role in helping alcoholics to rehabilitate themselves.

After treatment, many alcoholics have a very fragile belief in their capacity to survive without alcohol, others are over-confident and needlessly place themselves in situations of great danger to their continued sobriety. Knowledge by those involved of the dangers of too little or too much confidence will minimise these risks. Most alcoholics returning to the work-force are extremely apprehensive about the way their employers and workmates will react to their return, and this also affects their self-confidence. Their re-entry to the family circle is also loaded with apprehension and insecurity. Therefore, a full awareness of the difficulties experienced by the recovering alcoholic within the family and work-force is crucial to the recovery process. In Chapter 13 specific advice is given on how the family and employers can assist alcoholics, especially in the early weeks of their recovery.

Advice to families and others flows directly from the total theory of recovery, but parts of it are not self-evident truths, so it is recommended that the whole of this book be read carefully. For example, it will be explained why it is essential that the alcoholic does not continue to experience guilt feelings about the devastation he or she may have caused during the drinking phase. The reasons for this are complex; but basically it is claimed that guilt feelings about the past will wreck the present and possibly trigger a return to drinking. Alcoholics are advised that it is in their interests to make amends for past misdeeds where possible, and then to forget the past and concentrate on getting the present and future right. Self-feelings of guilt or attempts by others to throw the past in their faces because 'they should feel guilty' have exactly the opposite effect to that desired; guilt-feelings wreck the present and the future, and that is surely not in the interest of an employer, a wife or husband, a lover or anyone else with an interest in the welfare of the alcoholic.

Many of the problems with which alcoholics could not cope previously will still exist when they return to society. For example, even if an alcoholic's marriage has survived his earlier drinking, there are likely to be significant marital problems to be solved. As well as the usual trepidation about the return to work, the alcoholic may still be in the wrong job within the organisation or have a real problem with a direct superior, which needs to be resolved. A housewife may need to give up her domestic role and get a job in spite of continued opposition from her husband. A person with such problems can sometimes be helped by a personnel officer or a marriage guidance counsellor with a knowledge of alcoholism. Unfortunately the level of post-treatment care for alcoholics is minimal. The most readily available source is AA and its allied organisations, which do such a fine job. However, there is a definite place for those with specific skills in marriage, family, educational and vocational counselling.

The case for the use of skilled counsellors is very evident in the sexual area. Interruption to the normal sexual functioning of alcoholics is very common. Impotence among men and frigidity in females are significant difficulties, and often these conditions begin in the alcoholic stage, but they are caused by anxiety and not alcohol. Psychologists and sexual therapists specialising in the treatment of these difficulties do exist and should be consulted.

Alcoholism crosses all social boundaries and occupations. Doctors, judges, pharmacists, truck drivers, nurses, teachers, ministers of religion, university lecturers and public servants are all to be found in their ranks. Considering the enormous cost involved in training professionals and skilled workers, it is clear that anything an employer can do to assist the recovery process will benefit everyone. The crisis that leads to an alcoholic seeking help is frequently the threat of losing employment. Thus employers should understand and help in the recovery process as far as possible. The onus of recovery is, of course, on the alcoholic, because he or she is in charge of his or her future, but others can make recovery easier or more difficult.

It will become clear later on in this book that the advice given to recovering alcoholics and those who help them is to get back to living a completely normal life, with just one exception: complete abstinence from alcohol. The time it takes to reach this state will vary from individual to individual, but an alcoholic should not lead an artificial life in which everybody is on tip-toe, treading on egg shells, waiting for the 'inevitable break'. An atmosphere of suspicion and false accusations is precisely what an alcoholic does not need. Suspicion is understandable, given the probability of relapse, but those responsible for it need to understand that such suspicion may well cause the effects they least want.

Some programmes claim that a return to social drinking is possible for some alcoholics. The evidence for this claim will be examined later, but let it be said now that long-term evidence of contained social drinking is not forthcoming, and there is ample evidence from other programmes and from AA that abstinence is the only realistic goal. The programme put forward here depends very heavily on alcoholics thinking thoroughly and rationally about the everyday problems with which they are faced. Alcohol is a depressant, which interferes with the action of the brain, hindering the thinking process at relatively low levels of blood alcohol content. As rational thinking is an essential element in coping with life, anything that lowers this capacity is anathema. For this reason and for a host of others, recovery from alcoholism requires life-long abstinence.

Abstinence *must* be life-long because it is clear that *alcoholics have a proneness to uncontrolled drinking, which never disappears*, and which can be reactivated by a return to drinking even after twenty or thirty years of abstinence. Understanding this proneness to alcoholism is the outcome of the research into the brain chemistry of alcoholics as described in Chapter 2. In other addictions, such as smoking, the same phenomenon is frequently found. Give an addicted smoker a few cigarettes after years of non-smoking and his smoking habit is likely to be fully activated.

Many authorities on alcoholism refer to alcoholism as a disease that can't be cured but simply arrested and which may flare up at any time, given certain conditions. The writer prefers to think of the disease as *proneness to alcoholism*. The choice of words is based upon the conviction that recovery from alcoholism is dependent on changing the way we interpret our environment or, to put it another way, on changing our thinking and acting habits in quite specific ways in order to cope with specific problems. In other words, recovery is seen as primarily a psychological process once the biochemical action that is responsible for the physical compulsion to drink becomes dormant.

Given the emphasis on rational, clear thinking as a crucial component in recovery, it will come as no surprise to find evidence on recovery of cognitive skills. The conclusion is that most alcoholics recover their capacity to think to levels that are probably at or near their potential, provided that abstinence is maintained. Alcholics who return to heavy drinking risk the massive damage typical of those who refuse to or are unable to give up drinking and who repeatedly go in and out of treatment facilities. For those who give up drinking after their first hospitalisation or soon thereafter, the chances of an excellent recovery of cognitive skills are high.

This cognitive ability is seen as important in the development of control over negative emotions, such as anxiety, depression, anger, resentment, frustration, guilt and self-pity. This emotional control is seen in turn as being influenced by problem-solving skills, the level of self-esteem, confidence, assertiveness skills, and the level of need for approval by other people. All of these factors, their interrelationships and their relevance to recovery will be discussed in detail in the course of this book.

Most important of all for a recovering alcoholic is the development or restoration of feelings of *self-esteem*. This term covers the overall feeling we have about ourselves and our capacity to deal with the day-to-day occurrences of life. The way we do feel about ourselves is reflected in our behaviour. Those who feel that they are inadequate, are failures and are hopeless tend to have few successful ways of coping; and they behave in ways that inevitably lead to failure. People with high self-esteem tend to get things right; and even when they fail have ways of successfully coping with failure.

Evidence will be presented to show that alcoholics generally have very low levels of self-esteem. Further evidence will be presented to show how self-esteem rises and falls, and how the factors that govern this process rise and fall. The task for alcoholics is seen then as raising their personal sense of self-esteem by working on these various factors or aspects of their behaviour, so that actions that build self-esteem are maximised and those habits and ways of thinking that lead to a drop in self-esteem are minimised.

The programme for recovery presented here accepts the evidence that social, emotional, medical, biological and psychological factors all play a part in recovery. The evidence from current research is integrated into a single system that is easy to understand and to apply. We shall begin with an analysis of the disease of alcoholism so as to give some idea of the nature of the illness with which we are dealing.

2
The Disease of Alcoholism

Introduction

In Chapter 1 it was stated that building up a strong sense of self-esteem can be regarded as the central factor in recovery from alcoholism. That alcoholics are low in self-esteem is not surprising, considering the nature of the disease. This chapter, describing what alcoholism is, is placed early in the book because of the conviction of the author that *complete acceptance* of having *this disease* is essential for recovery. If people can accept that much of the alcoholic's bizarre behaviour and many of his or her personal, social, physical, emotional, legal and occupational problems can be directly attributed to having a disease, then it becomes much easier for her or him to cope with those past events and to ensure that such behaviour is not repeated.

In this chapter the memory changes and the distortions of reality that occur as the disease develops are spelled out in detail and integrated into a description developed by Johnson (1980). This outline clearly shows how alcoholics cross the line between social drinking and alcoholic drinking without being aware of it. The regular development of the symptoms of alcoholism are related to Johnson's 'mood stages'.

The final part of the chapter is based on very important recent evidence that shows that alcoholics have a different brain chemistry to non-drinkers, social drinkers and heavy drinkers. This evidence shows that compulsive, addictive drinking, which is a major symptom of alcoholism, is linked to a chemical that alcoholics manufacture in their brains. Once made and stored in the brain, this chemical makes it virtually impossible for an alcoholic to stop drinking without the medical treatment known as detoxification. While compulsive drinking lasts, for periods lasting from a few years to thirty or forty years, life is unmanageable, failure is the norm, and self-esteem drops to very low levels.

The two main implications of this research are that, once addicted, the alcoholic cannot stop drinking but, once treated, he or she can stop and that the responsibility for this is totally within each alcoholic's capacity.

The Onset and Development of Alcoholism

Alcoholism is a fatal disease for anyone who allows it to go unchecked. This disease affects the whole person, physically, emotionally, mentally, socially, psychologically and spiritually. It is a primary disease, which leads to other diseases, such as heart failure, cirrhosis of the liver, brain damage and many others: but it can be stopped. It can be arrested, so that desperately ill people can return to productive, happy lives, provided habits they have learned while drinking alcoholically are changed. These unadaptive and destructive habits are the ones that cause those in contact with practising alcoholics to shake their heads in amazement at the alibis that these drinkers dream up to cover their absenteeism, at the patently obvious 'reasons' they invent for their drinking, at the offensive behaviour they seem to have forgotten by the following day, at their memory lapses during blackouts, and at their apparent inability to see that their lives are disintegrating around them.

In part, the development of alcoholism is aided by the reaction to diseases that carry a social stigma compared with the reaction to conventional diseases. When someone gets pneunomia, develops an ulcer or begins to stagger from diabetes, it is expected that he or she will seek diagnosis and accept treatment. Family members and workmates will sympathetically encourage them to accept this treatment. However, when the symptoms of alcoholism begin to appear and start to affect the whole life of the alcoholic, he or she is told to 'pull yourself together', to 'exert some will-power' and to 'cut down on your drinking'. By the very nature of the disease, the alcoholic *cannot* recognise that heavy drinking is the major cause of his or her problems, and she or he *cannot* stop, even though he or she attempts to cut down on intake or to give up.

It is falsely believed that alcoholism is self-induced, self-inflicted and evidence of a lack of character. A lack of realisation that alcoholism is just another disease delays or prevents treatment being sought. Alcoholism is a disease that is treatable and capable of being arrested. Since alcoholism causes problems at work and within the family, it might be expected that pressure would be brought to bear on the alcoholic to accept treatment. In fact, the opposite occurs. As holding down a job is socially and economically desirable, the family covers up for absenteeism, it maintains silence about abusive drinking and matrimonial discord; and within the family the extent of the drinking is blamed on work stresses and ill health. At work, fellow employees cover up for the reduced productivity. Underlying this reluctance in both the family and work place to force the alcoholic to seek treatment is the stigma attached to alcoholism, because it is not recognised as a disease.

Quite often, unlike other diseases, alcoholism is left untreated. Sustained pressure from within the home or from within the work place comes only when the disease is well advanced and clearly apparent to all. The alcoholic, by this time, has undergone profound mental changes, which prevent self-recognition or admission of being an alcoholic. The major changes that occur can be seen in statements by alcoholics, which seem like alibis, but in fact represent changes in the thinking processes as the amount of intake increases.

There are three main ways in which an alcoholic attempts to conceal his alcoholism from himself, and these mechanisms must be recognised by the alcoholic during treatment. The first is *rationalisation, which is concerned with finding, using and believing reasons for excessive drinking*. This process is part of the disease and is a symptom shown by all alcoholics. For alcoholics whose drinking has got out of control, or is beginning to do so, it is essential to protect the ego, the sense of identity, the self-esteem from the knowledge that the evident chaos can be attributed to the alcoholic intake. Blame is placed upon a wife, on a husband, on financial loss, on problems at work and on the stupidity of other people for the problems that begin to crowd in upon him or her. This rationalisation process is unconscious, an automatic defence mechanism of which the alcoholic is unaware. It cuts in when the drinking has got out of control and there is a need to erect a wall between the self and the reality that is too threatening to be recognised.

The second defence mechanism is *projection, which occurs when the alcoholic has lost control of drinking and has begun to lose control of his or her life*. Stupid, irrational and destructive behaviour leads to a situation where the alcoholic is full of self-hate because of inability to control the way things are happening. Acceptance of this self-hate is too threatening to the ego, so a translation occurs: 'I hate myself for what I am' becomes 'I hate you for making me like this'. *This self-hate is frequently transferred to a wife or husband, a mother or father,* who of course is bewildered by these accusations, but frequently begins to search her or his own behaviour for the cause of the drinking.

The third mechanism that the self uses to protect itself from harm is *repression. Repression is the unconscious rejection of events that have occurred, but which are too horrible, too bizarre to be allowed to enter the conscious memory*. Thus a man who has publicly abused his wife at a party and described in lurid detail her failings as a wife and mother to horrified guests wakes up the following morning, and finding himself at home in his bed feels a sense of relief, which would immediately be drowned if he allowed himself to remember what has happened. Memories can be so horrible that the mind completely rejects them from consciousness; and they are repressed. To all intents and purposes the events never happened, so the man can face his wife and be amazed at the reception he receives, while she is so bewildered that she might begin to doubt her own sanity.

Rationalisation, projection and repression are unconscious psychological processes used by everyone from time to time to protect her or his inner being from harm. With alcoholics, these processes become habitual, pathological parts of the disease of alcoholism, which prevents the alcoholic from realising the extent of his or her problem. This leads to denial of any problem, and prevents him or her seeking treatment. During treatment and recovery, the alcoholic has to realise the extent to which these mechanisms have been brought into use and how habitual they have become. Almost certainly the high relapse rate for alcoholics is, in part, caused by the failure of alcoholics to see how these processes are part of the disease. Resistance to accepting the part played by these defence mechanisms leads to retention of these unadaptive methods of behaviour.

Memory Changes caused by Alcoholic Abuse

The three defence mechanisms described above are psychological in origin. They cause distortions to memory in very fundamental ways, which are usually beyond the comprehension of those close to the alcoholic. There are, however, two other memory changes caused by the poison known as alcohol. These are blackouts and euphoric recall.

Blackouts

Blackouts are not to be confused with the oblivion that occurs when so much has been drunk that the alcohol penetrates deeply into the brain and the drinker becomes unconscious. This type of extremely heavy, often fast drinking is very dangerous. Oblivion or passing out is, in fact, a safety device to prevent any further intake, which would penetrate to that part of the brain controlling the automatic processes of breathing and the pumping action of the heart. If this penetration occurs, and occasionally it does, death from an alcohol overdose is the outcome.

Blackouts are a normal part of the disease of alcoholism. They are the failure to remember events that occurred while the drinking alcoholic was talking, driving or otherwise seemingly engaged in the normal activities of life. They are caused by the chemical action of alcohol on the memory processes, so that remarks such as the following are common.

'I can remember leaving the party, but the thirty kilometres between there and home are a complete blank.'

'I wonder if I made a fool of myself at the office party. I can't remember anything after the early evening, but apparently I stayed a long time.'

'I have a vague idea I made arrangements to play golf with someone, but for the life of me I can't remember who it was.'

'My husband is looking daggers at me. I hope I didn't make a pass at anyone last night.'

'Well, I remember getting a taxi home last night, but where the heck did I leave my car?'

Blackouts not only cause confusion for the alcoholic, but throw others into situations where they cannot understand the behaviour of the alcoholic, because they assume she or he remembers all the details of the conversation or event that occurred. Anger at broken appointments can cause employment problems; and matrimonial strife follows these blackouts. The onset of blackouts tends to increase, but they can't be predicted with any certainty.

Euphoric recall

A feature of alcoholic memory is that whenever the alcoholic gets drunk he or she cannot remember all the details of the night before or of the party or of the hours in the bar. What does happen is that the memory acts selectively, usually by remembering the good parts and rejecting the bad. Thus a woman might say, 'I had a terrific time last night. My stories about those hilarious episodes on our holidays went over well. The music was great and I enjoyed the dancing. A beaut evening.' What she forgot was the boredom caused by her interminable stories, told in a slurred voice. She also forgot the embarrassment caused when she broke a valuable vase during a tipsy, staggering dance and the fact that her husband had to almost carry her out to the car when they were leaving. These events are not really forgotten. In a state of chemical change in her mind she didn't even know or notice her behaviour, but did retain the impression of a terrific night out.

The effect of the unconscious defence mechanisms and changes in memory processes is to place the alcoholic completely out of touch with reality, and this is the crux of the alcoholic disease. Not only can it not be cured at all, but it can't even be arrested until the alcoholic comes to understand the necessity for changing his or her way of thinking, so that contact with the real world is regained. It is no wonder that alcoholics cannot even see that there is a problem to be fixed and it is not surprising that they behave in a strange and bizarre fashion. It is understandable that the disease is difficult to treat successfully, because this disease takes the sufferer out of contact with reality.

In order to see how recovery is dependent on getting the alcoholic to make radical changes in her or his perception of the world and fundamental changes in behaviour, a simplified account of the change in moods and feelings that accompany the development of the disease follows. This abridged account is taken from an excellent book by Vernon Johnson called *I'll Quit Tomorrow*.

The Disease of Alcoholism: onset and progression

Johnson sees the onset of alcoholism becoming evident in mood swings. Moods, in this analysis, can be arbitrarily divided into three on a continuous feeling chart as in Figure 1.

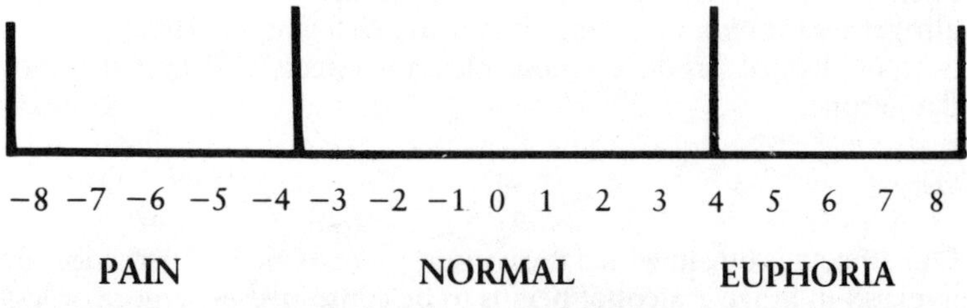

Figure 1. The Three Mood Stages

Most people have frequent mood swings in the normal band with occasional trips into the euphoric zone or down into the pain zone. The middle of the pain section of the scale might be represented by:

'This is terrible. I'm a no-hoper. I can't stand this.' The centre of the euphoric section might be: 'I feel terrific.' The progress of drinking for alcoholics is described in the following stages. This is a generalised account of a process that has as many variations as there are alcoholics, but the process is broadly the same for most alcoholics.

Stage 1

In Stage 1 the drinker is introduced to alcohol for the first time. He or she may or may not like the taste, but the good feelings that alcohol induces will be experienced. Feelings of being relaxed, warm, more open and elated are common, depending on the amount drunk. In short, it is a good, pleasant, rewarding experience, which she or he is likely to repeat. When the effects of alcohol wear off, the mood swing is back to the starting point, as seen in Figure 2.

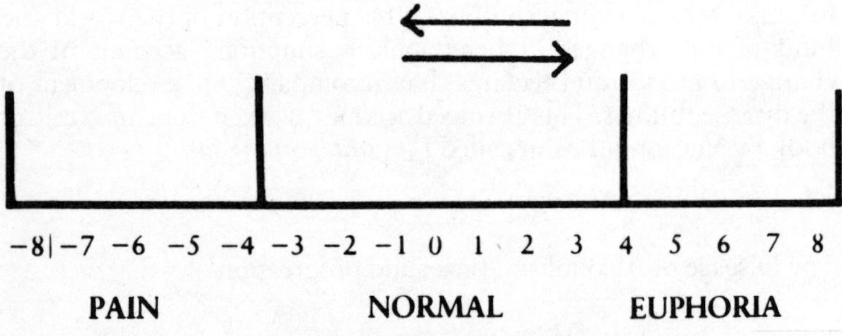

Figure 2. Stage 1: Early Drinking

Notice that the swing is towards the top end of the normal band and back to the starting point. No damage appears to be done, and altogether the experience is pleasant and welcoming. What is learned is that alcohol produces these pleasant effects and that it is not dangerous.

Stage 2

Our society is one in which the consumption of alcohol pervades our lives, so in Stage 2 alcohol begins to be consumed on a more or less regular basis, but on special occasions or when he or she feels a bit down the intake is increased to get that extra bit of a kick. While there may be an occasional excessive intake, the drinking tends to stay within reasonable levels and the rebound is back to zero with little or no damage done. Figure 3 illustrates this stage.

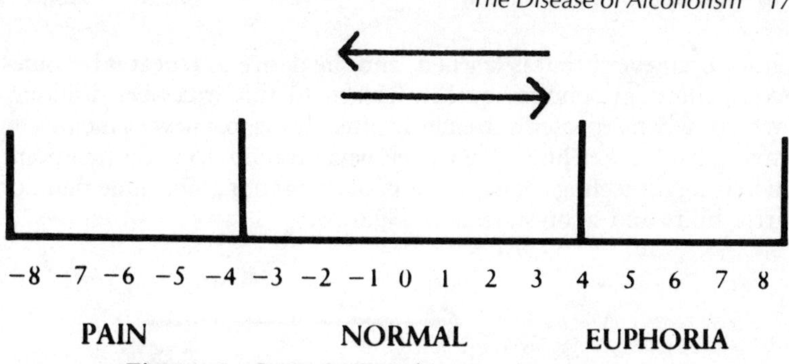

Figure 3. Stage 2: Drinking Begins to Increase

The time spent in this stage varies enormously. Many alcoholics pass through it at an enormous rate, all the time learning that alcohol is a reliable way of improving the way the world is perceived. Alcohol can be trusted.

Stage 3

In Stage 3 the knowledge that alcohol can be trusted to make one feel better without causing any apparent damage is put to the test. Occasional benders well beyond the normal limits begin to occur. These are often attached to important celebrations. Thus an undamaged alcoholic may drink very heavily at his or her twenty-first birthday party, to celebrate a promotion or the victory of a sporting team. This may result in a bad hangover, but the predominant recollection is of the terrific time the night before and the hangover is quickly forgotten. A small price to pay for such a night. The swing is still back to zero, as seen in Figure 4.

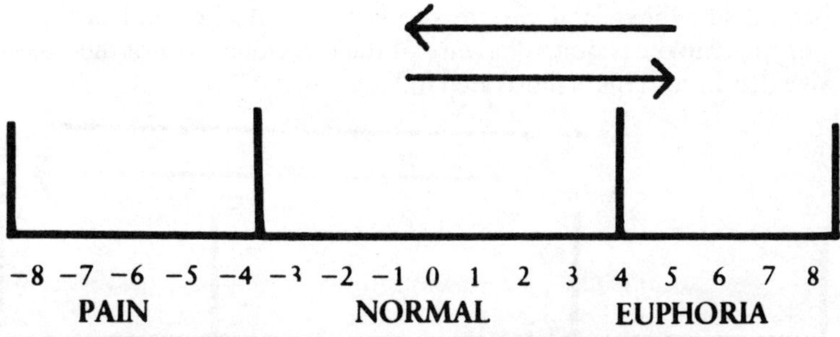

Figure 4. Stage 3: The Euphoric Stage is Reached

Stage 4

The euphoric feeling at the top of the swing in Stage 3 is the big emotional event that is learned, and the desire to repeat it becomes compelling. Alcoholics quickly return to this excessive drinking, which, when repeated sufficiently often, leads to a new element. The swing back takes him or her back beyond the zero point to a point where slight feelings of depression, of things not going quite right, of irritability and so on start, as in Figure 5.

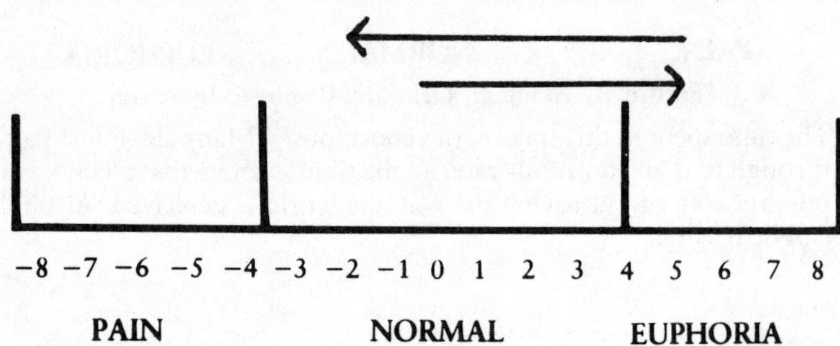

Figure 5. Stage 4: The Swing Back Beyond the Starting Point Begins

Stage 5

Our drinker, trusting to his or her experience of the beneficial effects of alcohol, now crosses, quite unknowingly, the thin line into alcoholism. In order to feel better the intake has to be increased to reach the same euphoric level as before. This, of course, causes the swing back to reach the pain zone, and chemical dependency on alcohol has begun. The inexorable progress to full-scale alcoholism has begun, but the drinker is quite unaware of the emotional cost of the excessive drinking. This is illustrated in Figure 6.

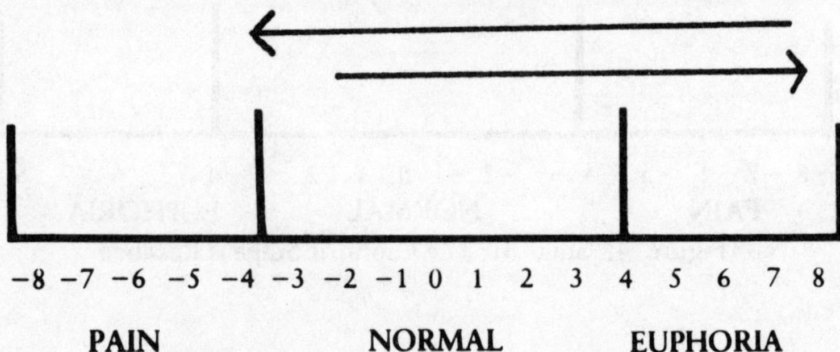

Figure 6. Stage 5: The Swing Back Increases

Stage 6

After Stage 5 the alcoholic problem begins to be recognised by others. The pattern of drinking changes. In order to recapture the euphoric feelings experienced in Stage 5, a great deal more has to be consumed, and drunkenness becomes the norm. The alcoholic is dimly aware that a problem exists, but the process of rationalisation takes over and ruthlessly suppresses awareness of just how emotionally hurt she or he is becoming. This relentless suppression of knowledge of the emotional crisis that is building up is done by the intellect blindly defending against hurt by rationalisation, by finding reasons for what cannot be denied. This fact that has to be explained away is the fact of excessive drinking. So remarks and internal dialogues like the following begin to appear.

'It's quite clear that I'm under a lot of pressure at work. Once this cash flow problem is beaten I'll be O.K.'

'The problem is my wife. If she would get off my back about these repairs to the house, I'd be able to cope.'

'The only reason I got drunk last night was because that waiter they hired kept filling my glass before it became empty.'

The problem with rationalisations such as these is that they work. The alcoholic *believes* these distortions and, having found a reason for his or her drinking, feels better. This leads to more drinking, to more and more bizarre behaviour, and eventually to Stage 6, where the pain area is entered for the first time, as in Figure 7.

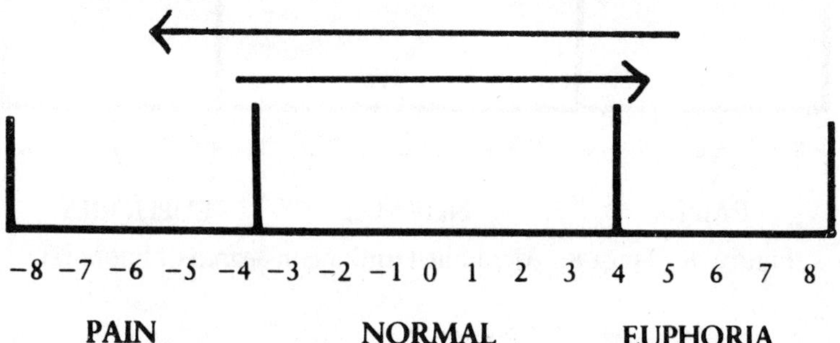

Figure 7. Stage 6: The Pain Zone is Entered

Stage 7

The alcoholic now feels distress, which is a compound of the psychological pain and the physical pain being experienced. At this stage, if not before, the alcoholic is likely to visit a doctor, but, being unaware of being an alcoholic, will present with symptoms of pains in the chest, impaired digestion and a general feeling of being off-colour. If questioned about drinking, the standard reply is: 'Yes. I drink a fair bit, but it's nothing to worry about. It's my digestion that seems to be the problem. I'm under a great deal of stress and I probably need some tranquillisers for a while to get me through this rough spot.'

Stage 8

During this stage the preoccupation with alcohol and with its supply becomes obvious. Liquor is hidden in garages, cupboards, in the garden, in storage areas, in the boot of the car. Morning and mid-day drinking commences. Occupations are changed, and moves to other suburbs, cities and countries are undertaken, but nothing works. Attempts to cut down, to fix the problem by drinking beer rather than spirits, and periods of abstinence are tried. Without alcohol, the alcoholic is lost. Awareness of some aspects of the drinking and a pervasive feeling of being a failure and a no-hoper lurk in the semi-conscious. These feelings also include thoughts of suicide as the bizarre behaviour, the lying and the deceit build up. To avoid these thoughts, more and more alcohol has to be consumed. Eventually the swing back takes the alcoholic deep into the pain zone, as in Figure 8.

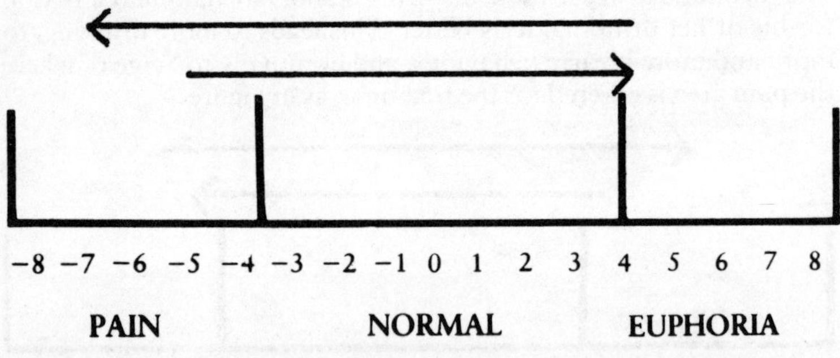

Figure 8. Stage 8: Alcoholic Drinking in Search of Euphoria

Stage 9

By this time blackouts have become common and the associated memory changes described earlier take over. Life becomes a shambles and unmanageable. Frequently the job is either lost or he or she is threatened with dismissal 'unless you get your act together'. Family life disintegrates into chaos, with the probability of verbal and physical violence increasing dramatically. Divorce either occurs or may be threatened. Sufficient of this penetrates dimly into the conscious mind of the alcoholic to cause an attack of self-hate.

The ego, the self-esteem are now so low that this hatred of the self and the depressive states can be solved only by self-destruction or by turning the hatred outwards, by projecting the hate onto someone else. Thus statements like 'I hate myself' are turned into 'You hate me and that's why you are picking on me all the time'. These insane projections combine with the repression of the most vile of the behaviour to take the alcoholic completely out of touch with reality. An impenetrable wall is built around the real state of the emotions, which cannot be borne, and this wall is the one that prevents the alcoholic seeing that he or she is destroying himself or herself.

Unless a crisis of some sort occurs to jolt the alcoholic into seeking help or unless hospitalisation occurs during a massive drinking bout, the final stage will be reached where contract with reality is lost, as in Figure 9. During this stage it is impossible to get back even to a normal state, no matter how much is consumed. When he is not drinking heavily, the alcoholic is distressed. When drinking, things are not much better, so the only way out is to drink to oblivion. Being unconscious is the only way to survive. Death follows shortly.

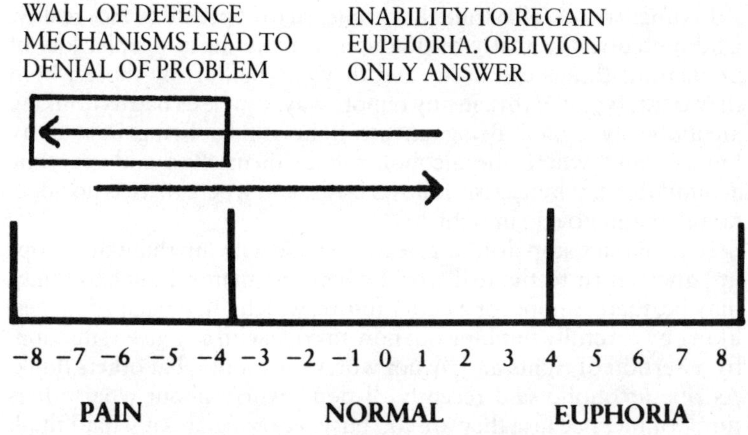

Figure 9. Stage 9: Alcoholic Drinking in Search of Oblivion. Complete Lack of Touch with Reality

Implications for Recovery

1. For the alcoholic

The more an alcoholic knows about alcoholism, the greater are the chances that he or she will show the insight into his or her own past behaviour so that it can be changed. While the processes of rationalisation, projection and repression are unconscious ones, reports of behaviour during the alcoholic phase by relatives will show that they did occur. These events, with the subsequent distortions in the perception of the world by alcoholics, have to be realised and accepted for change has to occur.

From the beginning of this book it has been made clear that alcoholics cannot blame anyone else for their behaviour. Recovering alcoholics have to stop rationalising, have to stop blaming others for their drinking or for their failure to cope. If they fail, if they make a mistake or if they can't solve a problem they have to admit to themselves honestly and directly that they have failed, they made the mistake and they couldn't solve the problem. They must accept that it wasn't the fault of anyone else, such as the boss, the system, the spouse or the nefarious practices of others. Rationalisation leads to greater chaos because it gives the user of the process a false picture of reality. This further chaos leads to projection of self-hate onto others and to a further distortion where repression and memory changes occur.

In other words, alcoholics have to learn to cope and to face reality. Undoubtedly, the real world contains many nasty people, lots of unpleasant things can occur and they can be hurt by those whom they trust. None of this, in any remote way, can be as bad as drinking alcoholically again. Being an alcoholic is like living in a nasty fantasy-land where the alcoholics hate themselves and everyone around them, where crisis follows crisis, and where there is no hope, no relief and no end in sight.

If alcoholics stop drinking, learn to cope with anything that crops up, and return to the real world where, no matter how bad things may be, there is hope for a better future, which can be shaped to their liking by carefully thinking out how to cope with any given situation, by assertion of rights and by not worrying about what others think. As one alcoholic said recently, 'I don't worry about what others think of me, because they are too busy worrying about what I think of them.'

The habits of rationalisation, projection and repression will have become strong over years of drinking and, because they are unconscious processes, can be recognised only by behaviour that flows from them. Thus an alcoholic rationalised the difficulty he was finding in getting a job in the following way: 'The reason I'm having a problem is that the word has got around that I'm an alcoholic. I'll never get a job.' In fact, the reason he was getting knocked back was a combination of a difficult economic climate and a very aggressive, abrasive approach, which alienated employers at first sight. When he changed his tactics, adopted a calm, assertive approach, found out all he could about the job from the personnel department prior to the interview, and carefully thought out what to say, he soon succeeded. The news of his alcoholism had not spread at all.

Learning to cope successfully should automatically do away with the need for projection and repression. By succeeding fairly often, as people do when they learn coping skills, self-esteem rises, so there is no need to protect the Self against the knowledge of continued failure. Self-hate will not build up, so it can't be projected onto others. In other words, for those who learn to cope these defence mechanisms do not operate as there is no need for them to operate. A return to drinking will mean a return to not coping.

2. *For the family and employers*

Advice to family and others associated with recovering alcoholics is given in Chapter 13. The main message is quite clear. It is that alcoholics are literally insane while they are drinking excessively. They are out of touch with reality. Acceptance of this will make it easier to accept the advice 'to forgive and forget'. There is no point in blaming alcoholics for the havoc and destruction caused while drinking, because they were living in another world, which is only dimly like the real world. At that time they were suffering and unable to comprehend what was happening.

Given the relapses that do occur, a gentle reminder of signs of any rationalisation process that might recur is called for to alert the alcoholic of the re-emergence of this habit. This is not to be read as advice to be suspicious, which is a very dangerous attitude. The main message is one of hope. No matter how bad things have been, there is hope that the alcoholic can return to full, free and happy relationships. He or she has been suffering from a disease that differs from many other diseases in significant ways. There is no permanent cure, but once arrested a normal life can be resumed after convalescence. The length of this convalescent period varies from individual to individual, just as it does in recovery from other serious diseases.

The Difference Between Alcoholic and Normal Euphoria

The preceding analysis of the onset and progress of the disease called alcoholism is based upon the fact that the drinking of alcohol leads the alcoholic to experience feelings of euphoria, a state that is so pleasant, so rewarding, so enjoyable, that the desire to experience the feeling again is overwhelming. The thing that marks off the rebound from alcoholic euphoria from the rebound experienced during normal euphoric states is the swing back past the zero point and into the pain area. Here feelings of distress are accompanied by actual physical pain caused by liver damage, hypertension, indigestion and the numerous other secondary diseases that are part of the primary disease of alcoholism.

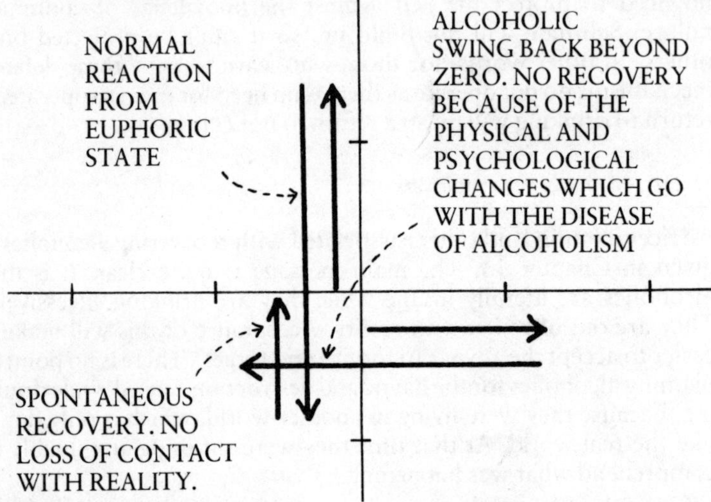

Figure 10. Response to Alcoholic and Normal Euphoric States

To illustrate this, Figure 10 shows normal euphoria on the vertical axis and chemically induced euphoria on the horizontal axis. There is no doubt that people experience highly intense states of euphoria without the use of artificial or chemically based agents such as alcohol and other drugs. Winning the final of the marathon at the Olympic Games, winning a large sum of money in a lottery, falling in love, and many other events can induce euphoric states that equal and indeed surpass the levels induced by alcohol. In some of these states there is also a swing back beyond the starting point. After winning the marathon, our runner may be on a high for a lengthy period but, quite commonly, this is followed by a period where the euphoria evaporates and a reaction sets in leading to a 'let down' that is obviously well below the normal state. Reports of vague feelings of despondency, of being out of sorts, of irritability and of inability to settle down to the normal routine mark this period. At least two major differences normally mark off this reaction from the euphoric state to that which happens to the alcoholic or drug taker.

(1) In his or her chemically induced state of euphoria the alcoholic is drunk, is out of touch with reality. During this period things are said or done that hurt other people and cause them to dislike or feel sorry for the alcoholic. The faint memory of these events poses a threat to the ego of the alcoholic, so the mechanisms of rationalisation, projection, denial and repression unconsciously become very active, taking the alcoholic further out of touch with reality as the swing towards and into the pain area occurs.

(2) The physical damage caused by the repeated excessive drinking begins to build up. Sleeping become difficult without a large dose of alcohol, pains in the chest and the stomach become a normal part of what rapidly becomes a semi-permanent state of distress.

The combination of actual distress caused by physical changes in the body and the knowledge, no matter how dimly felt, that their control over their lives is disintegrating causes the massive drop in self-esteem referred to earlier. These feelings do not disappear with time, so a wall of denial is erected to prevent the alcoholic from recognising the problem with any clarity, and drinking is resumed.

The winner of the marathon, on the other hand, has received a huge boost to his self-esteem. The let-down feelings may take him well down past the starting point as in Figure 10, but no damage to others is involved, and after some period of time there is usually an acceptance of living a normal life without the acclaim and without being the centre of attention, so the mood swings begin to start from zero again. At no stage are defence mechanisms needed to protect the ego from harm, so contact with reality is maintained. Spontaneous recovery from below the zero point prevents the damage that besets the alcoholic. This spontaneous recovery is shown by the third arrow on the vertical axis. For the alcoholic, who is suffering actual physical distress and acute mental distress, and who is becoming increasingly out of touch with reality, no such spontaneous recovery is possible. Some athletes and other celebrities do, of course, find the return to relative obscurity and the disappearance of the euphoric feelings that accompany their success too hard to cope with and become ill. Some of these take to alcohol, and some of them who have the disease pass into alcoholic drinking.

In order to illustrate the difference between heavy drinkers and alcoholic drinkers, it would be necessary to introduce a third dimension, which is implicit in all the above discussion. This is the reality-unreality dimension. Alcoholics have the disease that leads them to lose contact with reality. *This lack of contact with the real world persists even when they are sober.* Heavy and excessive drinkers may lose contact with reality while they are drunk, but do not suffer the changes in mental processes that prevent them seeing that they have a problem. They do not lose contact with reality, and they can stop drinking if they wish to, because they can see that it is their drinking that is causing the problem. Nobody will deny that heavy drinkers cause problems for themselves and their families, that they suffer some of the problems common to alcoholics, but because they control their intake, they do not become physically or psychologically dependent. The reasons for this are contained in the following section.

Biological Studies of the Causes of Obsessive Drinking

Even though Alcoholics Anonymous has always from empirical evidence described alcoholism as a disease, and even though the American Medical Association classified alcoholism as a disease in 1956, many people still refuse to accept this fact. Indeed there are at the present time misguided individuals and organisations trying to teach alcoholics to become social drinkers, despite compelling evidence that such enterprises are doomed to failure. Recent research findings should stop these practices.

The breakthrough in research began in Texas when Virginia Davis, who was conducting research into cancer, found a chemical that she thought was heroin in the brain tissue of recently deceased alcoholics. In fact the subtance was a highly addictive compound called tetrahydroisoquinoline (THIQ). This THIQ was used as a substitute for morphine in World War II, but was abandoned because it is even more addictive than morphine. Over the last decade or so research has centred on trying to establish how THIQ came to be found in the brain tissue of alcoholics.

The way the body normally deals with alcohol is well known. The liver breaks the alcohol into a very toxic substance called acetaldehyde; this is then broken down into acetic acid, which is vinegar; and finally the acetic acid is broken down into water and carbon dioxide to be eliminated through the kidneys and the lungs. It has always been thought that alcoholics break down all the alcohol in this way, but this is not correct.

When alcoholics get a lot of alcohol in their brain tissue following heavy drinking, something different occurs. A small part of the acetaldehyde goes to the brain, where it interacts with a substance called dopamine to form THIQ. The majority of the acetaldehyde is disposed of in the normal way. *Once the THIQ is formed, it does not go away, even if the alcoholic stops drinking.*

When alcoholics begin their drinking careers, they do not know that they are in danger of becoming alcoholics. By the time heavy abusive drinking begins, it is too late. The THIQ in the brain is formed, it is active and highly addictive, and it forms the basis of the physical compulsion to drink. It is just as difficult for an alcoholic to stop drinking as it is for a heroin addict to kick that habit. Incidentally, THIQ is formed also when an addict shoots heroin into her or his body.

The way THIQ is formed in the brain is known fairly precisely. Its properties, or at least some of them, have already been discovered. For example, it has been shown that when a certain strain of rats who normally shun alcohol like the plague have a minute amount of THIQ injected into their brains, they develop a liking and indeed a craving for alcohol and over a short period become alcoholic rats. When sacrificed and examined, large quantities of THIQ are found in their brains. If allowed to live and to dry out and go without alcohol for a period equivalent to many years in a human, the rats resume alcoholic drinking at the first opportunity.

These experiments have been repeated using monkeys, with the same sort of results, although not all the monkeys would drink alcohol, and so did not develop the disease. Myers (1978) has worked in this field and is among those who believe that it is an abnormal brain chemistry that marks alcoholics off from other drinkers. Taken in conjunction with the evidence of a hereditary basis to alcoholism, it seems likely that alcoholics are born with a predisposition to the disease of alcoholism. The AA insistence on treating alcoholism as a disease has been vindicated.

It is important to note that this discovery does not change anything directly for a recovering alcoholic. Presumably the THIQ in the brain becomes dormant after drinking ceases. It does not go away but, like a dormant volcano, lies there waiting for something to trigger it off and cause the compulsive drinking to start again. The catalyst or trigger, of course, is the first drink of alcohol. AA has a saying: 'One drink is too many and a hundred is not enough.' The wisdom of this cannot now be denied.

The problem for a non-practising alcoholic still remains that of learning to cope with life so well that under no stress, no strain, no abuse, no criticism and no circumstance will alcohol be used to 'help' in coping. AA has always made it clear that the responsibility for continued sobriety sits squarely on the shoulders of each alcoholic who has stopped drinking. This biochemical breakthrough has not changed that. It has resolved the question of responsibility quite definitely.

Summary

The disease of alcoholism can be analysed in terms of mood or feeling swings. Alcoholism becomes evident when the swing back of mood following drinking takes the drinker back beyond the zero point. At this time, larger and larger amounts of alcohol are necessary to enable the alcoholic to reach the euphoric stage where the world looks terrific and where anything can be fixed. As the drinking increases, defence mechanisms such as rationalisation, projection and repression — accompanied by actual memory changes associated with blackouts and euphoric recall — take the alcoholic out of touch with reality even while sober.

The fact that the alcoholics are out of touch with reality is the underlying reason why those living with alcoholics cannot understand them, why alcoholics cannot even see that they have a problem, and why others shake their heads in despair as the bizarre and destructive patterns of behaviour symptomatic of the disease of alcoholism begin to unfold. Alcoholics need to understand that they have developed the processes such as rationalisation to a fine art and to beware of the re-emergence of these processes in the recovery period.

Alcoholics have to be honest with themselves and honest in their dealings with others. They can no longer deny any weaknesses in their make-up, but have either to change these weaknesses or to accept them. Denial of being an alcoholic or refusal to accept that sobriety is the only way to arrest the disease of alcoholism is dynamite. Recovery cannot occur if sober alcoholics remain out of touch with reality by blaming others for their troubles or by using other defence mechanisms, such as denial or projection.

The phenomenon of euphoric recall is a potent source of danger during recovery. As physical health improves and as alcoholics move back into their old environment, the memory of the pain, damage and suffering associated with alcoholic drinking begins to fade and many alcoholics recall only the terrific times they had formerly, and remember the euphoric feelings associated with drinking. They are then and immediately at risk. An invitation to a party, the sight of others 'enjoying themselves' drinking and the presence of alcohol may be enough to set them off again on their destructive path.

This destructive path can be represented as a curve that rapidly accelerates towards the end, which — because alcoholism is a 100 per cent fatal disease unless total abstinence is attained — is death. Figure 11 represents this path. The important aspect to be remembered is that *the disease of alcoholism is irreversible.* It can be

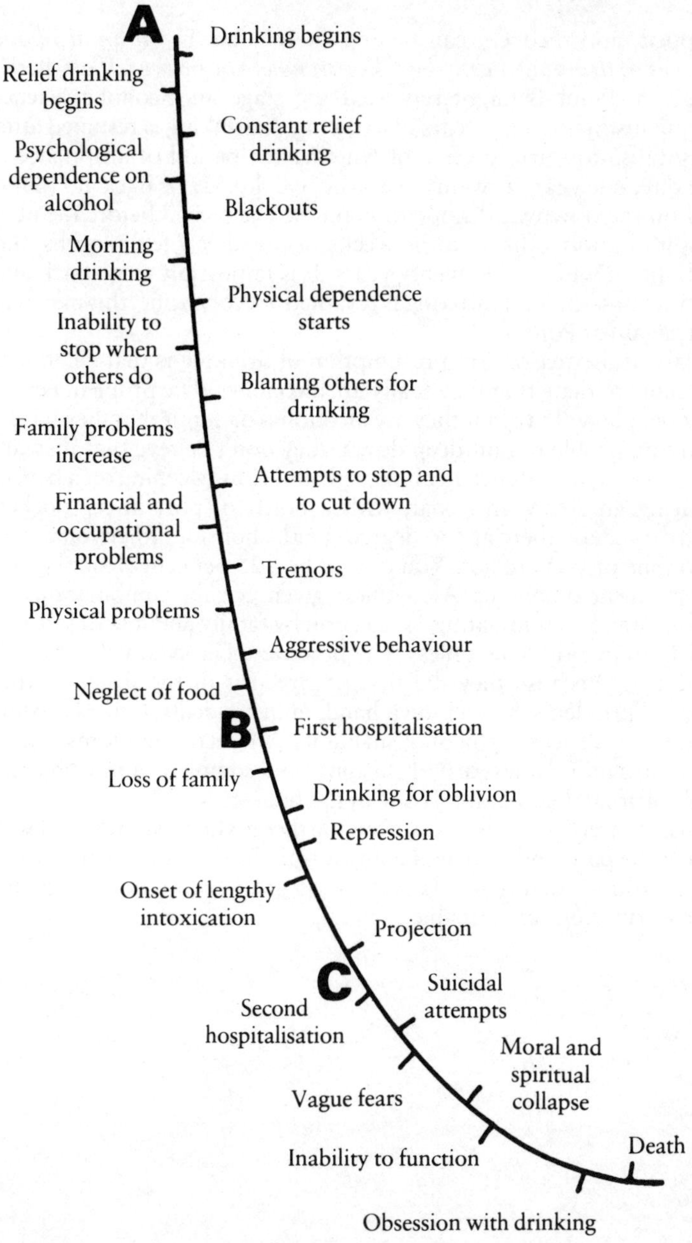

Figure 11. The Alcoholic Pathway

stopped, and recovery can be extremely good, but *if an alcoholic returns to drinking, he or she takes off where he or she left off*. In the diagram, Point B might represent the stage an alcoholic reaches during his first twenty years of drinking. If drinking is resumed after hospitalisation, irrespective of whether the period of abstinence is one day, one year or twenty years, he will quickly be back at Point B and on the downward slope to Point C. The period before the next hospitalisation is likely to be weeks or possibly a few months, but certainly it will not be twenty years. It is impossible to go back and start from scratch. If drinking is resumed a second time, this man will start again at Point C.

Part of the reason for a resumption of drinking is that alcoholics continue to deny that they really are alcoholics. The problem here is that people will say that they are alcoholics or admit that they have a drinking problem, but, deep down, they don't believe that they are the same as the derelict alcoholics in Skid Row, sleeping on a bench, wearing an Army greatcoat, with a bottle of port in the pocket. Unfortunately, there are no degrees of alcoholism. Either you are an alcoholic or you are not. You cannot be a 25 per cent alcoholic or a 99 per cent alcoholic. Alcoholics, given certain combinations of circumstances culminating in rejection by family and loss of job, can finish up in Skid Row unless they become sober. Many don't reach Skid Row because they die first of cirrhosis of the liver or other medical problems, by their own hand, or in accidents. Others become insane. The disease of alcoholism has its own set of symptoms, which occur in a more or less orderly fashion; and complete moral, physical and spiritual degradation is one of the final stages.

Fortunately, there is hope, even for those who have travelled well down the path and have had many hospitalisations. Provided drinking is stopped before the damage is too great, seemingly miraculous transformations are possible.

3

The Role of Self-esteem in Recovery

Introduction

In the previous chapter the disease of alcoholism was discussed. It was shown that, like other diseases, alcoholism has a cause, a course, a specific set of symptoms and a predictable outcome. The *cause* appears to be that alcoholics are born with a brain chemistry that predisposes them to alcoholism. Provide a suitable environment where alcohol is available plus the opportunity and motive to begin drinking, and the disease may start to develop. The *course* is well charted: it is downhill all the way. The *symptoms* are so well known that it is relatively easy to diagnose whether someone is in the early, middle or late stages of alcoholism. The *outcome* is equally predictable: for those who do not stop, death is inevitable.

For those who fully accept that they have the disease of alcoholism, the first step of building self-esteem is made easier. If individuals have a disease, and part of this disease is loss of contact with reality, loss of control of ability to think rationally and to make sensible decisions, then many of the crazy things that have been done were part of that disease. If part of this disease is loss of control over intake of alcohol, then alcoholics are not necessarily weak-willed, immoral creatures who lack the motivation to stop drinking. If the physical compulsion to drink is caused by a drug manufactured in our brains, then that provides an explanation for their obsession with alcohol. No longer need they feel guilty or ashamed of past excesses and violations of others' rights and feelings.

Building Self-esteem

The task of recovery from alcoholism is seen as being based on building up self-esteem by gradually achieving little successes. Not drinking for day after day is the main source of returning confidence, but success in every area of life is important. For many, returning to work is a traumatic event accompanied by anxiety. Once it is faced and overcome successfully, there is a great sense of relief and a huge boost to self-esteem. Other successes in family, social and occupational areas provide further increments. The stronger the sense of self-esteem becomes, and the stronger the habit of coping with life without alcohol becomes, the less likely it is that a relapse will occur.

The goal of all alcoholics should be to lead a completely normal life with just one exception: no alcohol. Alcoholics tend to regard themselves as quite different from other people, and to blame all their problems on their alcoholism. In fact, some of their problems would probably have emerged even if they weren't alcoholics.

Most people have trouble coping successfully with one or more of the significant areas in their lives. At times, many are angry and aggressive, others are selfish and dishonest, and get themselves into the same sort of problems as alcoholics. They too get divorced, they too get into legal and financial difficulties, and there are many lonely and friendless non-alcoholics, who have low self-esteem. Some highly paid, apparently successful business people are immature, dependent people whose personal lives are in a mess and who hate going to work because they have to act as if they are independent, resourceful, assertive individuals, when they are not. In other words they share many of the problems that beset alcoholics. They get depressed, angry and resentful. Their families suffer, and they have trouble sleeping. *The only thing different about alcoholics is that they cannot drink*. Alcoholics are not abnormal, they are not a separate and distinct group, they are not social pariahs. There is no reason why an alcoholic cannot become a fully functioning member of society, provided he or she stops drinking early enough and learns how to cope with life. The self-concept of alcoholics can become as high as that of non-drinkers and frequently becomes higher because of the tremendous feelings of achievement that accompany recovery.

Alcoholics frequently say that they are lucky because, once recovered, their enjoyment of even the simple pleasures of life is enhanced. In the alcoholic phase the whole of life is centred on alcohol, on ensuring that there are adequate supplies, on trying to prevent others from knowing just how massive the intake is, in denying that alcohol is a problem, and in actually drinking. The amount of time spent each day in drinking by some alcoholics is absolutely staggering. When they recover, they begin to take pleasure in waking up sober, in hearing birds in the trees, in being able to sit through a movie, in being able to entertain visitors, and in being treated with respect. These are things that most people take for granted. For alcoholics they are new experiences or ones that have not been experienced for many years. Recently, an alcoholic man expressed amazement and delight at the fact that, for the first time in his life, he had danced in public while sober. He was over fifty years of age! He had believed for his whole adult life that he could not dance without a heavy charge of alcohol. Such simple experiences add to the successes that raise self-esteem.

In the following chapters, ways of promoting the sense of self-esteem will be presented. These chapters will be about developing problem-solving skills, assertiveness skills, and about how to stop being dependent or, to put it another way, how to stop needing the approval of other people. Once we start to think carefully and rationally about our lives, once we begin to assert ourselves, and once we lose our emotional dependency or our need for approval by others, we will start making a success of our lives. This will lead to a rapid rise in self-esteem and in our confidence about our ability to cope.

Because self-esteem has been put at the centre of the recovery process, it is necessary to be quite clear what we are talking about. The major part of this chapter is given over to a discussion of two quite different ways of looking at self-esteem and suggesting that, for alcoholics especially, the second one is far preferable, because it provides a system for coping with some of the pressures that society places on everyone to conform to what is 'normal' in that society, at that point in time.

Since many of the problems that beset alcoholics arise from inability to cope with social pressures to conform, the second system seems preferable, because it is based not on social norms or what is expected, but simply on the decision of each individual makes about what sort of person she or he would like to be. If a person sees the demands of society as reasonable, then he or she makes an individual decision to accept that situation. On the other hand, if a man or a woman does not accept the values, attitudes and roles generally accepted by society, he or she can make an individual decision to reject them and aim at different goals.

For example, a woman alcoholic may be in trouble because 'society' has decided that women should bring up children, look after the house, cook, sew and clean, whereas she sees herself in the role of computer programmer and systems analyst. Under the first scheme, conflict would arise because of her frustration. Under the second, she is free to reject the social pressures and free to try to resolve the problem by attempting to get a job. It is to this discussion of the two concepts of self-esteem that we now turn.

The Concept of Self-esteem

The concept of self-esteem and adjustment have a great deal in common. Those who are high in self-esteem usually handle their day-to-day affairs with confidence and success. These people are also often described as well-adjusted. However, it is possible to be high in self-esteem and still behave in ways that lead to constant conflict with our friends, family and associates, or even with the law. Many would describe such people as poorly adjusted. For example, a man might typically behave in a very aggressive manner and see this as the appropriate reaction to a wide variety of situations. Despite the fact that this response alienates and upsets many with whom he comes into contact and perhaps leads to the loss of friends, his job or even divorce, he might deny his behaviour was the cause, attributing the losses to the stupid behaviour of others, and continue to think highly of his aggressive way of coping with problem situations. That is, despite what might seem to many to be clear evidence that his valued personality traits were non-adaptive and self-destructive, he might continue to see himself in a good light and blame others for the chaos surrounding him.

It should be clear from this brief description that being high in self-esteem is not necessarily a guarantee of leading a successful life, but it is abundantly clear that those who are low in self-esteem almost always lead chaotic lives, lack the confidence to think through problems and, even if they do, rarely assert themselves and put their solutions into practice. An example of the common experiences of those low in self-esteem is when he or she goes to a meeting with something he or she thinks is important to say and with the determination to speak up, but when the point in the meeting for speaking arrives, the fear of failure, the fear of being thought a fool prevents any speech, and the opportunity passes. Later, anger is turned against the self for saying nothing, and a depressive state may occur, further lowering the self-image.

The focal point of this discussion is the importance of self-esteem. Our lives have to be organised in such a way that our self-image is not only highly positive but also adapted to the situation that surrounds us. The adaptive part is crucial, because high self-esteem alone is not sufficient. In order to understand the two elements it is helpful to look at two entirely different ways of measuring self-esteem: the normative and non-normative.

Measuring Self-esteem

The normative approach

In most research studies and in common use a normative approach is adopted. Most of these methods are based on the 'adjective checklist approach'. In this method, the subject is presented with a long list of adjectives, such as happy, anxious, energetic, depressed, adventurous, aggressive, talkative, quiet, hostile, assertive, timid, submissive, extroverted, introverted, strong, and so on. The subject is asked to tick or check the ones that apply to him or her. The self-esteem score is arrived at by counting the number of *positive* items that are ticked or by subtracting the number of *negative* items from the number of positive items which are checked.

The two sets of items in the above list of adjectives might be said to be the following:

Positive: happy, energetic, adventurous, aggressive, strong, talkative, assertive, extroverted.

Negative: anxious, depressed, quiet, hostile, timid, submissive, introverted.

There are many problems with this method of measuring adjustment. For example, while most people agree that some personality traits or attributes lie in the positive or negative list, there is doubt about the placement of others, which are clearly important. If we take the extroverted-introverted dimension, this aspect can be highlighted. In personality research this dimension of introversion-extroversion is considered to be of central importance. However, it is not yet clear how this is related to success in coping with life. For example, Naylor (1972) has shown that the relationship between educational peformance and introversion-extroversion changes with the stage of education. In summarising the relationship between extroversion-introversion and school attainment, Naylor shows that stable extroverts tend to do well in primary school. In the secondary school the situation changes, with introverted boys and extroverted girls being high in attainment. Further changes appear at the tertiary level, where apparently introverts are the higher achievers.

The point being made is that there is no clear relationship between introversion-extroversion and academic attainment or, for that matter, with anything else — such as occupational, marital or social success. It is just not possible to place 'extroverted' in either the negative or the positive list. And there are many other adjectives that are equally difficult to place. For example, there is no evidence that rating oneself as *quiet*, *retiring* and *sensitive* indicates either lack of self-esteem or of adjustment.

The method described so far is the simplest and least sophisticated use of the normative approach. Basically, someone, usually a male psychologist, *decides* which adjectives belong in the positive lists. This judgement is often given respectability by asking a lot of apparently well-adjusted people to list or check the adjectives they think a well-adjusted person will display. Those adjectives that a large majority agrees are either clearly positive or negative make up the final checklist of items.

This approach can be further refined by arranging the adjectives in pairs such as dominant-submissive, sociable-unsociable, extroverted-introverted, happy-sad. Different patterns of scores can then be related to people who are successful in various occupations, and these profile-scores can be used to guide people in different vocational areas. Quite clearly, different personality skills and interests seem to be required to be successful in the selling occupations to those required in the investigative back-room research occupations, for example. However, two people selected with quite different profiles may be equally high in self-esteem and adjustment.

Problems arise when one set of attributes is deemed to denote high self-esteem or adjustment simply because this is what the majority agrees upon. At a given point in time the *norm* for high self-esteem for males might include aggressive, extroverted, not over-sensitive, forceful and adventurous, whereas it is at least possible that someone non-aggressive, introverted, sensitive, persuasive and non-adventurous may be even higher in self-esteem and better adjusted to cope with the daily problems of life.

The difficulties of the normative approach become even clearer when we come to sex differences. In many societies different roles and characteristics are deemed to be appropriate for males and for females. Thus the well-adjusted female may be expected to fill the roles of wife, mother, child-rearer, cook, housekeeper, provider of sex, and to be submissive, compliant, warm, affectionate and loving, whereas the male might be expected to fill the roles of breadwinner and protector and to be aggressive, dominant, stong and dependable. Males and females are often taught these normative roles from infancy.

Now, nothing is fixed or immutable about what society prescribes as being the norm. With the changing economic scene, with changes in values and expectations, and with the rise of groups challenging the currently accepted roles of women, quite marked shifts in norms occur. In some places the role of women is shifting so that many of the so-called male characteristics appear desirable. These changes in perception of women's roles are welcomed and accepted by some and resented and rejected by others.

Clearly the normative approach does not allow an acceptable way of measuring self-esteem or adjustment unless we define adjustment and self-esteem as *agreement by the majority at any point in time.* Those who are out of step with the prevailing climate of opinion are similarly assessed as poorly adjusted and lacking in self-esteem because they behave in ways perceived as 'abnormal' by the majority. Whereas some of these people in fact are so well-adjusted and high in self-esteem that they are capable of leading social change. Conversely, it is possible that those at the other end of the scale who are resisting changes may also be well-adjusted and high in self-esteem because they have the vision to see and resist changes that are detrimental to progress.

It is a brave or foolish man or woman who will state categorically that the possession of a certain set of characteristics or ways of behaving will necessarily constitute high self-esteem, and good adjustment on the basis that 'this is what society says', yet this is the very foundation of the normative approach.

The non-normative approach

Carl Rogers, a psychotherapist, has developed a way of looking at adjustment that is based not upon what society deems to be right and proper, but on the 'congruence' between how a person sees or thinks about himself at a given point in time (the Self) and what he would like to be (the Ideal Self). If there is large disparity between what he is really like and what he would like to be, then this constitutes a psychological disturbance. Such people will be poorly adjusted to life, unable to cope well and be low in self-esteem.

On the other hand, where the Self and the Ideal Self are similar or near-congruent, then adjustment and self-esteem will be high and the ability to cope will be enhanced. In this way of looking at adjustment it is possible for two people with two different and even opposite sets of characteristics and role preferences to be said to be equally well-adjusted and equally high in self-esteem. Consider two adult females who are quite different in terms of the way they see themselves but who also have quite different values and ambitions as set out below:

SELF — FEMALE A	*SELF — FEMALE B*
Assertive	Compliant
Extroverted	Introverted
Outgoing	Shy
Dominant	Submissive
Leader	Follower
Career woman	Housewife

Let us then imagine that both women's Ideal Selves are congruent with the way they actually are. That is Female A wants to be assertive, extroverted, etc., and active in a career, while Female B wants to be compliant, introverted, etc., and busily engaged as a housewife. Because there is a congruence between Self and Ideal Self for both, they appear to be perfectly adjusted, whereas according to the normative approach one of them would be classified as poorly adjusted.

Under the non-normative method of measuring adjustment, conformity to social norms is not a prerequisite for high self-esteem. This, of course, raises the issue that some people retain in their Ideal-Self image some characteristics, habits and roles that are harmful to themselves and to those who love them. Alcoholics, or at least a significant number of them, belong in this category. A few examples of the effects of retaining harmful characteristics in the image of the IDEAL SELF follow.

Many alcoholics will accept the fact that they are alcoholics, but refuse to accept that this means giving up alcohol consumption on a permanent basis. This is despite the evidence that the chances of a return to drinking at a social level are either very slim or non-existent on a long-term basis. This is shown in diagram form in Figure 12.

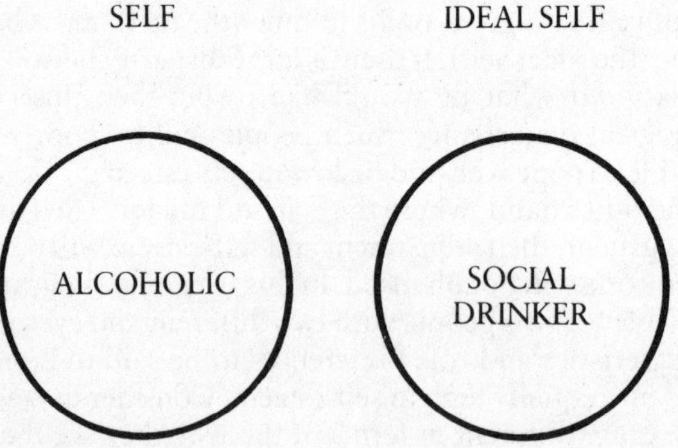

Figure 12. Incompatible Objectives for the Self

It is claimed here that there is little or no possibility that the Self can be made to move towards the Ideal Self in this case, that this failure will lead to a drop in self-esteem and probably to a major relapse. The sorts of changes that can be achieved with hard work are listed below:

SELF	*IDEAL SELF*
Dishonest	Honest
Angry	
Depressed	
Resentful	Calm
Envious	
Upset	
Guilty	Not-guilty
Cold	Warm
Distant	Affectionate
Aggressive	Assertive
Dependent	Independent

As far as acceptance of social, sex roles is concerned we need to look carefully at what *society* (possibly in the form of a parent, husband, wife or lover) says, and decide whether or not to accept the strictures of society or not. If we are happy to permit conventional wisdom to be the determinant of what we should be like, then we should allow it to do just that. If not, we have to appraise realistically the problems or dangers associated with bucking society and proceed with cautious assertiveness.

High self-esteem occurs when there is a high degree of overlap or intersection between the Self and the Ideal Self, as in Figure 13.

Figure 13. High Self-esteem

Low self-esteem is found where there is little or no intersection, as shown in Figure 14.

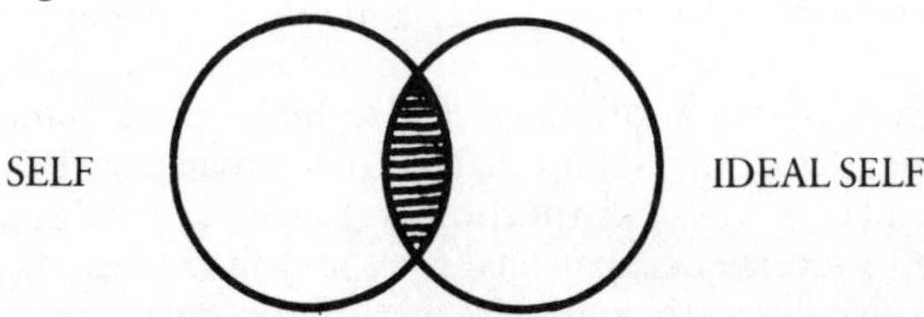

Figure 14. Low Self-esteem

The process of recovery from alcoholism — or from any other situation characterised by widespread failure to cope — is the movement of the Self towards the Ideal Self. Probably no human being is perfectly well-adjusted, but we can strive towards that end.

Choosing Between the Normative and the Non-normative Approaches

The normative approach stresses conformity to what the majority of people at any given point of time think is appropriate and proper. Thus, anyone who diverges too markedly from the norm in either direction is, by definition, abnormal. The term abnormal carries strong overtones of sickness, whereas all it really means is 'different'. This is easy to see on a dimension such as height, where people who are extremely tall (say above two metres) or extremely short (say below one metre) are not thought of as being ill. Transfer the scale to the happy-sad dimension and divergence from the normal range carries implications of sickness. Someone who is extremely happy is called manic and someone extremely sad is called depressed. While these departures from the norm may indeed point to psychological disturbance, the norms themselves shift from time to time, so someone who is deemed to be abnormal in one decade may be normal in the next. For example, men who openly displayed the positive emotions of love and affection in public a decade ago might have been classified as effeminate and therefore as poorly adjusted. With the current move towards recognising the crucial nature of the overt display of kindness and affection in human relationships, a different assessment might be made today.

Not so many years ago the notion of a male being a housekeeper and rearing the children while his wife earned an income was, for most, unacceptable. While still far from the norm today, such revolutionary concepts are accepted in some parts of society, even if they are still vigorously rejected by the majority. The point of view taken here is that there is a great deal of evidence to suggest that those who diverge from the norms of society and who are unhappy when they are forced to accept the normal situation should adopt the non-normative approach, provided it is to his or her advantage, and is therefore an *adaptive* solution. That is, if a man sees the value in the overt display of love and affection or decides after consultation with his wife to reverse occupational roles and she agrees, then these are the adaptive things to do despite the strictures of society.

For alcoholics, especially males, this rejection of the normative approach is essential. If the norm is 'there is something wrong with a man who does not drink' or 'it is not possible to enjoy yourself if you don't drink', then these irrational norms have to be rejected. For females, acceptance of norms like 'a woman's place is in the home', or 'women should be seen but not heard' are a sure recipe for renewed drinking bouts if she really believes the opposite. The best part of adopting the non-normative approach is that if your norms happen to coincide with the prevailing norms of society, then that presents no difficulty at all, as in this case the normative and non-normative approaches lead to the same Ideal Self position.

Planning for Recovery

One important step in recovery from alcoholism is to take a long, hard look at the Self as it is present. On the average, as will be made clear later, alcoholics tend to have a very low sense of self-esteem. Almost to a man and woman, alcoholics have been coping very poorly with their lives and usually have major problems in emotional, family, social and occupational areas and frequently in financial, legal and sexual aspects as well.

AA advocates a 'fearless moral inventory'; that is complete honesty in looking at the characteristics and abilities an individual possesses before looking at the characteristics and abilities that are preferred. In looking at the Ideal Self an individual needs to be careful not to include impossible attributes, characteristics or situations. While all may want to be rational, tolerant and calm, many people need to look closely at their pattern of abilities so they do not, for example, include occupations they do not have the ability or temperament for. Not all are suited to be salesmen or mechanics or computer programmers, and few have the ability to amass fortunes from small beginnings. Of course, the Ideal Self can be changed to meet changing circumstances. The important thing is for a person to identify quite clearly what the present Self is like and, as of that moment, what she or he would like to be. Below is a list prepared by a male alcoholic in conjunction with his wife:

SELF	*IDEAL SELF*
Alcoholic	Non-drinking Alcoholic
Irrational	Rational
Denial of Alcoholism	Acceptance of Alcoholism
Impetuous	Careful
Angry	Assertive

Dependent	Independent
Anxious	Calm
Distant	Affectionate
Cold	Warm
Inconsiderate	Considerate
Intolerant	Tolerant
Unstable	Stable
Unemployed	Employed
Stormy marriage	Loving relationship
Friendless	Having Friends
Intelligent	Intelligent
Good bricklayer	Good bricklayer

In this case, all but the last two attributes showed a disparity between the SELF and the IDEAL SELF. The man had lost his job because of abuse of his employer, frequent absences, drinking heavily on the job, and inability to get along with his fellows.

The method of trying to move the self-image towards the Ideal Self will unfold during the following chapters. Let it be said here, however, that many alcoholics fail because they think that after treatment for alcoholism their problems can all be solved in a short time. It must be remembered that habits such as intolerance, anger and especially irrational ways of thinking have been built up over many years and that it takes time to tear down these old habits while at the same time building up new habits of tolerance, assertion and rationality. Drinking has become an habitual method of trying to cope with stressful situations, and this habit, too, has to be unlearned and replaced with the non-drinking habit.

Changes in Self-concept During and After Treatment

When self-esteem is measured by normative methods, the usual finding is that both male and female alcoholics are lower in self-esteem than their non-alcoholic peers. For example, Beckman *et al.* (1980) measured 120 male and 120 female alcoholics undergoing treatment for alcoholism in Southern California. The average score for the female alcoholics was 2.83, for male alcoholics 3.26, and for female non-alcoholics 4.80, where the range of scores was 0-6. Armstrong and Hoyt (1963), Berg (1971) and Vanderpool (1969) in three separate studies showed male alcoholics to be lower in self-concept than male non-alcoholics.

Selby (1981) measured various aspects of change in the self-concept of male alcoholics during four weeks of treatment, comparing one group of patients, for whom the emphasis was on control of their own destiny and coping with stress, with another group, which had psychotherapy dealing with the harmful effects of alcohol on the body and on other people. For both groups there was a significant change in the general level of self-esteem on 9 of the 17 sub-scales. On 4 more sub-scales the group trained in internal-control procedures improved, while the others obtained lower scores. These scales were Family-Self, Social-Self, Sense of Identity and Absence of Conflict. Selby concluded that while both groups improved their self-concepts, the treatment stressing the importance of self-reliance and problem-solving showed improvement in other significant areas related to self-esteem within the family setting and in social situations, and that these were accompanied by less conflict and a greater sense of identity. The thrust of this book is a full-scale extension of this commitment to internal control and the advocacy of methods designed to overcome dependence on external props and reinforcement.

Beckman (1978) states the questionnaire was given again one year after treatment and both men and women shared highly significant gains in self-esteem, the women improving from 2.83 to 4.19 and the men from 3.27 to 3.94. From this study it seems reasonable to conclude that the initial low levels of self-esteem of both male and female alcoholics improved after twelve months. The results are not as clear as they might have been because although some of the subjects returned to drinking while others remained abstinent, all the scores were lumped together.

Brisset and his fellow workers (1980) compared 80 abstinent alcoholics with 30 alcoholics with renewed drinking problems forty-two months after discharge. Their self-concept was assessed by asking them how they felt at present compared with how they felt while they were drinking alcoholically. They were asked to indicate whether they strongly agreed, agreed, disagreed or strongly disagreed with the following seven items:

1. I am happier.
2. I find life more satisfying.
3. People act more positively towards me.
4. I feel better about myself.
5. I am able to accomplish more.
6. I am more optimistic.
7. People close to me seem happier.

The average percentage rating for each of four categories over the seven items is summarised in Table 1.

While 99 per cent of the abstinent group strongly agreed or agreed with the seven statements, so did 66 per cent of the problem drinkers. The unexpectedly high levels of the scores of the problem drinkers has been noted by others.

Table 1. Assessment by Abstinent and Non-abstinent Alcoholics and Life Changes Forty-two Months after Discharge

GROUP	STRONGLY AGREE %	AGREE %	DISAGREE %	STRONGLY DISAGREE %
ABSTINENT	54	45	1	0
DRINKING	11	55	26	8

Heilbrun and Schwartz (1981) investigated this phenomenon and concluded that some alcoholics seemed to have the capacity for the continuation of behaviour that they characterised as 'mal-adaptive' by over-valuing their own characteristics and under-valuing characteristics not claimed as Self-characteristic. They maintained that this distortion appeared to be brought about by the process of RATIONALISATION, where reasons are found to justify the maintenance of Self-characteristics that on any objective scrutiny are clearly factors in their continued problem drinking. Thus concepts such as 'aggressive' and 'social drinker' may be kept as part of the concept of what they really want to be like on the spurious grounds that men have to be aggressive to protect their own sense of identity, and they have to drink, at least socially, because they need alcohol to participate in their social activities. Some would even maintain that drinking is an integral part of their occupational activities.

Given this, it seems highly likely that some of the problem drinkers agreed that they were progressing well, when in fact an objective observer would have said that they were failing to cope. Hospitals and other treatment facilities that fail to convince their patients of the necessity to give up aggressive behaviour in favour of becoming assertive, and which do not accept abstinence as the only way to keep alcoholism dormant would seem to be encouraging their patients to retain goals in the Ideal Self that are not possible for alcoholics to attain and thus promote relapse drinking, because the proneness to alcoholism does not change. This difference in the aims of institutions may account for part of the difference in success rates. Because of the failure of most hospitals to conduct research into success rates, this is difficult to check.

Recent Research into Characteristics that Promote Good Adjustment and High Self-esteem

Recent research by Bem (1974), and by others following up his ideas, has challenged the way society readily accepts some characteristics and roles as being necessary for female adjustment and other characteristics and roles as necessary for male adjustment. This research is presented in some detail in the chapter about female alcoholics. For the moment it will be sufficient to point out that this recent work appears to show that *well-adjusted men and women appear to share the same characteristics, which are a mixture of what are usually deemed to be male and female characteristics*. This mixture includes being assertive, strong, dependable and direct, on the one hand, along with being calm, kind, considerate, supportive and affectionate on the other, but does not include being aggressive, dominating or submissive.

This research fits the ideas being presented here like a glove, because high self-esteem in both women and men is seen to depend on the same factors, unlike the normative approach where different characteristics are deemed to be appropriate for females than those for men. Men in our society tend to look down on males who are courteous, kind and considerate, and the former maintain their 'manly' image by being aggressive and dominant. Yet it is the calm, considerate ones who are coping.

Somewhere along the line, something has gone wrong. Men are often trained to be aggressive, females to be submissive, and neither is adaptive. High levels of adjustment seem to be related to the possession and display of all the positive emotions such as consideration, gratitude, kindness, love and affection. That is, adjustment is correlated not with an aggressive attitude but with an assertive approach in which people calmly size up situations, decide what to do, and take action to protect their rights and feelings. It is certainly worth considering this research when looking at what your Ideal Self might be like.

It is interesting to note that mature females prefer kind, sensitive men and that they avoid macho men like the plague. Yet many men still believe that aggressiveness is appropriate behaviour for a man, and act accordingly. Many male alcoholics have trouble with their recovery because they still believe that being kind or showing affection is inappropriate for a man, and they refuse to change despite the clear evidence that their former aggressive behaviour contributed to their alcoholism.

Females who are over-aggressive or submissive also need to look at this evidence. Many females are conditioned to believe that they have few if any rights, and behave accordingly. Submissive behaviour for a female alcoholic is an almost certain recipe for a return to drinking. It needs to be replaced with assertive behaviour to protect the rights outlined in the following chapters.

Summary

If we see ourselves as worthy people, if we are confident about our ability to cope and if we feel that we can adapt to changing situations, we are said to be well-adjusted and high in self-esteem. Those who are well-adjusted and high in self-esteem tend to act in ways that reinforce these characteristics and tend to cope with life quite successfully. Those who are not well-adjusted and are low in self-esteem tend to fail more often than they succeed, and do not cope very well. *We are what we think we are* to some extent.

Two different ways of looking at the concept of self-esteem were examined in this chapter. The *normative approach* was rejected, because it is not useful for recovering alcoholics. This method basically tries to find out what the majority of people believe is good adjustment, which will lead to high self-esteem. Anyone who differs markedly in either direction from the norm established by this method is said to be badly adjusted, abnormal and low in self-esteem.

The *non-normative approach*, on the other hand, takes no account of what society decides is right and proper. The emphasis is on each individual who decides for himself or herself what she or he really wishes to be like: this is called the Ideal Self. Each individual then tries to become like that. If the Self, at any point in time, coincides with or is reasonably like the Ideal Self, then he or she is said to be well-adjusted and self-esteem will be high. The process of recovery from alcoholism is seen to be the movement of the Self towards the Ideal Self. For alcoholics certain practices and characteristics seem to be forbidden. Alcoholics cannot include or retain 'social drinker', or 'being aggressive' in the Ideal Self, because being an alcoholic precludes this.

The work of Bem was outlined to emphasise the importance of not blindly accepting the values of society as being appropriate for everyone. This research suggests that a mixture of the so-called masculine and the so-called feminine traits leads to good adjustment. Research evidence was also presented to show that alcoholics are low in self-esteem, but that the level rises with abstinence. In the following chapters, procedures designed to promote self-esteem are outlined.

4

Anxiety, Alcohol and Failure to Cope

Introduction

In this chapter a model is introduced that shows what is involved in 'failure to cope'. The model shows how anxiety, low self-esteem, a low level of confidence, poor problem-solving, a high level of dependency and a low level of assertiveness are linked in this failure-to-cope cycle. Finally it shows how alcoholic drinking emerges as an attempt to cope with this situation and how the drinking actually makes failure even more inevitable.

Anxiety and Behaviour

The whole of the following discussion is designed to show, firstly, that anxiety is something we can do without because of its disastrous consequences, and, secondly, that it is possible to control our anxiety levels. In discussions with alcoholics it is clear that initially almost all believe that it is impossible to control anxiety because it is a 'natural emotion' and 'we are born with it and can't change it'. A favourite saying is some variation of: 'I'm anxious, my mother was anxious and her mother was anxious. How can I change that?'

These statements are usually based upon the failure to distinguish between *fear* and *anxiety*. Fear *is* a natural emotion and it is *adaptive*. If we are being attacked by someone with an axe or a hammer, it is sensible and adaptive to be afraid. We are born with the capacity to become afraid because this fear releases adrenalin, enables us to run faster or makes us stronger if we decide to fight. Babies who touch fires develop fear responses and are thus less likely to reach into the flames again. These are adaptive responses and essential for our survival.

Anxiety is very like fear and is probably a derivative of it. The difference lies in the fact that with fear there is *real, objective danger*, whereas anxiety is a learned response to situations where there is apprehension of danger, where the threat is *subjective*. Thus a young boy approaching a girl to ask her to go to a dance with him may feel anxious. There is no threat to his physical well-being. The subjective threat is that she might say no. If this happens, the danger is to his psychological well-being and to his self-esteem. The apprehension he feels when he approaches the girl is what we call anxiety.

The nasty emotion we may feel when we are asked to make a speech, when we have to walk into a room full of strangers, when we wonder whether we will be able to cope with a new job, when we enter an examination room, or as we are about to return to our jobs after being in hospital for treatment for alcoholism is anxiety.

State Anxiety

State Anxiety refers to the complex emotional reaction a person has when she or he interprets a stressful situation as being personally threatening. With this notion *it is possible for an individual to interpret a very stressful situation as non-threatening or, on the other hand, to interpret a low-stress event as highly threatening*, because the degree of threat attributed to any given situation or problem will be determined by an individual's past experience.

If we take as an example two students walking into a mathematics examination, we can see this in operation. One, who has a past history of success in mathematics, who has studied hard, and who does not feel a need to get very high marks will probably be quite calm. The second, with a poor record in earlier mathematics examinations, and who thinks he must do well to please his parents, is probably agitated, starts to sweat a little, to feel apprehensive and to have other unpleasant bodily reactions. In other words, he responds with a large elevation in State Anxiety. So, while the situation contains the same amount of stress for both, there is more threat for the second student. Stress refers to degree of objective danger. Threat refers to our own personal subjective appraisal or interpretation of the situation as dangerous. In our mathematics example, there is potentially the same amount of stress in the situation for both, but the situation is appraised by the second student as highly threatening to him.

State Anxiety responses, as we will see, prevent people solving problems effectively and efficiently, and lead people into emotional chaos and illness, including alcoholism. We can change State Anxiety responses simply by altering the way we interpret situations, but this will be discussed later on.

The Effects of Anxiety

A massive amount of research on anxiety levels and various measures of performance supports the following conclusions:

1. High levels of anxiety lead to low levels of performance whenever the task to be done is in any way difficult. It follows that we could expect high anxiety to lower the standard of performance in examinations, interviews, in many social situations, in sexual performance and in occupational areas whenever the stress factor is high and is evaluated as a threat.
2. High levels of anxiety often lead to failure.
3. High levels of anxiety that lead to failure also lead to a drop in self-esteem, which leads to a drop in confidence.
4. Success lowers anxiety levels and raises self-esteem. Failure raises anxiety levels and lowers self-esteem.
5. Stress is neutral. Only if we interpret it as a threat does it cause anxiety.

Anxiety and Failure to Cope

The evidence given above suggests that if a person assesses a task as threatening, he or she becomes anxious, and will probably make a mess of it. This failure will make her or him more anxious and result in a drop in her or his level of self-esteem. The next time an individual meets this situation or one like it, she or he will assess it as very threatening. The anxiety level will rise even more, failure will be more likely. A circle of failure will have been started, as shown in Figure 15.

The problem with this analysis is that it does not tell us what makes a person anxious in the first place. What are the characteristics of the task, the problem or the situation that have the potential to arouse anxiety? Why do some people perceive the stress that is inherent for all as threatening to them, while others do not? In other words, what are the characteristics of situations that provoke anxiety?

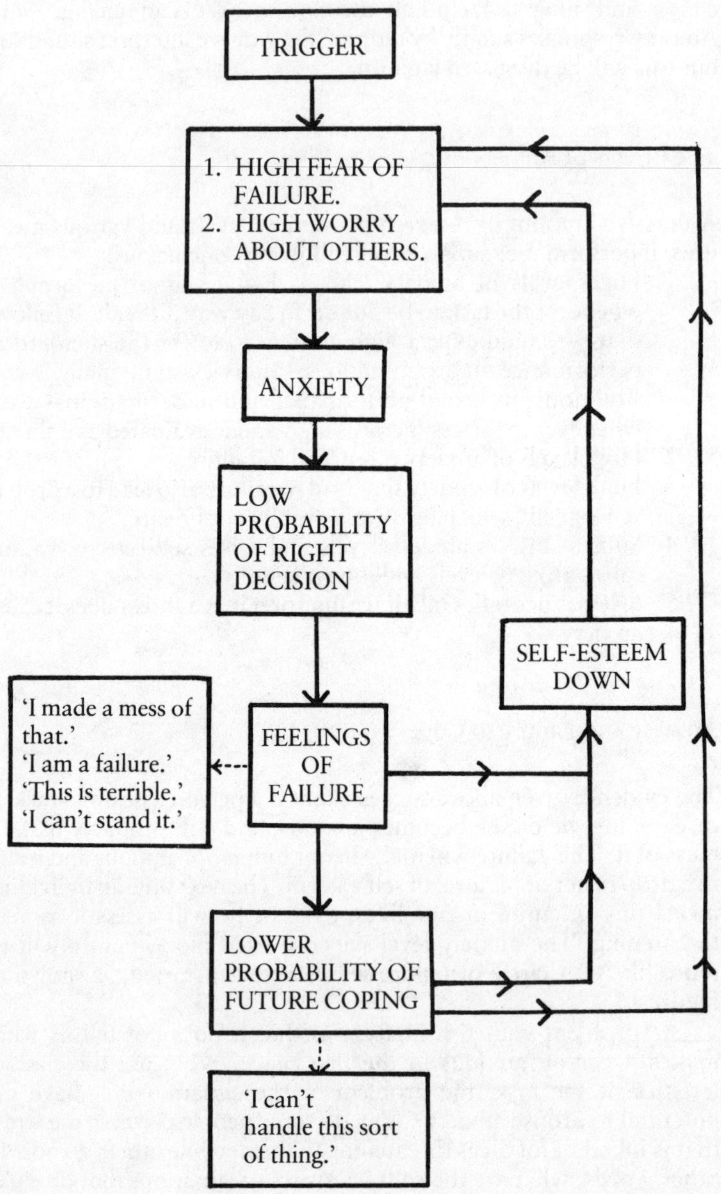

Figure 15. How Anxiety Starts Off the Failure-to-cope Circle

Characteristics of Anxiety-provoking Situations

The main method of assessing stress reaction has been to take people who are high or low in Trait Anxiety (a measure of how anxious they *generally* are) and subject them to different sorts of situations in order to identify areas where there are dramatic differences in aroused State Anxiety between the two groups. After a great deal of research, it is now crystal clear that there are two completely different types of stress situations, which produce quite different results. The first type is where all subjects are threatened with harmful physical punishment, such as electric shock, if their performance is not good. When the State Anxiety level is measured under these circumstances, both low and high Trait Anxious groups respond with high levels of State Anxiety, but there is no differential reaction.

The other type of situation is to tell the subjects that their performance will in some way be compared with that of others or evaluated by other people or groups. This has been done by stressing the importance of the results, by telling the subjects that their results will be compared with the results of the others who have done the test or by telling them that their performance will be watched, analysed and criticised by their own group or by another group. The essence of these procedures is to make it clear in one way or another *that someone else or some group will be evaluating and making judgements about the adequacy of their performance*. Unlike the situation when physical punishment was threatened, there is a huge effect upon the performance of the highly Trait Anxious but little or none on the group with low Trait Anxiety, as shown in Figure 16, where the two situations are compared.

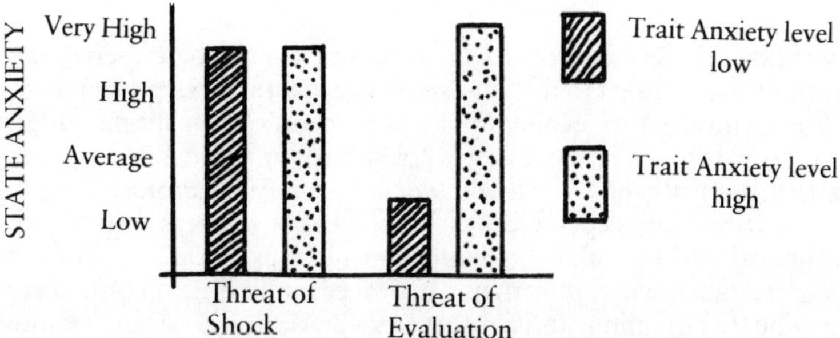

Figure 16. Comparisons of State Anxiety Levels Following Physical or Psychological Threat for People with Low and High Trait Anxiety Levels

There is no doubt about the characteristics of the situations that make people highly anxious. *The difference occurs when we subject people to situations that contain the possibility of negative evaluation by other people, where there is the possibility of failure and of a consequent blow to self-esteem.* The anxiety reaction that people have in such situations seems to reflect a fear of failure in these interpersonal situations where self-esteem is involved.

One of the most anxiety-producing situations is having to make a speech before an audience. This contains all the elements already discussed.

1. Threat to self-esteem.
2. Fear of failure.
3. Possible evaluation by other people.
4. Worrying about what other people think of you.
5. Being a 'people pleaser'.

A man suddenly asked to get on his feet to make a speech may respond with many of the anxiety symptoms, including physiological ones and the psychological feeling of apprehension. These very conscious bodily reactions flood the brain with messages essentially saying: 'Things are pretty bad down here. Do something about it quickly.' The brain starts searching for ways of coping with these demands and has little or no capacity left to deal with what to say, how to say it, and how generally to cope with the problem that originally led to the sudden surge of anxiety. The end-result is bound to be a poor solution. Neither refusal to speak nor a nervous, halting, incoherent speech can be classified as confidence-building.

Anxiety and Dependency

As State Anxiety is aroused in those situations where there is an appraisal of a threat to the self-esteem because there is a possibility of failure and negative evaluation by other people, then another interpretation is possible. That is, it is possible to say that *it is our need for approval by other people that is the cause of the rises in State Anxiety level.* If we are dependent on other people for reassurance, for approval and for constant reinforcement of us as capable, worthy people, then it will follow that, when faced with a difficult task, there may be fear of failure and a threat to the sense of self-esteem because of the possibility of our adequacy being appraised by others.

Thus alcoholics faced with the necessity of returning to work after treatment lasting many weeks frequently become extremely anxious because they are worried about what their employers and fellow workers will think and say about them. They may feel guilty and ashamed about their past behaviour, where their productivity may have fallen off, their attendance may have been erratic. They may have said things that could alienate many. Their alcoholism may even have contributed to industrial accidents. This anxiety about resumption of work leads them to construct imaginary barriers, to think that people will be nasty to them, call them names and so on. *All of this is based upon the fear of negative evaluation by others.* In reality, it hardly ever happens. Accounts of return to work usually result in the alcoholic saying. 'It was a breeze. Everyone was glad to see me back in good health. I feel terrific. Why did I punish myself all those weeks?'

We now have another link in our chain. If we have a high need for approval by other people and are always worried about what they will think of us, we will assess the situation as threatening and become anxious. Adding this to our diagram, we are really adding an important factor, which causes the anxiety that leads to failure. We can call this factor *dependency* or *high need for approval*, as shown in Figure 17. That is, emotional dependence or high need for app-

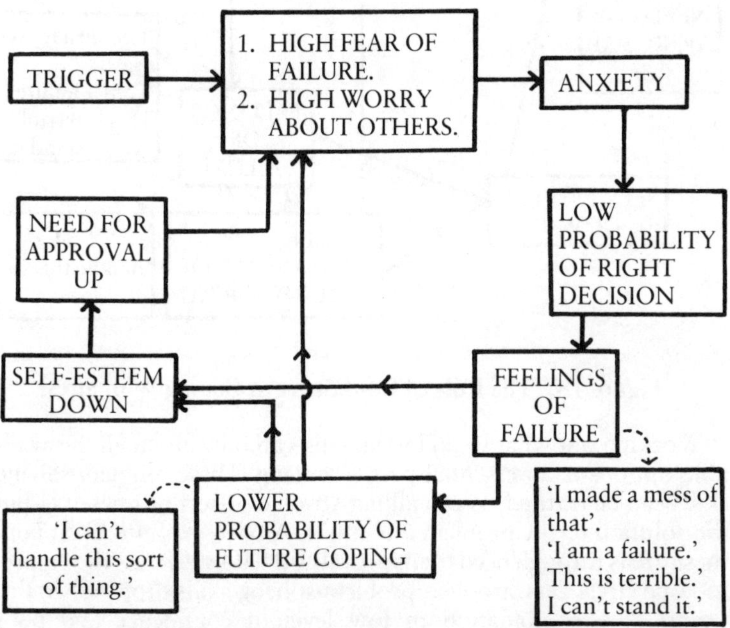

Figure 17. The Role of Need for Approval in Failure to Cope

roval by others causes the anxiety that leads to failure. The failure leads to a drop in self-esteem, which in turn increases the need for approval, which feeds back into the circle, increases anxiety and so on round and round the circle. The existing level of self-esteem and the existing level of need for approval by other people jointly determine the level of confidence we feel about dealing with this sort of problem. If our level of confidence is low, the problem will usually be evaluated as very threatening, and this will generate high levels of anxiety. This aspect is shown in Figure 18.

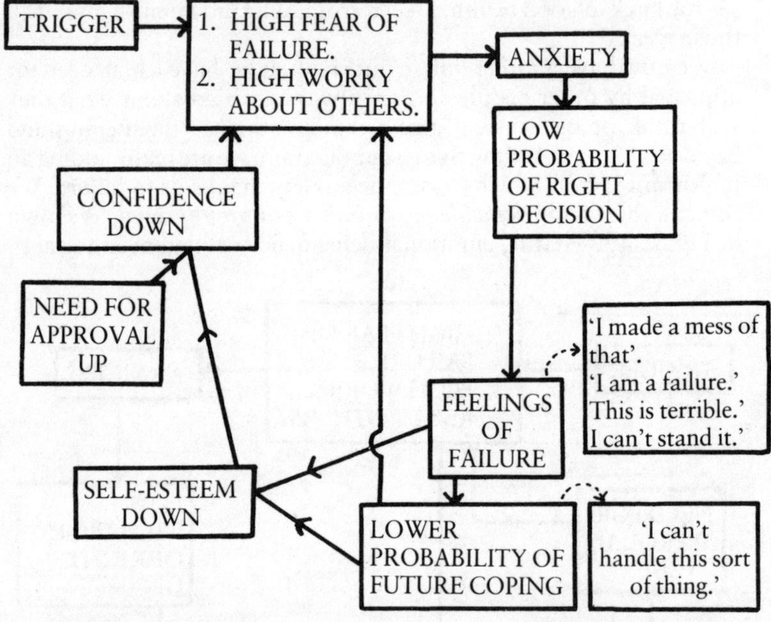

Figure 18. The Role of Confidence in Coping With Stress

Working out what to do by thinking carefully about all the available options is an essential part of coping. These problem-solving skills can be learned, as can taking action or asserting oneself to put the solution to the problem into effect. Anxiety has effects on both these areas through need for approval and self-esteem. As the failure-to-cope circle gets stronger, problem-solving skills drop. When this occurs, the combination of low level of confidence and poor problem-solving skills gets people to the position where they can't work out what to do. Even if they do reach a sensible decision, the level of confidence may be too low to allow them to assert themselves and take the action necessary to protect their rights and feelings. They will begin to act impulsively or not act when they should.

Impulsiveness and little thought about various ways to solve the problem lead to irrational decisions. These combine with low levels of confidence and result in low levels of assertiveness. Low levels of assertiveness lead to assessment of the problem as a threat. These connections are shown in Figure 19.

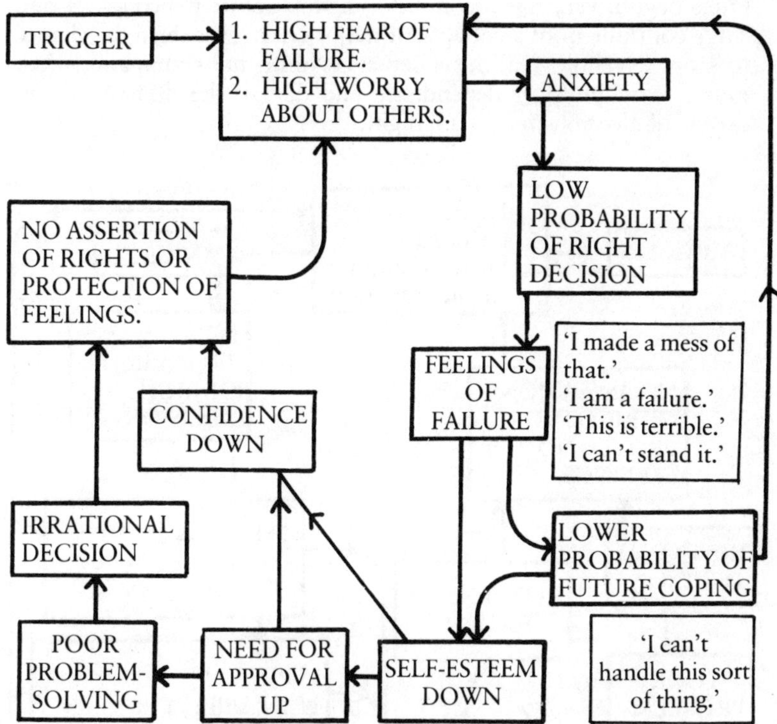

Figure 19. The Role of Problem-solving and Assertiveness in Coping With Stress

If individuals are exposed to a sufficient number of experiences of this kind, their self-esteem becomes so low that they begin to think in the following ways. 'I have failed. I can't cope with things. This is awful. This is terrible. I can't stand this any longer. I am a failure. Life is not worth living. I'm hopeless and no use for anything.' Faced with this, people try different ways of coping with what is quite clearly a desperately unhappy state of affairs. Most try alcohol because it temporarily changes the perception of the world so that it becomes bearable. While under the influence of alcohol, they often construct grandiose plans to fix the situations. They feel in control of their lives again. Unfortunately, alcohol does not change the situation, except to make it worse. Next morning, the euphoria has gone, the solutions are seen to be impossible, impractical dreams — and now they have a hangover as well.

The real disaster is for the group of people prone to alcoholism. Once begun, very few alcoholics can stop before the course is run. They continue until a collapse or major crisis gives them the chance to stop. Psychological dependence gets into full swing and, when joined with physical dependence and denial, the disastrous syndrome of alcoholism is in full flight.

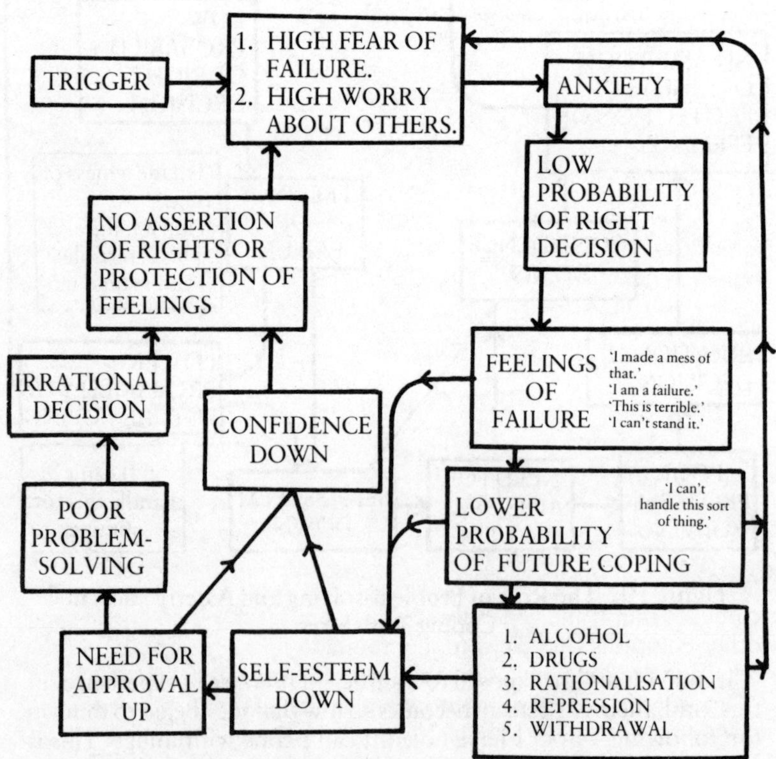

Figure 20. Drinking Alcohol, Taking Drugs and Other Habits as Inefficient Attempts to Cope With Failure

Now a large proportion of our society is unhappy and does not cope very well with life. Many take to alcohol, but they do not become alcoholics. Others attempt to cope by swallowing vast quantities of tranquillisers, anti-depressants and sleeping pills. Others try to rationalise their problems out of existence by finding 'reasons' for their inability to cope, usually blaming others for their own inadequacies. Some take to illegal drugs and others physically move to other suburbs, cities, states or even migrate to another country. Rarely do these coping attempts succeed, because the basic problem is not solved. Someone who is immature and dependent will soon become anxious in the new environment, and this will ultimately cause a fresh cycle of failure. Alcoholics, of course, often try all of these methods of coping.

The second-last stage in the failure-to-cope chain can now be added. This is these inefficient attempts to cope, which include alcoholic drinking, as shown in Figure 20.

It should be noted that the habit of drinking alcoholically begins in order to cope with feelings of failure and worthlessness. This habit, too, lowers the sense of self-esteem and feeds back directly into how similar tasks are appraised in future. They are seen as more threatening. This leads to greater levels of anxiety and to less efficient coping. This is the crux and the paradox of alcoholism. *Alcoholics drink to feel better because they are failing to cope. The result is that their level of coping drops even further and their lives become even more unbearable. Then they drink to feel better, this leads to worse failure, and round and round they go on the alcoholic treadmill.*

Changes in Thinking Processes as the Alcoholism Gets Worse

The more people drink on any occasion, the less rational they become, because alcohol depresses the action of the brain. As they begin to drink more and more because they cannot cope with significant areas of their lives, the less capable they are of making sensible decisions. They begin to act impulsively, doing the first thing that comes to mind, and generally act irrationally. Of course, anxiety and other emotions lead to irrational thinking in the first place, but the resulting drinking makes the thinking processes more irrational.

In order to cope with their lives people have to *think clearly and rationally*, instead of impulsively doing the first thing they think of. Furthermore, having worked out what to do, they have to have the *confidence* to do it and the *assertiveness* to say or do what they have decided. People who get in the failure-to-cope circle begin to think irrationally. Furthermore, even if they do work out what should be done, they lack the confidence and the assertiveness to act to carry out their decisions. Figure 21 completes the analysis of the meaning of 'I'm not coping'.

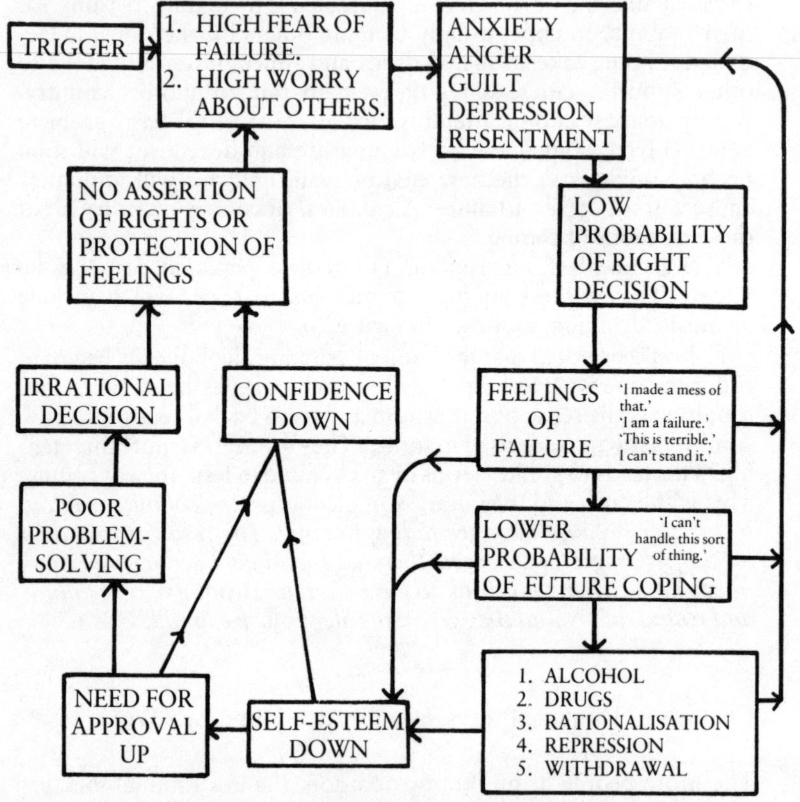

Figure 21. The Failure-to-cope Cycle

The word in the very first box stands for 'problem to be solved', 'choice to be made', 'environmental event' and many others. What is meant is that these are the problems to be solved, the choices to be made, or the decisions to be faced in our daily lives. The word 'trigger' has been chosen to stand for all of these. A trigger on a gun, like the choice, decision, problems or task, is harmless. It is what we do with the trigger that counts. According to this analysis of failure-to-cope, if people assess the situation, choice or decision as difficult and threatening to them they will get anxious. Once this happens they will almost certainly fail to cope. For recovering alcoholics, failure-to-cope is dynamite, and can lead to relapse drinking.

At a later stage the emotion of anger will be discussed at great length, because most alcoholics display a great deal of anger and the aggressive behaviour that follows. It will be shown that what has been said about anxiety applies to anger and that, like anxiety, anger is under our control, has harmful effects, but can be replaced by safe, assertive behaviour. The other negative emotions of depression, resentment, frustration, self-pity, jealousy and intolerance have the same disastrous effects on behaviour, and are included with anger and anxiety in the final model.

Summary

The discussion so far makes it clear that if individuals allow themselves to become anxious, angry or depressed, if they are full of resentment, self-pity, frustration, guilt or jealousy, they are likely to start to think irrationally and make a mess of their lives by saying and doing stupid things. This failure to cope will lead to a drop in their level of self-esteem and make them more dependent on others for approval. The tendency to think impulsively and irrationally will increase, and more and more failure will become likely. The inevitable end is that life will become so unbearable that a return to drinking will occur in what always is a futile attempt to make things better.

The recovery process is centred on finding ways to break this failure-to-cope chain, on examining the social pressures that are involved, on discovering whether biological inheritance plays a part, and on examining in detail how people who play significant roles in the lives of alcoholics can help. The role of prescribed drugs in the recovery process will be examined and the evidence about recovery rates and their relation to attempts to return to social drinking will be presented. However, let us define the recovery process as consisting primarily in learning how to cope with life without alcohol or other sedatives.

5

Coping with Stress

In the previous chapter it was claimed that failure to cope with the stresses of everyday living is the basic cause of alcoholics returning to drinking. The chain of events that can end in a serious relapse was outlined and the various factors that contribute to and determine why this chain runs an almost inevitable course were isolated. The inevitability begins early in the chain. Once one of the negative emotions of anxiety, anger, guilt, resentment, self-pity, depression and others, such as jealousy and frustration, arises, the possibility of a progress through the failure chain is high.

The key to coping with stress and avoiding a relapse clearly lies in preventing these negative emotions occurring at all. An inspection of the flow chart shows clearly that there are only two areas preceding the emotional arousal. These are the environmental events, which have been labelled as the trigger, and the evaluation or assessment phase, where these life situations are appraised. It is in one or both of these areas that the answer to coping with the stress that can lead to a return to drinking must lie. Either men and women change the problems that end up making them anxious, angry, depressed and so on or they change the way they interpret and evaluate these situations.

Changing the things that cause arousal of intense, unpleasant emotions is a possibility in some situations, but is not possible in most, because the behaviour of most other people is not under our control. Nor can we prepare for all the situations that can threaten our sense of well-being, because the list is infinitely long. People can and do perceive most situations as containing threats. All social situations contain areas of stress that can be perceived as threatening. Most people feel a need to perform well in their jobs, as husbands and wives, while meeting strangers, when asked to make a speech, in bringing up children, at school, in making things, in being a housewife, in planning a holiday, in earning a living and so on. Quite clearly we cannot be so totally prepared for everything that might happen that there is no event that will pose a threat to us. There will always be some situations that will catch us unaware. Thus, we must turn our attention to the way such situations are assessed or interpreted. This is the crux of this discussion. In order to prevent relapse drinking occurring, *alcoholics have to change the way they look at and interpret problem situations*. The way they interpret problem situations is determined by past experiences, is stored in the memory so that responses to situations become habitual. For alcoholics these habitual ways of thinking have led to disaster; so change is necessary.

This habitual way of responding, like all other habits, can be unlearned and new habits substituted. New responses do not call for a radical change in personality, and are relatively easy to do. They do call for constant practice, and the more help one can get in adopting the procedures the better. Since the way people think is under their personal control, so the way they go about recovering from alcoholism is under their control. With the exception of major events such as whether a war will begin, whether bank interest rates will rise or fall, or whether it will rain or not, people are in control of their own destiny. It is not these uncontrollable factors that cause them to return to drinking, but the way they react to the things that happen in their everyday lives. People get angry because they are criticised, they get depressed because they make mistakes, they become resentful because they are passed over for promotion, they feel sorry for themselves because of the wasted years spent in alcoholic drinking, and they become desperate because they cannot see how to overcome their loneliness.

All alcoholics are capable of rational thinking once they dry out and recover from the symptoms of physical dependence on alcohol. This programme assumes that this stage has been reached. *The very first step in recovery is to make a conscious decision to begin to think rationally about one's behaviour*, to give away the impulsive, irrational, emotional ways and to adopt a problem-solving approach to life.

Rational Problem-solving

Later, a whole chapter will be given over to problem-solving skills and their application to the recovery process. For the moment, it is necessary only to discuss the first two areas of the six that are involved in successful problem-solving. These are the *orientation* to the total process and the *generation of options*.

Earlier it was claimed that alcoholics become impulsive in their attitude towards the solution of the tasks, problems and decisions that crop up in their daily lives, and frequently resort to alcohol as a solution. The following points are a recommended orientation for alcoholics to bring to bear upon each and every situation, decision or problem that may arise. It really is a mini-philosophy to guide the day-to-day activities of alcoholics.

Orientation

1. My life has become unmanageable because of my alcoholism.
2. Complete abstinence is the only way to keep my alcoholism in check. Therefore I will not ever resort to alcohol as a way of helping to solve my problems.
3. The best way to solve problems is to keep calm and think clearly about ways of solving them.
4. I must protect my own rights and feelings at all times. However, if I insist on my rights I must also be tolerant of and consider the rights and feelings of others.
5. Life is just a series of problems to be solved.
6. I am in control of my own destiny. The choices I make will decide whether my future is happy or not.
7. I will consider many possibilities before I act.
8. When I have carefully decided on a course of action, I will act without worrying about what others will think of me.
9. If my action is unsuccessful, I will rethink the situation and try again.
10. There are some insoluble problems. These I must accept as insoluble.
11. I will ask for help whenever it is necessary.

The evidence for some of these points has not yet been presented. For example, the evidence for the necessity for life-long abstinence will be found in the chapter dealing with follow-up studies of alcoholics. The reason for including some of the other points should be self-evident. Anyone who has reached the stage of being treated for alcoholism and will not admit that his or her life has become unmanageable is deluding himself or herself. Denial of the fact of being an alcoholic before treatment is foolish but understandable. Continued denial after treatment is insane. The necessity for remaining calm even during a crisis raises from the previous evidence that getting upset in any of the ways previously discussed leads to failure and drinking. Keeping calm raises the probability of success.

Generation of options

Instead of acting impulsively, good problem-solvers try to think of every possible way the task could be tackled. Usually there are dozens, even hundreds, of ways to tackle a problem. The more possibilities that are generated, the more likely we are to come up with a viable solution. Even far-out, bizarre solutions should not be too easily discarded because they can sometimes be combined with more conventional ones to generate a good answer. Some of the problems with which we are faced demand quick solutions. Alcoholics have to have an immediate answer for what to do when offered an alcoholic drink, for example. However, many serious problems give us plenty of time to think up a whole series of options, to consider them carefully, and to act on the one most likely to succeed.

The choice of the best option will be guided by the points listed in the orientation phase. Thus any action involving drinking cannot be considered. Getting angry, anxious or depressed is overridden by the necessity to remain calm. The decision must take into account the rights and feelings of others, but failing to put a sensible decision into action out of fear that someone will pull the emotional rug out from under us, because of emotional dependence on others, because of a need for love or approval is a recipe for disaster. Once a rational solution is reached, it is necessary to act, be assertive and not fail to act because of dependency on others. Individuals who fail to assert their rights feel like worms and plunge back into the failure-to-cope chain.

The Coping-with-life Chain

The way for alcoholics to cope with life is to build up their sense of self-esteem so that they feel confident in being able to handle most of the problems of life that arise. In order to do this, it is necessary to think clearly about each situation, using the orientation points outlined above, to generate as many solutions as possible and to choose the one most likely to succeed. Having done this they must then put this plan into action without worrying two hoots about what other people will think about them and their actions. The aim is to remain calm so that they can think clearly. Once they remain calm, the success-with-coping chain will follow. Self-esteem will rise, confidence in handling this sort of situation will increase, and they will be more likely to be successful in this area in future. When they discover

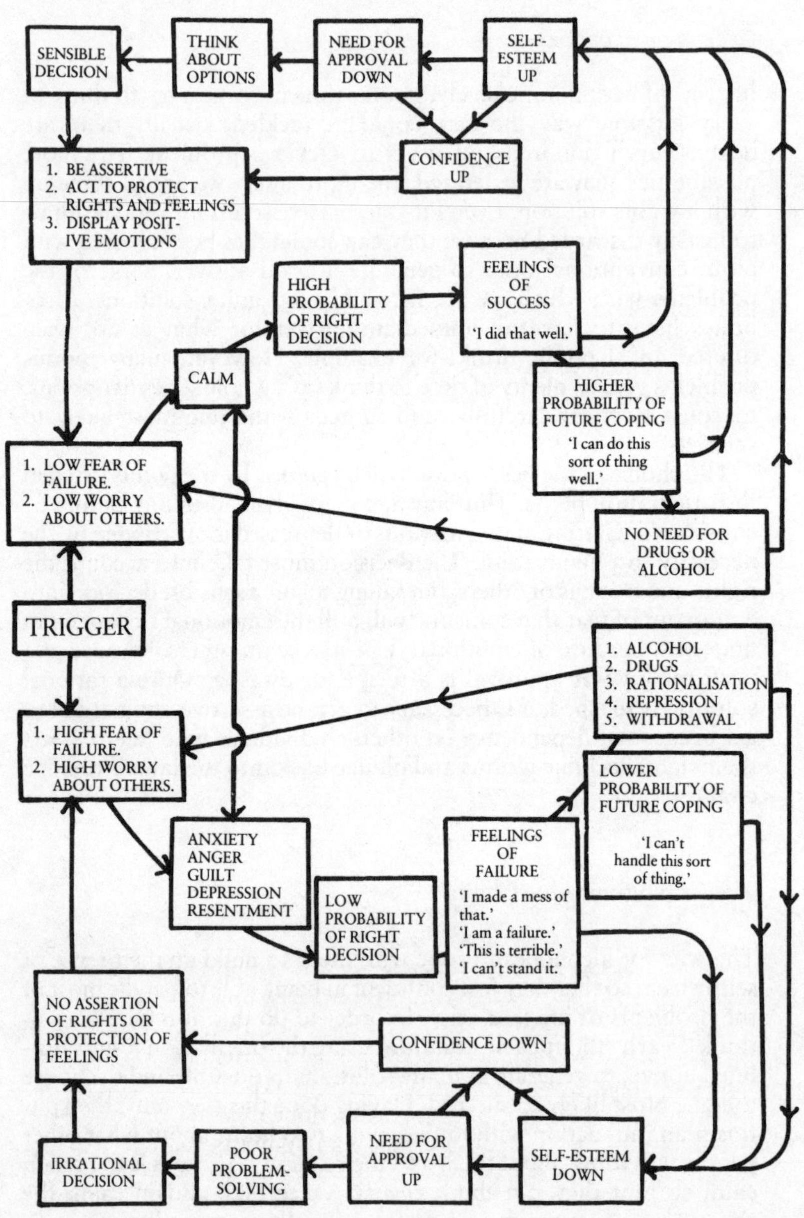

Figure 22. Coping Compared with Not Coping

that not worrying about what others think about them leads to success, they begin to understand the paradox of negative emotions. *The more they worry about pleasing other people, the less success they have and the less they please others. The less they worry about other people's reactions to them, the more success they have and the more they will be liked.* We will return to this paradox and make it quite explicit that this is not a self-centred, selfish approach, but exactly the opposite. But, first, Figure 22 shows the success-with-coping chain, which is the mirror-image, the opposite of the failure-to-cope chain. It shows in broad outline the steps necessary to cope with life. Notice that the final box shows a situation where alcohol is no longer needed at all. People who cope successfully do not need tranquillisers, sleeping pills or anti-depressants. Nor do they need alcohol.

The Difference Between Coping and Not Coping

Those who are likely to cope well remain calm. Those who fail to cope get anxious, angry, guilty, depressed, are full of resentment, self-pity, envy and jealousy. Once they learn to remain calm, the chances of making the right decision increase dramatically. If they succeed, they have feelings of success, this raises their level of self-esteem, and pushes up their level of confidence. They begin to feel that there is hope, and the future begins to look inviting. When their self-esteem is up, this is reflected in their future behaviour and increases the chances of future success. The chances of going back to drinking begin to recede and diminish. What, then, leads to these feelings of calmness? What steps do they take so that they get on the coping pathway?

Coping involves making a very deliberate attempt to think clearly and rationally at all times about the problems they have to solve, the choices they have to make, the tasks they have to do, and the actions they have to put into effect. Having made a decision after considering all the elements of the problem, the decision has to be put into effect without worrying about the reactions of others, because if they do worry about the responses of others, they may do nothing or choose another course of action less likely to solve the problem.

The crux of the problem lies in the distinction between WANTS and NEEDS. We all WANT others to like us, to appreciate us, to love us and to reward us in various ways for our actions and that is healthy. What is unhealthy and the factor that leads to anxiety and failure to cope is when we NEED others to like us, to appreciate us and to pat us on the head for our efforts. Emotional need for approval prevents rational thought, leads to emotional upset, to failure, and opens up the possibility of a return to drinking. Our lives should be directed at achieving the greatest possible happiness and towards bringing happiness to others. The paradox is that if we have an unhealthy need for approval by others, this leads to unhappiness. The distinction between INTERNAL versus EXTERNAL sources of rewards and satisfactions is related to WANTS and NEEDS.

The task for adolescents is to move from a state of childhood dependency where their actions are shaped by external reinforcements and rewards from parents, to a situation where they are prepared to make independent decisions and to carry them out because they have thought through the problem and feel sure they have made the right decision. *Reinforcement comes from an internal sense of satisfaction* in achieving success. If they get external approval, this is great; it is a bonus that makes them feel even better, but *they do not need this external approval.*

This is what maturity is all about. When an adolescent reaches the stage when he or she is emotionally independent of the parents in decision-making, maturity has been reached. He or she is an adult. This has nothing to do with rejection of the parents. The best families, the ones with the closest ties, are those where there is love, affection, mutual consideration of the rights and feelings of the members, but where all the members have outgrown the adolescent need for approval. They are all emotionally independent. They WANT the others to display affection towards them and to help them where necessary, and thrive and blossom with external praise, but they do not NEED these external forms of approval.

Those who do not outgrow their need for approval by others, who are externally directed and constantly need these external sources of reward may get into trouble when faced with difficult decisions. For example, take the case of an alcoholic woman whose main problem in life was that her husband worked eighteen hours a day even though they were well off financially, whose social life was non-existent, and who became so lonely and depressed that she began to drink heavily and finally landed in hospital for treatment for alcoholism.

On her return to the home she finally decided to do something about her workaholic husband by describing the situation and her desperate feelings of loneliness, and by asking him to work less and give her more companionship. On his return from work she became so afraid that he would tell her she was stupid and that he might abandon her that she said nothing. A few weeks later she was carried back to the hospital after returning to alcoholic drinking. This failure to act was based on emotional dependency. As is common, the need for approval led to an irrational action, or rather failure to act, and produced exactly the effect she was trying to avoid, because he did abandon her by seeking divorce because of her continued alcoholism. Her internal monologue may have gone like this. 'I know I have to fix this situation, but if I say anything he might get angry and tell me that I should be able to cope on my own and that I have no right to interfere in his business. He will probably say that we need the money because I have spent so much on alcohol. I couldn't stand that. That would be terrible. I'll keep quiet.'

Now in this case we have no way of knowing with any certainty what the outcome would have been if she had asserted her rights to share in the decision about this issue. In many similar cases, the men have been unaware of the results of their work habits, and when approached calmly and rationally have agreed to change. Certainly, in this case, assertion of her rights could hardly have produced a worse result. *Her failure lay in the assertion area*, which has three aspects. The first is that once we have come to a reasoned decision about the issue at hand, we must *act upon that decision* without worrying about the reactions and thoughts that other people might have. The second and very fundamental aspect is that at all times we must *protect our rights and feelings*. We have to learn to say 'No!' to requests, commands, invitations where agreeing would not be in our interests or cause us distress. The very first right an alcoholic has is the right to refuse to drink alcohol no matter how great the pressure. We have to learn how to handle criticism without getting upset and how to assert ourselves, to protect ourselves if we are criticised unjustly. Under no circumstances can an alcoholic let anyone walk over him or her because the result will be a feeling of inadequacy and anger and depression. Because of their low sense of self-esteem, alcoholics tend to lack assertion and rely on submission or aggression, neither of which work. Both submissive and aggressive behaviour need to be replaced by assertiveness, the socially acceptable but forceful expression of personal rights.

The third aspect of assertion is centred on the necessity to *publicly and overtly express positive emotions to other people*. These are expressions of *gratitude* to those who help us, *consideration* for their rights and feelings, *tolerance* of views with which we may not agree and the display of *affection* and *love* to those who are close and dear to us. Many alcoholics are very low in these areas. Many have been brought up in families where the overt expression of these emotions is rare indeed. Many, especially men, have come to believe that the expression of such emotions is evidence of unmanliness, and they regard men who openly display such emotions with grave suspicion. This is despite the evidence that the pay-off for those who learn to genuinely express these emotions is high indeed.

People like being thanked, praised and told that they have done a good job. When someone helps us and we express our gratitude, they feel good, and this makes them respond more positively towards us. The greatest single factor in divorce is the failure to consider the rights of the partner and to let him or her know by our behaviour that he or she is loved. It is not sufficient to know that you love someone. You must tell them so and behave in such ways that demonstrate your feelings.

This assertion of positive emotions is not restricted to the immediate loved ones. Even at work, consideration of the rights and feelings of others, kindness, consideration and gratitude are essential elements in recovery. People, both higher and lower in occupational status, will respond to this expression by feeling more positive about you. This aspect of assertion counters the possibility of not seeking the approval of others or being dependent on their approval. Taken together, independence of others' approval and the expression of positive emotions form the ideal mix.

Some Implications of the Model

1. It is quite clear that when problems arise that result in us getting angry, we cannot blame the problem, the event, or the person for our anger, no matter what he or she did. The reason is that the event has to be assessed; the impressions or perceptions of the incident enter our brain, are processed and evaluated. Only if we evaluate them as a threat to our sense of self-esteem, to our very being do we get upset. If we think rationally about what is happening and try to work out a way to deal with it and do not worry about what the other person will think, we will remain calm and probably succeed in dealing successfully with the problem.

What is being implied here is that *we are in control of our own emotions*. We decide whether to be anxious or calm, resentful or accepting, angry or placid. No person, event or situation can make us angry unless we decide to get angry. The level of State Anxiety will rise only if, in our evaluation of the situation, we are afraid of negative evaluation or fail to assert ourselves. It is not the strangers in the room that causes the surge in anxiety, but the way we interpret or evaluate the situation; and that evaluation is under our control.

2. For alcoholics, this line of reasoning can be extended to the

conclusion that *he or she cannot blame anyone else for their alcoholism or for any relapse that might occur*. No one or no event can cause an alcoholic to return to drinking. Men frequently blame their wives for their relapses. This is illogical because no matter what the wife may do, this is evaluated by the alcoholic. If his assessment is: 'This is awful. This is terrible, What's the use?' he may go back to drinking, but it is his evaluation of the situation that leads him to choose to return to drinking. The adoption of a different strategy, such as: 'Her behaviour is ridiculous. How can I get her to change?' followed by a rational, calm way of trying to solve the problem might well save the day. Individuals are in charge of their own behaviour, including the decision to resume drinking, and cannot blame anyone or anything else for a crazy decision to return to alcohol.

Both male and female alcoholics who have not learned how to cope successfully with life are expert at inventing plausible and implausible excuses (usually called reasons) for their relapses. Women blame their husbands, their obstetric and gynaecological problems, their children leaving home and their loneliness. Men blame their health, their work and their children refusing to leave home for their return to alcoholic drinking. There is never a valid reason except that they haven't learned to cope. Anyone can learn to cope with anything including death without recourse to alcohol if she or he tries hard enough. Emotions of sadness, disappointment and even desolation are normal and natural as they do not make people behave in the stupid ways that anger and resentment do.

Living in the Past — Guilt and Resentment

Recovery from alcoholism is a day-to-day process, starting with the final drink. It occurs in the present with some planning for the future. In our analysis of failure to cope, guilt belongs with the negative emotions that lead to failure. Let it be admitted that the lives of most alcoholics have included many shameful, illegal, immoral and stupid actions. The advice to alcoholics is to repair any damage, physical, financial, legal, personal or whatever that can be fixed, make amends for what can be amended and then forget the past. The fact of being an alcoholic must be accepted, because that has important implications for what can and what can't be done in the present and in the future.

Dwelling on the past, feeling guilty about the devastation that was caused, feeling guilty about being an alcoholic or allowing anyone to make him or her feel guilty is not only a waste of time but is actively destructive. What has happened in the past is now history and nothing can change that. Guilt and resentment about being an alcoholic are extremely common. These emotions are harmful because they lead to irrational action in the present and increase the chances of relapse very markedly.

The problem of guilt can come from external sources. Spouses and families are the main culprits. Statements such as: 'If only you hadn't spent a fortune on alcohol we would now own a car and a house' are commonly made to the alcoholic. These remarks can lead to guilt feelings and trigger off the relapse behaviour, which of course leads to even worse financial situations. Families of alcoholics need to accept the fact of alcoholism, to accept that what happened in the past cannot be changed and that they, too, need to live in the present, making it as happy as possible. Making the alcoholic feel guilty is not likely to achieve this end.

Tolerance for Failure

The procedures outlined here are designed to increase the rate of success in dealing with problems and situations encountered by alcoholics. However, no matter how calm they remain, how clearly they think about the problem and how assertive they are, they will sometimes not succeed. No-one in this world succeeds all the time. The point about this system is that it guarantees a high degree of success and this builds up a sense of self-esteem and confidence. Once this point is reached, it is relatively easy to tolerate incidents of failure. They have to think in the following way if they do not succeed, even after taking all the right steps. 'Well, that did not work. Stiff luck for me. I'll go back and re-think the problem and try another solution. I have simply made a mistake.' Everybody makes mistakes, and this has to be accepted as a fact of life. One way of handling lack of success is never to regard such an event as a failure. If a person has thought the problem through carefully and done her or his best to solve it, then he or she has not really failed, and certainly lack of success cannot rationally be translated into 'I am a failure', a common habit of alcoholics.

Some alcoholics have minor relapses where they become upset over some failure or criticism and have a few drinks to enable them to cope. This is crazy and dangerous, because these actions contain the possibility of a major return to uncontrolled, full-scale alcoholic drinking. If it is a momentary, short-term relapse it belongs in the mistake category. The best advice is as follows:

1. Stop drinking.
2. Admit that you have made a serious mistake in dealing with the problem.
3. Analyse the situation carefully to see what *caused* the relapse.
4. Seek help if necessary, especially from AA sources.
5. Learn from the mistake, so that you don't make the same mistake again.
6. Carefully review the 'coping-with-life programme', don't feel guilty about the break and start again.

Tolerance for the Mistakes of Others

If an alcoholic insists on his or her right to make a mistake, he or she must grant this right to others. Few people will know as much as the alcoholic about what is involved in recovery from excessive, uncontrolled drinking. Many, with the best intentions in the world, will do stupid things in an attempt to protect the alcoholic. One of the rights an alcoholic has is to decide if and when the knowledge of the alcoholism shall be made known to others. However, if a family member tells a host or hostess at a party not to give the recovering alcoholic a drink 'because he is an alcoholic', this should not lead to a flare-up of anger and resentment, and certainly not to a defiant decision to accept a drink. The family member should have respected the alcoholic's right to decide whether to make his or her alcoholism public. But the alcoholic should also simply accept what has happened as the the simple mistake it is, and draw the family member aside to explain his or her rights. The advisability of making the fact of alcoholism public knowledge will be discussed fully later.

Acceptance

One of the greatest hurdles that an alcoholic has to jump is to accept the fact that he or she is an alcoholic. The second hurdle, which follows immediately, is to accept the fact that this means that the remainder of life must be lived without the prop of alcohol. Now the AA philosophy is that the alcoholics should resolve not to have a drink for the next twenty-four hours. The next day they commit themselves not to drink for the next twenty-four hours. Days stretch into weeks, weeks to months, and months to years. This method is of great help to many, but the aim is the same: life-long abstinence.

The chances of anyone landing into hospital for treatment for alcoholism and not being an alcoholic are so remote that they can be dismissed as impossible. People without the disease of alcoholism do not lose control over their intake or become dependent on it. Non-alcoholics do not lie about their drinking intake, hide their liquor in sheds, cupboards, hedges and boots of cars. Nor do they get upset when someone suggests that they might have a drinking problem. Normal drinkers don't drink two drinks where the others in the party have one. Social drinkers don't need a few stiff ones in the morning to get their 'heart started', nor do they drink in toilets. Proneness to alcoholism leads to some or all of these signs of alcoholism. The main thing, however, is that alcoholic drinking causes significant problems in the family, in marriages and at work; it results in legal and financial problems. Any drinker whose drinking has led to such problems and continues to deny that he or she is an alcoholic is crazy and bent not only on self-destruction but on ruining the lives of many others as well. *The first step in recovery from alcoholism is to accept the fact that you are an alcoholic*, that you are prone to alcoholism, and that the disease can be arrested but never cured.

If an alcoholic begins to drink again, he or she will almost inevitably return to uncontrolled alcoholic drinking. The evidence from AA and research studies clearly supports this conclusion. *The second step is to accept the fact that this means that life-long abstinence is the only solution.* The difficulty with the second step lies primarily in the fact that our society is structured around alcohol. Births are celebrated by drinking; so are engagements, marriages, arrivals and departures. We celebrate when our team wins, we drown our sorrows when it loses. If a friend visits, the immediate response is: 'What will you have to drink?' And we don't mean tea or coffee. For a large proportion of the population, life is centred on alcohol.

Yet there are significant sections of our society where alcohol either provides no problem or it is not used at all. The Jewish population uses alcohol, but drunkenness is virtually unknown; it is unthinkable in their way of life. Mormons and Moslems and Baptists and Seventh Day Adventists forbid the use of alcohol and survive happily without it. The excessive use of alcohol in our society is a habit, a custom, but *it is not necessary to drink to be part of society*. Fully recovered alcoholics join in everything, go to parties, join in celebrations, and live full and happy lives without drinking alcohol. One of the reasons AA works is that recovering alcoholics can see others leading healthy, happy, alcohol-free lives. Yet the stories of other alcoholics' past lives are horrific and often bear a strong resemblance to their own. Acceptance of the fact of alcoholism and acceptance of the fact that this means that you the alcoholic can never drink again are the first steps in recovery.

Denial

Denial involves self-deception. Whenever an individual knows deep down that she or he has made a mess of things by his or her actions or lack of action and refuses to voice this knowledge or even to accept that the cause lies in his or her own fear, hatred and resentment, then she or he is attempting to cope by denial. Denial as a defence mechanism probably starts early in life when the child does something that makes him or her feel guilty. For example, he may break a window with a ball and say to his parents, 'It wasn't my fault, was it?' If he can get his parents to agree, then he feels safer and more comfortable. The habit of denial then grows stronger and reaches the stage where a person can lie to herself or himself and to others without feeling guilty.

In adult life denial is much more subtle, as the following examples demonstrate. A man who was constantly passed over for promotion was very resentful, but blamed the success of these younger men and women on worming their way into favour with their superiors by drinking with them after hours. This man was denying the actual reason, which lay in his inability to get along with others because of his personality traits, which included an angry, abrasive manner. A female executive blamed her lack of promotion on sex discrimination, whereas in fact she lacked the skills involved in the import-export business in which she was involved and constantly refused to accept advice to take courses to acquire these skills.

Before admission to treatment for alcoholism most alcoholics deny that the problems that are mounting up are caused by their drinking and maintain that the problems are causing the drinking and once the problems are solved the need to drink will disappear. As they are alcoholics, they will continue to drink even if the problem does vanish; and other excuses will be found or invented. Almost certainly, the reason for the denial is the same as that of the child. They know that they feel bad and have to deny that there is a problem in order to feel better. The alcoholic must deny he or she has a drinking problem because the prospect of trying to cope with life without dulling the senses with alcohol is highly threatening and even unthinkable. *Alcoholics are failing to cope*, cannot see how they will ever cope and this makes them see life as awful, terrible and something that can't be faced without alcohol, which allows them to see the world in a much more rosy light and to see some hope for the future. When the effect of the alcohol wears off, the despair returns, and a further plunge into a sea of alcohol becomes necessary.

After treatment, many alcoholics continue to deny the fact of their alcoholism. Once they are physically fit, have recovered their health and have begun to eat properly, they try social, controlled drinking. The reasons for the return to drinking and the denial of the alcoholism are the same as before. They have not learned how to cope with their jobs, their wives, husbands or children; they have not learned what actions to take to counter their feelings of loneliness and so on. They believe they can have a few drinks because *life without alcohol and the activities they associate with drinking cannot be tolerated.* Instead of working at solving their problems, they drink. Because of their proneness to alcoholism and their denial of it, they soon revert to full-scale alcoholic drinking. This can and does occur repeatedly for some alcoholics, who go in and out of treatment repeatedly. A few survive relatively intact after as many as fourteen or fifteen admissions. Many die from cirrhosis of the liver, suffer massive brain damage or suffer from the other diseases that accompany chronic alcoholism. In order to survive, alcoholics cannot continue their denial, because recovery is dependent on continued sobriety, and sobriety will not occur while denial of the fact of their alcoholism continues.

Summary

Recovery from alcoholism has been shown to depend on learning how to cope with stress. This means alcoholics have to keep the following principles firmly in mind.

1. Alcoholics have to accept the fact that they are alcoholics.
2. They have to accept the fact that they must become permanent non-drinkers.
3. They have to adopt a rational, clear-thinking approach to life where they calmly work out what to do by considering all the options.
4. They have to assert themselves and carry out their decisions.
5. They have to protect their rights and feelings. They should not be submissive on the one hand or aggressive on the other. They should take the middle ground and assert themselves so that no-one ever tramples on their rights or upsets them.

6. They should stop worrying about what people will think of them. If they carefully consider all the options and then carry out the best plan they can think of, people will come to approve of them. *Need* for approval is dangerous.
7. They should express kindness, gratitude, love, affection to others quite overtly and show consideration for the rights and feelings of others, which makes others feel good and makes them respond more positively towards them.
8. Above all, they should choose not to get angry, anxious, depressed, resentful, jealous, envious or full of self-pity. These are destructive emotions, which lead to relapse.
9. The secret lies in alcoholics changing their ways of thinking so that they concentrate on ways of fixing the things that cause them to get upset. If they are impulsive, dependent and unassertive, they will almost certainly fail. Failure leads to anxiety. Anxiety leads to failure. Failure leads to a drop in self-esteem. Low self-esteem can lead to a relapse.
10. Alcoholics are in control of their own destiny. Nothing that happens to them can *make* them drink. If they cope there will be no need to drink, and coping can be learned.

In the next chapter the role of anger and aggression will be taken up together with the allied emotions of frustration, resentment and depression. The dangers of anger will be shown by describing situations within the family setting and within the work place that commonly lead up to anger and resulting aggressive behaviour.

6
Anger and Aggression in Alcoholics

In the preceding chapters it was stated that anger and the aggressive behaviour that often follows feelings of intense anger are luxuries that alcoholics cannot afford, because anger often precedes and in fact precipitates a return to drinking. Fortunately, anger can be controlled, it is a habit that can be discarded and replaced with the adaptive habit of being assertive.

Anger, like anxiety, is a reaction to circumstances that arise. Anyone can have a high proneness to anger and this is called Trait Anger. The anger felt in a given situation is State Anger, and this can be controlled in the same way that State Anxiety can be controlled. Anger has devastating effects on the capacity to think clearly and profound effects on problem-solving capacity. Anyone who is frequently angry will attest to their continual frustration at not performing at their best because they lost their temper, allowing others who may have known less about the issue to win the day.

Anger probably is even more damaging than anxiety because it is so highly visible to those around us and it upsets them. Anger not only interferes with problem-solving but anger and the accompanying aggression also alienate those who are forced to witness it. Anxiety is less visible in many instances and will have fewer of these bad side-effects. However, both anxiety and anger can be controlled by the same process, by choosing not to be angry or anxious.

The Effects of Anger

1. Irrational thoughts

When we are angry we begin to think irrationally because the brain becomes flooded with the bodily sensations that accompany being angry. A recovering alcoholic, falsely accused by her husband of drinking while he was at work, became so angry that a violent argument developed in which many hurtful things were said. The damage caused by her previous drinking was thrown in her face. She responded with damaging comments on his sexual inadequacy, leading him to storm out and her to seek the nearest bottle to 'calm her down' and remove the guilt feelings aroused by the fight.

A frequent cause of anger is criticism of any kind. Few people have learned how to handle criticism and behave quite irrationally following the anger it has aroused. Two basic types of criticism have the capacity to make us angry, and each can be divided into two. The first is criticism that is *fair and just*. This sort can be subdivided into situations in which mistakes can be fixed and those in which the mistake can't be fixed. The way to handle criticism of any sort begins with calmly assessing whether it is fair or not. If it is fair and the error can be fixed the way to handle this is easy. The error is admitted and fixed. For example, you may say, 'Sorry. Yes, I did make a mistake. I'll fix it up right away.' No one gets angry and the problem is solved. Alcoholics, like everyone else, make mistakes and have to learn to accept fair criticism. If the criticism is fair, but the damage can't be repaired, the way to handle it is not by getting angry or depressed because of the mistake but simply to admit the error and try not to make that same mistake again. You might say 'Yes, you are right. I did make a mess of that. I'll learn from that and try not to make that mistake again.'

Handling *unfair criticism* is harder, but if anger is allowed to surge, the outcome can be disastrous. Again, there are two sorts of unfair criticism. The first is where the person making the criticism is wrong and genuinely believes you have gone wrong when you haven't. The second is nasty, vicious criticism, aimed at blaming you when you have done nothing wrong. In both these cases, not only do you have to think calmly and rationally about the problem, but you have to be very assertive to protect yourself from the unfair criticism. If you look closely at the situation and decide that you have not made the error for which you are being criticised, but decide that the other person doesn't understand or has just made a mistake, the thing to do is to assert your rights, to protect your feelings by trying to convince the other person that he or she is wrong. 'I understand what you are saying, but I think you are wrong. I've looked at it closely, but there doesn't seem to me to be anything wrong. Perhaps you didn't take into consideration these other issues.' Proceed to try and convince the other that he or she is wrong.

The most difficult situation, in some ways, is dealing with nasty, deliberately vicious criticism. Assertive behaviour is needed to throw the criticism firmly but calmly back at the person doing the criticising. In a work situation a product might be criticised as follows, 'You idiot. That's a shoddy job. You alcoholics are all alike. You shouldn't be given a job.' Instead of flying into a rage, you might calmly say, 'O.K. I've had a good look at this and I can't see anything wrong. Four times in the last week you have criticised me unfairly. Let's get an independent opinion from the boss. You obviously know nothing about alcoholism or you wouldn't say what you said. Let's see if you know more about the job.'

The general way of handling criticism has to be adapted to fit particular situations, but the principles are clear. In order to handle these situations, you have to think carefully and calmly, assess what category the criticism falls into and, at all times, protect yourself from unfair criticism not with anger and aggressive behaviour, but by a cool, assertive approach.

2. People who get angry alienate whoever is on the receiving end of their aggressive behaviour and those who witness it

During their alcoholic lives most drinkers succeed in losing friends, alienating their wives, husbands and children to some degree, because excessive drinking is frequently accompanied by either or both physical and verbal abuse while the alcoholic is angry. Families of alcoholics suffer the most from physical assaults or angry, sarcastic, irrational, verbal attacks, and the families resent it. Friends, relatives and workmates who sometimes witness these attacks are embarrassed or revolted by what they see and hear and frequently opt out altogether.

Few, if any, people enjoy watching an angry person or two angry people. Angry scenes often erupt at parties where large quantities of alcohol are being consumed, people mishear and misinterpret conversations and fights and rows flare up. Those unfortunate enough to witness these scenes are unlikely to come again, because there are social sanctions against the open display of anger and aggression in almost all levels of our society. The stupid, irrational behaviour that flows out of anger is more than most people can tolerate.

3. Those who become angry and aggressive often feel guilty about it when they calm down

After an outburst of anger, most people regret what they have said and done because they see how stupidly they have behaved. Usually, however, the other person has responded in an equally irrational way, and neither will admit error; and they may not speak for days, months or even a lifetime. Both feel guilty, but this guilt has the same effect as anger and anxiety. It leads to further irrational behaviour. Many marriages where there is still love and affection break up following such an angry, stormy and aggressive encounter. The feelings of guilt are very damaging to emotional well-being.

4. *The angry, aggressive person will almost always lose if he or she comes up against a cool, rational opponent*

There are some people who are expert at getting others angry. This is frequently seen at meetings, where someone pushing a certain line will deliberately bait the opposition. Once the opposition gets angry, he or she loses track of the argument, becomes personally abusive, says stupid, illogical things and finally loses out.

5. *One of the quickest ways to return to drinking is to continue to get angry*

Accounts given at AA meetings of relapses are frequently about people losing control, becoming angry and aggressive, and then heading for the nearest supply of booze. They have failed to cope, know that they have failed, and cannot cope with their feelings without alcohol.

Blane (1968), who worked with alcoholics in the USA, puts forward the claim that most, if not all, alcoholics are angry people. No matter whether they behave as if they are or not does not matter according to Blane. As he puts it, 'we also know from the psychotherapeutic experience that the angry wishes and aggressive impulse of alcoholics are intense, no matter how they behave'. The reason why many alcoholics appear to be calm and mild is that they bottle up their anger. Either they feel that their anger makes sense to them, but it will not make sense to others; or they are afraid to vent their anger openly because of the public sanctions that exist against the expression of anger in aggressive behaviour. The cause of this anger, according to Blane, is frustration of dependency needs or need for approval. When people go through their adolescent years without achieving the emotional independence from their parents that is the major task of adolescence, they still depend on parents or drinking groups, or a spouse for support. This causes conflict between dependency needs and the need to be independent, and anger results. For many, the anger can be expressed only covertly: in sarcasm, teasing, provocation or in aggressive driving of motor vehicles. The other result, of course, is to turn the anger inwards to blame the self. We become critical of ourselves, full of self-disgust at our inability to cope with life: this is called depression. Chronic depression, of course, is a profoundly painful and unpleasant emotion, which many try to drown in alcohol.

When we are angry, the possibility of solving the problems that confront us in any satisfactory way is absolutely minimal, because the anger floods the whole body, including the brain, with unpleasant demands for immediate action. Depression, which can be thought of as the inward-turning to anger, has the same ultimate effect, but has the added elements of a sense of futility, lack of control over what is happening and of hopelessness that rules out virtually any reasonable attempt to solve the problem. Aggression against the self can hardly be regarded as a rational solution to any situation.

Arguments Against Giving Up Anger and Aggression

Some of the alcoholics exposed to these ideas during their recovery period in hospital resist strongly the idea of giving up anger, even though they concede that it is necessary to give up the other negative emotions. Almost certainly, as Blane argues, all alcoholics are angry, and they have used their anger and aggression as a way of trying to cope with the frustrations of life. Until they are convinced that there is another and better way of coping, that is by being assertive, they advance a number of arguments against giving up their anger.

1. *Bottling up anger is dangerous*

A common argument is that if anger is bottled up it may erupt in a massive blowout, like a volcano. This argument is easily countered, because the advice given here is to *remain calm and not to allow yourself to get angry. If a person does not get angry, then it is not bottled up*, so there is no volcano waiting to explode.

2. *It is natural to be angry and aggressive*

This argument is based on the premise that anger and aggression are necessary to protect ourselves. There is no doubt that man is a very angry animal. Anger is evident from birth, if dependency needs for food, liquid, warmth and shelter are not met. Removal of a bottle or nipple from a feeding child usually evokes an instant response, which looks very much like rage. Thus many alcoholics claim that it is *natural* to be angry and aggressive, and that it is *unnatural* not to be so. The same argument is used about anxiety, when reference is made to the adaptive function of anxiety. In fact, the only adaptive function is where there is a threat of physical harm. Now undoubtedly the release of adrenalin where physical danger threatens is adaptive, because it allows for greater speed in escape. This is the only adaptive function present. However, it is very rarely that threats of physical danger are claimed to be the primary source of alcoholism or of relapse drinking. We get angry because of perceived threats to our sense of psychological well-being; because we think we are failing in our jobs, or in our various roles in the domestic scene, or in countless trivial day-to-day problem situations. In every one of these areas negative emotions such as anger and the consequent aggression are likely to be unadaptive and to create more problems than they solve. Anger leads to ineffective problem-solution in almost every area of our daily lives. If anger is adaptive it is only in the rare cases of actual threats to *physical* well-being. Even here it is doubtful if anger is the best response. A rapid, calm assessment of threats to physical well-being may lead to a better solution, a coolly planned counter-offensive is more likely to succeed than a plan constructed while angry.

Many of the claims for aggression being natural stem from the work of ethologists such as Konrad Lorenz, whose work with animals suggests that aggression in the defence of territory and of the sexual partner is instinctive. This instinctive aggressive behaviour has then been attributed to man by writers such as Robert Ardrey, a playwright turned science writer, Desmond Morris and Raymond Dart. This attribution fails to take into account the highly developed brain of man, which, theoretically at least, enables mankind to work together in groups for the common good, to develop co-operative behaviour rather than competitive behaviour for the better life of all, and to use his rational powers to plan for the future. Undoubtedly animals develop some spectacular forms of co-operative behaviour also, but mankind has infinitely more capacity for this through the use of his highly developed capacity to think of the future. Whether mankind is actually using this capacity for rational thinking in order that life is coped with happily is very debatable. Certainly a lot of thought is given to acquiring money and material possessions, but these do not guarantee happiness. The best chance we have of happiness is to lead our lives rationally, and this rules out anger and aggression.

3. People who are not angry and aggressive allow others to walk all over them

This is a ridiculous argument in view of what has been said previously. It is quite clear that we must not let others walk over us, but when we get angry that is usually what happens. We lose control over the situation, and the others win. In order to win we must keep calm. The argument that we must be aggressive probably means that we need to be aggressive if someone is trying to kill us or physically injure or maim us. What people do in the face of insane behaviour is best left to their own judgement. If you have to fight to protect your life, do so. This is not what we are talking about. The thing we are talking about is the necessity of keeping calm during the daily affairs of our lives. The anger and aggression that ends in people going back to alcoholic drinking is almost always a response to some relatively trivial family, social or work situation where we lose control. Sometimes these are more serious, like the threat of divorce or the threat of losing a job, but even these are not helped and usually made worse by losing our temper.

4. *It is also claimed that children need to be taught to be aggressive or their fellows will bully them*

This is a harder argument to counter because children are not capable of the same level of reasoned thought as adults. They cannot see that being aggressive is not in their interests. Furthermore, many experience bullying, which cannot be tolerated and has to be stopped. The best way of countering bullying, if it can be done, is to organise a group of the smaller, weaker ones to collectively threaten the bully. This has worked very well in many such occasions. The problem in teaching children to respond with anger and aggression is that these learned habits will carry over into adult life, where they create trouble because they are applied to situations other than those involved in physical attack by others. However, we are not concerned here with children but with the recovery of adults from alcoholism. For them, anger and aggression have enormous potential for harm and a return to the misery of alcoholic drinking.

Anger and Changes in Thinking

The changes in the way way we think while intoxicated or very angry are quite similar to the well-documented research into intoxicated aggression. As well as a lowering in general ability to cope effectively with anything but the simplest situations, there are two quite specific changes that occur. These are:

1. An increase in risk-taking behaviour

There is clear evidence from studies of risk-taking that the greater the state of intoxication the lower the capacity to assess risks accurately. In the area of psychology devoted to the study of risk-taking behaviour, techniques of measuring risk-taking have been devised. The results show that, like any other human characteristic, individuals vary in their willingness to take risks. Like anxiety, for example, this risk-taking behaviour varies with the circumstances. When people are studied under various levels of intoxication, the risk-taking behaviour rises, as in Figure 23.This is seen in everyday living when a man staggers out of a bar or a party, brushes aside the efforts of his friends to restrain him from driving, gets into his car insisting that he is competent to drive. Off he goes with what seems like a reasonable chance of being involved in an accident where he and others may be killed or seriously injured. This is an extremely aggressive act and bears out the risk-taking theory. The risk may even be acknowledged but the driving continues.

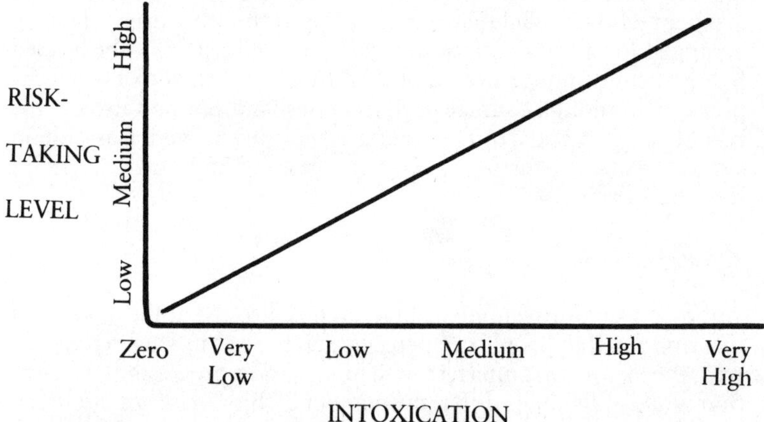

Figure 23. Risk-taking Depending on Level of Intoxication

Similarly, risk-taking increases as anger increases, even without the presence of alcool. Quite sober people take the most incredible risks at times when they experience a sudden surge of anger. Car driving seems to be an area where this is most clear. Many normally calm people go quite berserk if another driver cuts sharply in front of them, pulls suddenly out from the kerb causing them to brake sharply or steals a parking space under their nose. High speed chases, heated verbal exchanges and physical fights following such incidents are common. These exchanges sometimes end in someone, perhaps an innocent third party, being injured or even killed, in expensive legal actions and general chaos. The level of thinking involved here is hardly rational.

For alcoholics, especially, control over such surges of anger is essential as the following illustration shows. This woman, an excellent driver with an unblemished driving record, had recently left a hospital where she had received treatment for her first bout of alcoholic drinking. Her husband was so relieved to see her free of her compulsive drinking that he bought her a new car. Three weeks later, while stopped at a traffic light, a car ran into the rear of her car causing considerable damage. To use her words, 'I went off the planet with anger, burst out of my car and began to abuse the other driver.' After a short time, the other driver backed up, roared past and was never seen again. The woman then realised that, in her anger, she had forgotten to take the elementary steps required in such situations. She had no note of the registration number of the car, she had not asked for the driver's name, she had not found out if he was insured, and she had failed to enlist the aid of a witness to the accident who left while she was shouting at the other driver. Having arranged for a tow-truck to take her car to be repaired, she headed for the nearest liquor store and was stupefied with vodka when she plucked up enough courage to ring her husband. She had also run the risk of being attacked by the other driver during her verbal assault. In similar incidents, further deliberate ramming and physical assault have occurred.

2. *Changes in input-processing*

Another area of psychological research is directed at the amount of information that people can perceive and process in a given time and with the factors that interfere with information-processing. It is clear that while individuals differ, the number of 'bits' of information that can be processed by the brain in a short time-span is quite limited, and that many factors can make this processing capacity even less. When we are working under stressful conditions or are angry, our capacity to process incoming information declines markedly. Research into driving capacity under various levels of blood alcohol content shows that even experienced healthy drivers, racing drivers and so on decline in driving performance after drinking. Simple tasks such as reacting to simulated traffic lights are performed less well. Steering and braking skills decline as more and more stimuli have to be attended to and processed and as the blood alcohol level increases. The common belief that we drive better with a few drinks is just not true, because driving demands the constant processing of a vast amount of information. As long as everything is normal we may cope, but a sudden emergency makes demands that are unlikely to be met by a brain working at well below its peak capacity.

If a man jumps into a car and speeds off following a domestic row, his driving skills will decline markedly because his intense anger will limit his capacity to process information. He may fail to notice, or at least to interpret as dangerous, a ball rolling out of a gateway onto a road and run the risk of killing the child who suddenly appears running after the ball. Driving demands a high degree of concentration on the hundreds of constantly changing bits of information to be processed. While angry, our capacity to process drops markedly.

In the domestic scene, anger is loaded with danger, because while angry we fail to perceive the danger signals and continue to say and do things that lead to domestic chaos and even to divorce. Recovering alcoholics need domestic brawls like they need a hole in the head, so they have to push aside feelings of anger whenever they start to surge and try to remain calm and to think how to fix the problem that has led to the anger.

Controlling Anger

Repeating the main point, anger is not caused by others, by car accidents or anything but by the way we react. *Anger is a habit* that we can decide to give up here and now. *Being calm is a habit we can learn and practise.* Once we make a firm decision to give up getting angry, it is not necessary to become despondent if the emotion reappears. Anger is a habit developed over a lifetime, and it can be expected to reappear in all the old situations that previously led to its upsurge. The thing to do is to consciously push it away, consciously refuse to get angry and be determined to keep calm. (The vertical arrow in Figure 22 shows the possibility of changing from being angry to being calm.) Gradually the habit of remaining calm will replace the anger habit. Even so, the anger gets so intense at times that it takes over and causes chaos.

An account of a male alcoholic's progress with controlling his anger, which had figured prominently in his alcoholic life, is interesting. In a three-year period, his anger got out of control on three occasions and on each occasion there were unfortunate consequences. The first occurrence was centred on a motor vehicle. The transmission on his car was playing up intermittently, so he took it to be repaired, which was a major and fairly costly job. The next day he left on a holiday with his family to a beach resort some 600 miles away. During this holiday the problem returned, so three weeks and 3000 miles later he took it back to the service station. When he went to pick up the car, he received another account for the repair. He argued, calmly at first, that he had already paid for the repair and insisted on a free service. When the serviceman argued that it could be a fresh problem because 3000 miles had been travelled, he refused to listen and became abusive. The serviceman lost his temper and made a rash statement that the firm could not guarantee the work (meaning not in these conditions). The supervisor was called, insisted on payment because of the time lapse, and the distance travelled since the service, but threatened to sack the serviceman for what he had said, because the firm did guarantee its work.

Thinking the matter over later, the driver could see that there was some merit in the firm's argument, recognised that his anger had led to the possible loss of employment for the serviceman, so he apologised for losing his temper and paid the bill. The next day, the problem recurred, and he rang the supervisor, who this time did get the problem fixed without cost.

On another occasion he lost his temper over a trivial family incident, which led to a six-month period where one family member would not speak to him. The final occasion happened at work where he was blamed for something he did not do, failed to assert himself, became angry and depressed, and was almost dismissed from his job. Fortunately he came to his senses quickly and explained the situation calmly and was reinstated. For the remainder of the three-year period he managed to keep calm, pushing away any feelings of anger as they arose. He has now been promoted, his family life is serene, and he has apparently adjusted fully to life without alcohol, having survived these three danger points without going back to drinking. Perhaps the anger may come back again, but it seems unlikely, because he has seen quite clearly what devastation can result from its arousal.

It is also important to review the unfortunate outcome of the woman whose car was damaged to see how her behaviour fits into the advice being offered here. For a start *she forgot the orientation to handling problems*.

Firstly, she did not remain calm and think what to do. Her first action should have been to get the number of the other car. Then she might have tried to enlist the support of the witness before talking to the other driver, trying to get him to admit fault in the presence of a witness. Then she could have made inquiries of his name, insurance status and so on. Secondly, she did not protect her rights because she got angry and made a mess of things. Thirdly, when she failed to cope with the situation, this actually became a new problem. 'What do I do now?'

At this stage she tried to cope with the situation by drinking. Almost certainly this was because of her unresolved dependency on her husband. Even though the initial crash was not her fault, the mess she made of the situation was, and she was frightened of the criticism she might get from her husband. This led to anxiety and then to drinking, hardly a result likely to please her husband. Apprehensive about a *mistake*, she should just have admitted the mistake and, because there was no way to fix it, just learned from the error in case a similar situation occurred again. Maybe her husband would have been critical, but everyone makes mistakes and perhaps he would have come to understand that.

Let us return now to the alcoholic who became angry only three times in a year and tell of his latest and successful attempt to push away his anger. On Saturday of one week his wife was using the automatic clothes washing machine while he was in the kitchen doing the cooking. Hearing a scream from her, he raced in to find the water pouring out of the sink adjoining the machine and rapidly running towards expensive carpeting in an adjoining room. Keeping calm, he switched off the machine to stop it pumping further water into the sink, pulled out some underwear his wife had left in the sink and which was acting as a plug, and asked his wife to grab towels to build up a barrier at the door to prevent the water soaking the carpet. Working together, they quickly mopped up the water and saved any major damage. By keeping calm and thinking rationally, not only was the situation saved, but he had managed to keep down his anger and a matrimonial dispute was completely avoided.

On Sunday, the very next day, the same situation was repeated, when the wife left the plug in the sink and water poured out. This time he did let his anger rise for a few seconds before he pushed it away and concentrated on fixing the problem, and some water did get on the carpet. While mopping up the water and drying the carpet he thought carefully about the momentary failure to control his anger. His conclusion was that in his anger he had failed to take into account not only that his wife, like anyone else, was not to be blamed for making a mistake, but that people do make the same sort of mistake twice in a row occasionally. His flash of insight came when he said to himself. 'Well, I made the same mistake every day for twenty-five years, and she tolerated that. Surely I can understand and tolerate her making the same mistake on two successive days. After all, twenty-five years is more than nine thousand successive days of mistakes.' This man had discovered the importance of a concept central to AA philosophy, and one important in this book: TOLERANCE.

This true anecdote of a seemingly trivial event in the life of a three-year-sober alcoholic who now seems to be functioning effectively in all areas of his life leads naturally to a discussion of a whole range of family situations that seem to occur in the homes of alcoholics, and which lead to angry, aggressive actions and to drinking.

Anger in Family-life Situations

There is no doubt that the most difficult area for recovering alcoholics, the one where failure to cope is most common, lies within the family. This is the hub around which everything else revolves. Getting along with wives, husbands, lovers and children is a dicey business for most people. For alcoholics returning sober to the family home, probably after fifteeen to thirty years of alcoholic drinking, or even after just a few years, the situation is loaded with danger. If the alcoholic knows what to do, he knows what is required, and if the family too understands about alcoholism and recovery from the disease, then the process can be made easier and the probability of a return to drinking minimised. The problems that can arise within a family and which lead to anger are endless. The same way of coping applies to each and every one of them, but there are some that are so frequent that they deserve special treatment.

1. Decisions about keeping alcohol in the house

Usually alcoholics are advised not to keep supplies of liquor in the house in the early days of their recovery. The reason for this is that it takes time to build up the non-drinking habit, and furthermore it takes times to build up the calm, rational approach to living to replace the impulsive, irrational ways that lead to drinking. One of the major reasons for the advice about making booze less readily available is centred on this impulsive behaviour. The idea is that if an alcoholic does get upset and reactivates his or her old habit of trying to cope with the anger by reaching for the bottle, he or she will at least have some time to calm down if there is no liquor at hand and may not take the action necessary to get supplies.

The advice offered in this book is the same. Do not keep alcohol in the house until the sober behaviour becomes strong. However, there are some alcoholics who are so strong in their desire to stop drinking that they insist on having alcohol in the house to show that their control is absolute. Others, quite correctly, say that they have no right to stop other members of their family drinking socially, so they have to learn to live normally, except for not drinking alcohol. This is an individual matter and should be decided by a free and full discussion by everyone involved. Ultimately, alcoholics have to return to normal living. In our society, alcohol is used freely and found everywhere. Sooner or later, recovery depends upon being able to live with it without drinking. Many of the most successful recoveries include those who keep alcohol in the house for the social drinking of others, and who can mix and pour drinks for others without feeling the slightest desire to drink.

2. Responsibility for decisions

During the alcoholic years the partner of an alcoholic often takes over the complete responsibility for decision-making, because the alcoholic is so frequently drunk that he or she is incapable of making responsible decisions. The wife takes over the management of finances, the raising of children, the educational decisions, decides where and when to go on holidays, drives the car and generally becomes very independent. Her growth of independence is probably the only good thing associated with the problem, but it can cause problems when the sober alcoholic returns and wants to resume what he perceives to be his role as chief decision-maker.

Now there is no logical reason why a male, because he is a male, is better at making decisions than a female because she is female. In a good marriage or partnership, there is full and free communication between the partners and they discuss their problems and come to joint decisions. Alcoholics tend to be impatient. They want to solve all their problems in one week, and that can't be done. Each case has to be treated on its merits, but clearly the aim should be to obtain or resume family decision-making as soon as possible. An atmosphere of calm must be built up so that differences of opinion can be aired and discussed without anyone flying into a rage. Whether to buy a car or not, and if so what sort to buy, can cause chaos in any household. Arguments about the amount of freedom that should be allowed to teenagers lead to friction in many homes. Where there is an alcoholic in the house, it is even more than usually essential to discuss and evolve policies about bringing up the children, so that arguments between the parents at least are under control.

3. Apprehension, suspicion and accusations about drinking

Many alcoholics claim that they have returned to drinking because they got angry when those close to them created an atmosphere of apprehension, when there's an expectancy that at any moment drinking would start again. There is no doubt that many partners and other family members secretly search for hidden supplies, try to smell the breath in some subtle way or betray their suspicion that drinking is occurring again. Others openly ask if the alcoholic has had a drink. Altogether there is a lack of trust, which the alcoholic resents, and which leads to anger and often to the very drinking that the family so fears. This suspicion and apprehension, these accusations and the lack of trust are dangerous. They will not stop the drinking if it is about to occur, and in fact are more likely to cause intense anger and the very drinking that has to be avoided. Trust is essential, even though some will abuse the trust and start drinking again.

4. Jealousy and resentment of AA activities

The role of AA has been mentioned from time to time in the preceding pages. Attendance at AA meetings has been the only programme shown to work for many alcoholics, and the advice of this book is that all alcoholics should give AA a long trial. Most who do so find it invaluable in helping with their sobriety and recovery. One of the unfortunate by-products is resentment within the family because of the time spent on AA activities. As one woman put it, 'Well, we have spent eighteen years living in a sea of booze. Now we look like spending another eighteen talking about it. Surely, now he is sober and his health is O.K. we could forget it and live a normal, family life.'

The fact is that many alcoholics derive tremendous benefit from seeing and hearing other alcoholics who have been sober for years and learn from others who are struggling to live without alcohol. They see and hear others who mess up their lives by returning to alcohol, and they help one another in their search for a happy, alcohol-free existence. When criticised for AA attendance, many alcoholics become angry because they believe that this is one place where they can get the help and support needed to recover. It is therefore in the short-term and long-term interests of everyone concerned with recovery that this attendance be completely accepted as being necessary.

Alcoholics are usually advised to go to AA as often as they feel the need. Some go many times a week, others weekly and some even less often. Criticism of this activity is ill-founded and should be abandoned. This is not to say that AA attendance should be the sole interest of the alcoholic. Alcoholics have to get back to leading a normal life. Their wives and families do have rights, and these might have to be respected. Wives need to be taken out to social functions, and the children need support with their problems and their homework. Marriages falter if those rights are forgotten by complete absorption in AA. (AA is fully discussed in Chapter 12.)

5. *Publicity about alcoholism*

Two stories about alcoholics who thought that giving up their habitual telling of lies meant that they had to announce the fact of their alcoholism to all and sundry will make the advice on this issue clear. The first young man had been fired from his job because of his alcoholism. After treatment he began applying for jobs and on each application he stated that he was an alcoholic. After a long series of rejections he went back to the hospital for advice. He was told to leave out any reference to his alcoholism and to concentrate on his fine qualifications and experience as a fitter and turner. He succeeded in getting the next job for which he applied and has since been promoted. Now this young man's confidence and self-esteem were being shattered by the repeated rejection; he was becoming angry and on the point of drinking again. Most employers do not understand alcoholism and shy away from it. Nobody would dream of making a big deal of having had other diseases. No one would put in an application form that he had been treated for smallpox, pneumonia or venereal disease, so why tell people that you have been treated for alcoholism when you have it under control?

The second case centred on a woman holding a middle-level executive position in a large organisation, who was successfully coping with her job after treatment. She took her husband to a social function where her husband broke in when she was offered a glass of champagne by saying to her, 'You can't do that. Alcoholics can't drink alcohol. Ask for a soft drink.' The report of this got back to her immediate boss, who had strong views about the 'evils of alcohol' but who knew nothing of her problem. After this unhappy incident, she was never ever given the tasks for which she was trained, and her career, which had looked so promising, came to a full stop. Frustrated and angered by the lack of opportunity, she resigned.

These two incidents make it clear that, in some circumstances, making the knowledge of alcoholism public can have effects that might lead someone back to drinking. It does not matter whether it is the alcoholic or someone close to him or her, the principle is clear. *Never admit the fact of being an alcoholic or allow anyone else to announce it wherever there is a possibility of it doing harm to the alcoholic or anyone close to him or her.* There are certainly occasions where most of the people with whom you work know of the alcoholic problem, and there are sometimes good reasons to let someone know you are an alcoholic. Certainly your doctor should be informed and your close friends may need to know, although most will know already.

6. *Blaming the alcoholic for past mistakes*

Living with an alcoholic is no picnic, and the trail of devastation caused during the years of uncontrolled drinking can be a long one indeed. Legal, financial, occupational, social, family and personal problems of horrendous proportions are common. It is very understandable when those closely involved privately blame the alcoholic for the chaotic conditions, and even when they throw the blame right in his or her face. Not unnaturally, this often leads to a surge of anger, to a feeling that life is hopeless and that the only way out is via a bottle. Laying blame on a recovering alcoholic is not only useless, it is positively dangerous.

7. *Failure to learn about alcoholism*

The more a family knows about alcoholism and about the factors involved in recovery from its effects, the less likely they are to make the mistakes that result in the recovering drinker getting angry. Getting angry, of course, is a mistake on his or her part. However, an effort should be made by the family to learn and practise the procedures that aid recovery rather than provide situations that might lead to an angry response of the sort, 'If you knew anything about alcoholism you wouldn't say that.'

Anger in the Work Place

Practically all of the situations that can lead to an angry response in the home can occur at work, but there are some others that are common enough to merit special attention. These are listed below where the anger arises because of:

1. Having been passed over for promotion.
2. Being returned to a job below his or her level of skill.
3. Non-acceptance of her or him as a normal person and provision of special conditions to protect him or her.
4. Sarcasm and rejection by a supervisor.
5. Not being invited to staff functions and parties.

Coping with these problems is no different to coping with other problems, except that where there is a clearly defined authority structure it is sometimes necessary to be very careful about asserting his or her rights. But assert them he or she must.

As a result of alcoholism some things have to be accepted as problems that can be solved only by the alcoholic proving that he or she is worthy of promotion now that the desire to drink has been mastered. It is not unnatural for others to be sceptical of the alcoholic's ability to keep off the grog, but this lack of trust will disappear with continued sobriety. It is useless for him or her to get angry about and to resent the promotion of others, because no employer in his right mind would promote a practising alcoholic if the problem is recognised. The work place and the home are places where the alcoholic has to prove that his or her level of skill is as high as ever and that he or she can be trusted not to hit the booze again.

Summary

In this chapter the effects of anger were shown to include:

1. Irrational thinking.
2. Alienation of those on the receiving end as well as witnesses.
3. Feelings of guilt after getting angry.
4. Almost always losing when getting angry.
5. Increasing the chances of a return to drinking.

The following arguments in favour of continuing to be angry were examined and found to be *false*.

1. Choosing not to be angry leads to dangerous bottling up of anger. FALSE.
2. It is natural to be angry and unnatural not to be. FALSE.
3. It is right to get angry and aggressive when others try to walk over us. FALSE.

The changes in thinking that occur while we are angry were shown to include:

1. An increase in risk-taking behaviour.
2. A decrease in capacity to process the information entering our brain.

Control over anger was shown to depend upon:

1. Substituting calm assertion for anger.
2. Thinking rationally.
3. Learning how to handle criticism.
4. Having a low need for approval.

Finally, a number of family and work situations that commonly evoke anger were described. Anger, like anxiety, is dynamite for alcoholics. However, like anxiety, anger is under our control. It is a habit that we can get rid of by choosing to be calm instead.

7

The Other Negative Emotions

This will be a short chapter because the other negative emotions are basically other forms of anger. Frustration, resentment, envy, self-pity, intolerance and jealousy form one group of emotions, with guilt and depression forming the other group. Most alcoholics experience a high level of all of these feelings; and they all have to be discarded in order to cope successfully with life and recover from alcoholism.

Frustration

Frustration occurs when we have set our sight on an objective or a goal, and someone or something blocks or appears to block our progress. The common reaction to frustration is anger. Now *alcoholics are impatient,* and wish to solve all their problems quickly, so they tend to get frustrated easily. Problems that took years to develop are unlikely to be solved in a few days. *Learn to be patient.* If something should get in the way, then it should be regarded calmly as another obstacle to be overcome. It is necessary to think calmly and rationally about the best method of removing or getting around the obstacle, then to act without worrying about others and what they may think.

One young alcoholic, a boilermaker by trade, found work hard to get after a long period of hospitalisation. He tried an unusual solution to his problem by going to a psychologist for occupational guidance. Now he is making a great deal of money because he followed the advice given by the counsellor. He changed his hobby into a major occupation by joining a rock-band as a drummer, and he started making metal sculptures as a hobby. His hobby is now producing more money than the lucrative music career. His only problem now is paying his accountant to keep track of his rapidly expanding income.

Resentment

Resentment is the hurt someone experiences when feeling injured, overlooked, rejected or insulted in some way. Resentment is virtually indistinguishable from anger. Another young male alcoholic resented the fact that his wife had left him during his alcoholic phase, taking the children with her, and had obtained a divorce, moved to another state and was about to remarry. His distress and resentment about this were at such a level that he kept going in and out of hospital. Once out, he would drink huge quantities of alcohol, be carried into hospital, dry out and head straight back to the liquor store.

This brings us to an important issue in problem-solving technique. *When faced with an insoluble problem, recognise it and accept it.* For this young man there was absolutely no chance of getting his marriage going again. He had tried everything possible and failed. When faced with an insoluble problem, all we can do is to accept it as insoluble and then forget it. This advice was finally accepted by the young man and he is now concentrating on rebuilding a life without his family.

The incidence of divorce is very high, especially for female alcoholics, because their husbands are not as supportive as the wives of male alcoholics, a fact that we will return to in the chapter about female alcoholism. No matter how distressing divorce may be, it must be accepted if the partnership has no chance of revival. Some alcoholics may actually be better off without their partners, and some find consolation in the fact that if they remarry, it will be a new experience, because they have never tried marriage while sober.

Resentment about failure of a former employer to rehire is another source of trouble. Sometimes it is possible to persuade the employer that the alcohol problem has been brought under control and for the alcoholic to get rehired on the understanding that any relapse will mean instant and permanent dismissal. This can sometimes be organised through a counsellor contacting the personnel officer and assuring him or her of the state of recovery. This intervention by a third party is at least worth trying if it can be arranged.

Fortunately, industrial programmes dealing with alcoholism are becoming more common. Management and unions are involved in working out programmes for early detection and help for alcoholics, who are kept on the payroll on the understanding that they seek help for their drinking problem and on the condition that they get the problem fixed. For management there is a clear pay-off, because of the enormous cost involved in training its employees, in reduced absenteeism and industrial accidents, and improved personal relationships.

Resentment about failure to gain promotion is also frequent. The productivity of alcoholics falls off as their condition worsens. They become prone to accidents on and off the job and their absenteeism rate is very high. It is little wonder that others are promoted and they are passed over. On return to sobriety it is useless for an alcoholic to resent this fact. All he or she can do is to accept it, remain sober and get life back in order so that they can prove that they are now worthy of promotion. For some, of course, the opportunities will have passed and this too must be accepted.

Envy and Jealousy

These are closely related to resentment. Within the family, recovering alcoholics are often envious when they see brothers and sisters who have achieved success in the various areas of their lives. One man became envious of the fact that his brother, a non-drinker, had built up a successful business, was happily married and owned an impressive house, had a holiday home at the beach and the various material possessions that go with a high income. He refused to visit his brother and refused all the offers of help his brother made. Now, these offers were made with the best possible motives, to help his brother who has financial, emotional, legal and family problems. The rejection had no logical basis, but was based solely on irrational feelings of envy, jealousy and self-pity.

Self-pity

Self-pity or feeling sorry for oneself is also common to alcoholics. It is usually accompanied by attempts to blame the unpleasant features of life on someone or something else. The point to remember is that each alcoholic is in control of his or her own destiny and that it is useless trying to put the blame elsewhere. Furthermore, feelings of self-pity serve only to prevent rational thought and action that would improve the present and future. No purpose is served by thinking about how hard done by in life she or he is. It is useless to wallow in feelings of self-pity. When an alcoholic looks at the wreckage that his or her alcoholism has produced and says 'Why me? What have I done to deserve this?' he or she is avoiding what should be his or her prime objectives: To make the present as happy as possible for himself or herself and to give happiness to others close to him or her.

Intolerance

Intolerance for the views, ideas and behaviour of others, and lack of respect for the rights and feelings of other people is also frequent. In Chapter 9 it will be made clear that assertive behaviour is essential to recovery. Part of being assertive is to protect one's own rights and feelings from harm. People have a right to their own views and ideas about things, they have a right to behave in ways that lead to their recovery and happiness, and they must protect these rights.

Other people will have different ideas, and behave in other ways, and even where one does not agree one has to be tolerant of these differences. Intolerance often leads to violent arguments and to angry, aggressive behaviour. One has to recognise that other people's attitudes are just as hard to change as one's own, and even if one disagrees with them, at least one can understand and tolerate these views and attitudes. This is particularly important, because many people will have little or no knowledge of alcoholism and recovery from alcoholism. Many do not understand that social drinking is not possible for alcoholics and believe that it is just a matter of physical recovery and the exercise of a little will-power. 'One drink can't hurt you; take this' is an expression of this lack of understanding. Alcoholics have to learn to be tolerant of this misinformed attitude and learn how to refuse the drink without upsetting others by becoming angry and abusive.

Guilt

Feelings of guilt, like feelings of anger and anxiety, prevent a person from dealing effectively with the real problem. That is, blaming oneself and feeling guilty because of something that is in the past prevents effective action in the present. Most feelings of guilt are not concerned with acts that have legal aspects, but are of the interpersonal sort. Parents make children feel guilty with remarks like: 'If you cared for me then . . .' or 'you don't love me. I'll get it myself.' These childhood guilt feelings are carried over into adult life. Children manipulate their parents using guilt in phrases like: 'I hate you. Why can't you be like Johnny's father. He always takes him out and he plays with him.' All sorts of people make us guilty and it is usually centred around statements that say or imply that our actions mean *we do not* CARE *for someone whom we* SHOULD CARE FOR.

A second common form of guilt is when we break a code of conduct we have set for ourselves. A woman who gets drunk and has a casual affair may reproach herself for years for having breached her own code of behaviour. A man who gets angry and shouts at his daughter for being late home may feel guilty for having broken the good relationship he had assiduously built up, because of his commitment to a way of bringing up children which ruled anger out. Now no form of guilt will change what has happened in the past. Throw guilt out. Make any reparations that can be made without causing further problems and don't make the mistake again. That is the only function of the past. We should learn from our mistakes. Guilt feelings prevent us from acting wisely in the present and serve no other useful role. Choose not to be guilty. We all make mistakes and have to learn to accept that fact. Feeling guilty about a mistake is irrational. No one should convict himself or herself for making an elementary error. Admit the mistake, apologise and forget it. If someone else tries to make a big deal out of it, assert that it was just an error. The worst aspect of guilt for alcoholics is the fact of the alcoholism. It is useless and dangerous to feel guilty about the wasted years or about the devastation you may have caused during the long downhill road.

Another source of guilt comes from a least expected source. Recently, an alcoholic male who was really booming along in his recovery was made to feel guilty by his AA sponsor, who berated him because he was attending AA meetings only twice a week. After a telephone conversation with his counsellor, who had helped him earlier in his recovery, he decided to forget his guilt feelings and to assert himself. He met his sponsor and calmly told him that he considered that AA attendance was an individual matter and that he thought that twice a week was the optimum number for him. He went on to point out that, because he was feeling so well, he had taken up his photography hobby again and that he was really enjoying that because he was sober and could appreciate the work of others and learn new techniques more readily than before. He also told of the extra time he was putting in with his children and of how his wife was responding to his efforts in helping her with the domestic chores and to the gradual resumption of a social life involving her.

Faced with this clear account of progress the sponsor agreed that his criticism was unfounded.

There is no doubt that some alcoholics need very frequent attendance at AA meetings early in the recovery process, while others seem to cope without alcohol with less frequent visits. It is an individual matter, which needs careful consideration, probably erring on the side of heavy attendance rather than light, if there is any doubt.

The most frequent source of guilt, however, is leftover guilt. Feelings of remorse and guilt about the events that occurred during the alcoholic drinking are common. So many stupid and hurtful things were done, and some are hard to forget, while others tend to be remembered by others and referred to in moments of stress. For example, a young female alcoholic was getting along well with her recovery and was into her third year of recovery when an argument erupted over a visit by her mother-in-law. Her husband lost his temper and claimed that she hated his mother, citing as evidence a stormy scene when the drunken wife had poured a cup of coffee over his mother, who was attempting to sober her up. This attempt to make her feel guilty actually failed, because she had already apologised to her mother-in-law for this specific act and a lot of others, and because she realised the dangers of allowing guilt feelings to arise. She remained calm and pointed out that the reason for not wanting the visit was a previous engagement, which ruled out the suggested date. Faced with this calm logical approach, the husband's anger subsided and his mother's visit was arranged for another time.

Depression

When we make a mess of things and get angry, this anger is sometimes not expressed in aggression against someone or something else but is turned inward against the self. We kick ourselves for not speaking up and for not having taken certain steps, and the memory of the failure runs round and round in our heads and makes sleep difficult. This is a simple state of depression, which can be treated in the same way as anger or anxiety. Unfortunately, some circumstances lead to deep depression, which pervades the whole life of the sufferer. These people feel that they are completely hopeless, that life is not worth living, and that nothing they can do will change this catastrophic state of affairs. In the worst of these depressive states suicide is contemplated, and sometimes real or half-hearted attempts are made at self-destruction. Some of these are successful.

Now, people suffering from these deep endogenous depressions find it extremely difficult, if not impossible, to carry out the rational analysis that is needed to control the anger and self-pity that led to the depressive state. Such people may need urgent medical help and prescribed drugs to break the depression. There are drugs available that can alleviate these profound depressions, so that psychological approaches such as those outlined here or other treatments can be undertaken to get at the underlying cause of the depression. In all cases of extreme depression medical help should be sought as a matter of urgency. Fortunately, the depression that often accompanies alcoholism is relatively minor in degree and is susceptible to the same treatment given for anger and anxiety.

Depression is probably one of the worst sicknesses and should be treated as a serious matter, but quite clearly the way to handle depression is not to allow yourself to get depressed in the first place. Alcoholics get depressed because their families are not responding to their efforts at recovery, because they can't get a job, because their sexual potency has vanished, because they are lonely, and because they can't make friends. The list is endless. Most of these situations can be solved if the right steps are taken.

One woman whose alcoholic drinking was accompanied by severe depression solved her problem by coming to realise that she had been submitting to her husband who believed that a woman's place was in the home and behaved accordingly. While in hospital she attended a group therapy session that centred on the social pressures associated with female alcoholism. On her return home, she began to assert herself, insisted on returning to the work-force, where she soon became immersed in her old job and used some of the money she earned to pay a housekeeper to do the jobs she could no longer do at home. Her depression vanished, as did her need for alcohol.

Another young woman, whose descent into alcoholism had been very speedy, came to the conclusion that her depression was associated with the disappearance of love and affection from her marriage. She too had learned the value of assertive behaviour, and went to a marriage guidance psychologist. The husband became involved and soon came to see that unless he began to display the love and affection he did in fact feel towards her, either she would drink again or a divorce would occur. He changed his habits and all is now well.

Summary

The following emotions were seen to have the same effects as anxiety and anger. They can all lead to crazy irrational thinking and to a return to drinking. These were feelings of:

1. Frustration.
2. Resentment.
3. Envy and jealousy.
4. Self-pity.
5. Intolerance.
6. Guilt.
7. Depression.

During the discussion other important points emerged:

1. Learn to be patient. An alcoholic's problems take time to fix.
2. When faced with an unsoluble problem, recognise it and accept it as unsoluble.

8

The Six Steps in Problem-Solving

Coping with the stresses of life, with the day-to-day events, with the environmental circumstances, with the decisions we have to make, and with the choices we have to face has been labelled as the TRIGGER. This could equally well have been called the PROBLEM. These events, problems and choices are not unique to alcoholics because they share with non-alcoholics the common problem of earning a living, bringing up children, making friends, deciding where to go on a holiday and an infinite number of others. Every non-alcoholic brings a different set of lifetime experience, skills and memories to bear on each problem with which he or she is faced. Some are expert problem-solvers, some are average and some aren't very good and make a mess of things fairly often. Alcoholics are the same as non-alcoholics, except that most have a long history of unsuccessful coping that has culminated in seeking oblivion through alcohol to blot out the highly unpleasant feelings generated by their failure to cope. The very clear evidence of inability to cope with life very well makes this chapter and the next two chapters on assertiveness and need for approval of critical importance, because these three interlocking chapters show how to break the vicious circle of alcoholic drinking as a response to failure to cope.

The system outlined here is a variant of a scheme popularised by Dr Thomas Gordon (1955). The system has six steps:

1. Orientation to the problem.
2. Defining the problem.
3. Generation of many options.
4. Selection of the best option.
5. Putting your choice into action.
6. Assessing the success of your action.

In Chapter 5 the eleven aspects of a suggested orientation to the problems we have to face were presented. The first two are included because alcoholics need to have them in their approach to problems because they are alcoholics. Similarly, a person who bleeds profusely even after a slight graze and whose bleeding is difficult to stop would need to include special conditions for his or her special case.

The chaos that surrounds the lives of practising alcoholics is well documented. Personal, legal, family, sexual, and social problems are an integral part of the alcoholic pattern. To give some idea of this, part of a questionnaire answered by all the patients who were admitted to Montclair Hospital, Brighton, Melbourne, Australia during a six-month period was analysed. An average of 93 per cent of the patients agreed that during their alcoholic period:

1. Their family life had been seriously disrupted.
2. They had frequent blackouts when they could not remember what they had done while drinking.
3. They frequently drank early in the morning.
4. They attempted to hide their supplies.
5. They had made attempts to give up drinking.
6. They drank to calm their nerves.
7. They often drank alone.

An average of 75 per cent said they had shaking hands in the morning and that they resented comments about their drinking. 46 per cent had had the police called because of their drinking. Between 30 and 40 per cent of them had lost at least one job because of alcoholism, had been divorced or separated, had been arrested for drunkenness, had been charged with drinking while intoxicated and had delerium tremens, while 10 per cent had been involved in industrial accidents. Given this sort of picture, it is not necessary to go further to prove that alcoholics are not coping very well and that they need to change their habits. Every single one admitted to 'drinking to calm my nerves', so keeping calm without artificial aids is the aim of this programme. *The first step in keeping calm when faced with a difficult situation is to TO WORK OUT WHAT TO DO TO SOLVE THE PROBLEM*. An attitude or an orientation likely to lead to a successful solution is also necessary.

Step 1: Orientation

1. My life has become unmanageable because of my alcoholism.
2. Complete abstinence is the only way to keep my alcoholism in check. Therefore I will not ever resort to alcohol as a way of helping to solve my problems.
3. The best way to solve problems is to keep calm and think

clearly about ways of solving them.

4. I must protect my own rights and feelings at all times. However, if I insist on my rights, I must also be tolerant of and consider the rights and feelings of others.
5. Life is just a series of problems to be solved.
6. I am in control of my own destiny. The choices I make will decide whether my future is happy or not.
7. I will consider many possibilities before I act.
8. When I have carefully decided on a course of action, I will act without worrying about what others will think of me.
9. If my action is unsuccessful, I will rethink the situation and try again.
10. There are some insoluble problems. These I must accept as insoluble.
11. I will ask for help whenever it is necessary.

1. Life unmanageable

Once an alcoholic gets fully into the alcoholic pattern, life becomes centred on alcohol. The overriding concern of alcoholics is to ensure that adequate supplies are available at all times. Booze is usually hidden in garages, in hedges, in tool-sheds and even in toilets, so that a heavy intake can be maintained while trying to hide this fact from other people, families and spouses. A flask is packed with lunch, so that even while at work the alcohol level can be kept up. While driving long distances, excuses are found to stop, raise the lid of the boot and swiftly gulp down some spirits. As this pattern develops, it is not surprising that problems occur in the home and at work, and it is inevitable that family and social life begins to disintegrate. Even when not drunk, the chief concern is about when the next drink will arrive, so the normal pressing problems associated with being alive and having to fulfil many roles are not solved very well at all. At social functions alcoholics tend to drink quite heavily in order to get there in the first place, drink much more quickly than others while they are there, and often are among the last to leave. Not surprisingly their wives or husbands and the other guests resent and are embarrassed by their drunken behaviour. At work, productivity decreases and absenteeism increases. Even when work attendance is good, this complete absorption with alcohol interferes with productivity.

The massive intake of alcohol, combined with irritability and the self-centred approach typical of alcoholics, joins with the aversion of sexual partners to the smell of alcohol and to the aggressive behaviour that often accompanies the drinking to upset the sexual life of the partners. Children react negatively to specific acts and to the general feelings of chaos and begin to exhibit symptoms of their unhappiness. In other words, life becomes unmanageable because of loss of control over alcohol. The first thing an alcoholic has to do is to admit that it is his drinking that has caused many of the problems that beset him or her and to stop blaming bad luck, other people or fate for the troubles that abound.

2. *Abstinence*

The second point in the orientation is admitting that the overwhelming bulk of evidence points to the fact that alcoholics cannot drink at all, ever again. Evidence for this comes from two main sources:

(1) Prior to the formation of AA no one seemed to be able to help alcoholics at all, although ministers of religion, the medical profession, social workers, psychiatrists and psychologists and others all tried. The fact that alcoholics have a condition that predisposes them to loss of control and to dependence on alcohol was not recognised, and it was thought that this continued drinking was a sign of lack of will-power. As we have seen, most alcoholics make desperate attempts to stop drinking, but their addiction gets in the way. With the spread of AA throughout the world, alcoholics who alone understand the nature of their problem began to help one another to live without alcohol, because they alone understand that *complete and life-long abstinence is the only way to arrest the course of their alcoholic lives.*

(2) The second source of evidence comes from long-term follow-up studies of alcoholics. They show that those who attempt to return to controlled drinking do not succeed, and that, despite assertions to the contrary, there is not a single, properly documented case of an alcoholic returning to a lifetime of social drinking. Therefore, alcoholics can never resort to alcohol in an attempt to solve a problem. Alcohol is a depressant that affects the action of the brain. The more they drink, the less capable of rational thinking they become. Clear, logical thought is essential to work out the best possible way to solve any given problem, so alcohol must be avoided. Most people drink because they are not coping well, but the drinking only makes the situation worse.

3. *Remaining calm*

Evidence shows clearly that when anxiety surges, the performance-level on all sorts of tasks drops markedly. The same is true of anger, depression, frustration, self-pity, resentment, envy, jealousy and guilt. In order to solve problems well, it is necessary to remain calm and think clearly about the various ways in which the problem can be solved. The negative emotions listed above have to be pushed aside and the problem attacked calmly and logically instead of in the emotional, illogical and impulsive way typical of many alcoholics.

4. Protection of rights and feelings

A list of the rights of alcoholics is in the chapter on assertion. It includes the right to be treated with respect, to say no without feeling guilty, to refuse to drink alcohol, the right to demand time to think and many others. The point about rights is that they are not given to anyone or granted to anyone as a favour by other people. These rights apply to everyone regardless of sex, race, age or religion. Alcoholics have the same rights as those who have had the measles, chickenpox, pneumonia or have lost both legs. These rights and feelings must be protected as far as possible, because if someone allows others to dominate, humiliate or hurt her or him, then he or she is likely to get emotionally upset and this starts off the failure-to-cope chain and may lead to a relapse. Most alcoholics believe that it is necessary to get angry and aggressive to protect their rights and feelings, but nothing could be less true. Being assertive is the way to achieve this.

Once someone claims to have certain rights and feelings, then she or he must allow that others have similar rights and feelings, and in working out the best way to solve a given problem, these must be taken into account. If people grant themselves the right to make mistakes, they must be tolerant of the mistakes of others.

5. Life is a series of problems

When we open our eyes each morning, we have to decide whether to get out of bed or not. Then in rapid succession we may have to decide whether to shower before or after breakfast, choose which clothes we will wear to work, what to have for breakfast, decide whether to get angry or not about being criticised for always running late and so on throughout the day and evening. In any single day we make thousands of decisions and choices and solve countless problems, all of which contain stress and which may be interpreted as a threat to the sense of self-esteem. If we choose to remain calm, to think rationally and to act on our choice of option, then we are likely to be happy and cope successfully. Life is just a series of choices that determine our future.

6. Control of destiny

Implicit in the preceding section is the notion that we are in control of our own destiny. Our future is largely determined by the choices we make and not by what people do or say to us, by fate or circumstance or by things that happen. If we get angry when someone criticises us, it is because we have chosen to get angry instead of choosing to remain calm and handle the situation as just another problem to be solved. If we become depressed because we have made a bad mistake, we have chosen to be depressed instead of remaining calm and achieving success. In Chapter 4 it was shown that it is the way we assess situations that is critical. If we assess being criticised as a threat, then we will be quite likely to get angry, but it is not the person criticising us who makes us angry, it is the way we evaluate the situation. Therefore we make ourselves angry. Some people blame fate or circumstances for their problems. Alcoholics make remarks like 'If only I hadn't gone to the party . . .' 'When I came in there was the bottle sitting on the table' and 'She was in a hell of a temper when she came home from work' for their relapses. This is rubbish. The only way an alcoholic can go back to drinking is if she or he decides to do so. Certainly we do not have control over major happenings such as earthquakes, wars or the decisions of governments or huge companies. However, these rarely cause the problems that lead to relapse. It is dealing with the family, the job and the trivial everyday affairs of life that causes problems, and we exercise control over the way we respond to these situations and therefore control our own future.

7. Generating options

There are usually many possible ways of solving each problem that comes up. The more options we think up and consider, the more likely we are to come up with a good answer. If, on the other hand, we act impulsively and do the first thing that comes to mind, we are more likely to fail. Alcoholics generally have a long history of failing to cope very well and have developed non-adaptive ways of handling their problems. We have already discussed how many react with anger and become aggressive because that is the way they have reacted in the past. Angry and aggressive solutions may result in short-term gains but, in the end, they cause others to resent us and to plan revenge. We have also seen how other alcoholics are submissive and allow others to walk all over them. For both, other assertive options have to be learned and used in seeking solutions.

8. A decision should lead to action

It is useless for a person to spend time working out what to do, if when the time comes to act she or he does nothing, or does something else, which has previously been rejected. A woman decided that the best way to solve the problems that led to her alcoholism was to tell her husband that she was seeking a divorce. However she cancelled the visit to her solicitor on several occasions because she was apprehensive about her husband's reactions, became angry with herself and then depressed. Many people make correct decisions, but fail to act for various reasons, which are described in the next chapter.

9. Making the wrong decision

No matter how carefully the problem is thought about, and no matter how many options are generated, people sometimes make mistakes and choose the wrong solution. If the chosen solution does not work, this is really not a failure. They have done their best and the only way to think is as follows. 'Well, that didn't work very well. Stiff luck. I'd better go back and try again. Maybe I forgot an important factor while I was sizing up the situation.'

10. Insoluble problems

There are a few, but very few, problems that are insoluble. Recovery from alcoholism is NOT one of these. Recently a young, attractive female alcoholic well on the path to full recovery was involved in a car accident in which she received injuries that resulted in her becoming paralysed from the waist down. She contemplated suicide during a brief relapse into massive drinking. On her recovery she accepted the fact that she was injured and that nothing could be done about it because it was an insoluble problem. She is now a fully employed, reasonably happy young woman getting as much out of life as she possibly can. The Serenity Prayer of Alcoholics Anonymous sums up the advice better than any other words can: 'God grant me the SERENITY to accept the things I cannot change, COURAGE to change the things I can, and WISDOM to know the difference.'

11. Asking for help

An important part of recovering from alcoholism is becoming emotionally independent. This means that an alcoholic has to learn to make his or her own decisions and act upon those decisions without worrying about what other people will think. In arriving at a solution, however, it is often advisable to ask others for their opinions, advice and help because other people may come up with options that would never have occurred to the person most concerned. The alcoholic is free to reject their advice if it doesn't seem productive. Unfortunately, an alcoholic often finds it difficult to ask for help, and this is a habit that has to be learned. One of the many reasons that AA works is that it provides a source where 'help is but a phone call away' and helping one another is a cornerstone of the whole process. In fact, most people like being asked for help because it makes them feel good.

Step 2: Defining the Problem

Some problems are quite clear-cut and fully defined from the beginning. If an eleven-year-old says, 'Mum, I want to get my ears pierced so that I can wear these ear-rings', there is no doubt what the situation is. At the other extreme a female alcoholic might come home after being to an AA meeting and find her husband apparently asleep in bed. The next day he speaks to her in monosyllables and then only when asked a direct question. The silent treatment is on. This leaves the source of the problem quite unclear. Perhaps he thinks she is not helping enough with the children's homework? Perhaps he has got the sack and is afraid to tell her?

Now, *unless the problem is sorted out and defined quite precisely, it is unlikely to be solved.* In this case the definition of the problem might proceed as follows. Quite clearly the wife has a right to know what the problem is. She has to assert herself, so she might say: 'Bob, you seem to be very unhappy and I don't know why. Since I arrived home last night you have barely spoken to me, and you haven't touched or kissed me and that makes me unhappy. I want you to tell me what the problem is so that we can sort it out together.'

'Look, Sue, the whole alcoholic deal makes me mad.'

'What do you mean? Tell me specifically what it is that is upsetting you.'

'Well, we never seem to have much time together any more. We don't go anywhere together or talk to anyone and I'm sick of it.'

'Is it my going to AA meetings that is the problem?'

'Well, I suppose that's part of it. Then people ring you up and ask for help and I just don't seem to be part of your life at all.'

Now, Bob, although not an alcoholic, is quite clearly not a good problem-solver. Not only has he not really worked out what is making him upset, but at first the only way he can communicate his unhappiness is by not speaking at all. Sue, on the other hand, having learned to be assertive, describes the situation clearly, and tells him that she wants to find out what the problem is so it can be sorted out, because she doesn't want him unhappy.

After further discussion the dimensions of the problem became clear and the outcome was as follows:

(1) Bob resents Sue going to AA three nights a week. After a long discussion about AA she convinces him that it is in his interests as well as hers for her to conquer her alcoholism, and that the AA visits are essential for this. She makes arrangements to go twice a week during the daytime while he is at work and to attend only one night meeting.

(2) Bob likes going out to dinner occasionally and also likes jazz concerts. They agree that they can use the nights formerly given to meetings to go to these places. Sue asks if they can avoid licensed restaurants for a while until her non-drinking habits become stronger and he willingly agrees.

(3) Sue asks him not to bottle up his feelings in future and to speak honestly and directly to her about them. He agrees to try, so the immediate problem is fixed and future benefits also become a possibility. It is clear that nothing was achieved until the difficulty was defined quite clearly.

A quite different problem faces Jean, who notes that her alcoholic husband, Harry, appears to be losing his interest in sexual activity. After his return from the hospital where he received treatment, their sex life had been resumed to the satisfaction of both, but now Harry seems to be losing interest. Jean becomes quite apprehensive about the situation and thinks that he might be having an affair with another woman, that he might be becoming impotent as a result of his alcoholism, that he is depressed and all manner of other things. She tries all sorts of remedies with no success. Finally, she decides to ask him quite directly what the problem is.

She calmly describes the situation quite clearly to him, tells him that she is unhappy because of it, and asks him to tell her what is causing the problem. Before treatment Harry was a tax consultant who worked on a contract basis with various firms. He is very good at his job, but cannot bring himself to ring his former clients to tell them he is available because he believes the word about him being an alcoholic has got around. His income has dropped alarmingly and he is concerned that they can no longer afford to send their children to the private schools that they attend. He sees his whole life disintegrating.

Knowing now what the problem is, and feeling great relief that it is not centred on her or the marriage, Jean says that she will immediately go back to work to relieve the financial pressure. Harry goes back to a counsellor, who helps him to relieve his anxiety, writes out what he should say, and persuades Harry to call one firm from the counsellor's office. This succeeds beyond Harry's wildest dreams, because the firm leaps at the chance to employ him, for he had been very good at his job while sober.

Alcoholics and non-alcoholics alike make a mess of things when they go through life living with unbearable situations that they never really define. They know in a general way what is causing the problem, but until they face up to it and work out exactly what the dimensions of the problem are, it is unlikely that they will ever get it fixed.

Step 3: Generation of Options

Having decided what a given problem is, so that it is no longer fuzzy and vague but clear-cut and definite, individuals have to work out what to do to solve the problem. The way to go about this is to *list all the options they can possibly think of without judging at this point whether these are good solutions or not*. Gordon suggests six things they might say to themselves or anyone else who is involved.

1. Let's list some of the possible solutions to this problem.
2. Let's see how many ideas we can come up with.
3. What are some things we might do?
4. There must be a lot of different ways we can solve this problem?
5. What ideas do we have for solving this problem?
6. What are some solutions we might try?

If we take an example of an everyday problem we can see this need for clear definition of the problem more easily. A woman with a husband and two children lives one mile from the shopping centre. Sometimes she walk there to buy supplies, but at week-ends she uses the family car. In emergencies her husband uses public transport and leaves the car at home. One or both children help with the shopping during holidays and occasionally after school.

Consider the following situation. The woman goes to the refrigerator and notices that there is a low supply of various articles and says to herself. 'Well, I need to do some shopping as things are getting low.' That is, she recognises that there is a problem and makes a first attempt to define it. However, even in this mundane aspect of living, it is clear that the formulation of the problem is not very advanced, because it is not clear what action should be taken to solve it. The first step is to define the elements in tangible terms. Probably in this case the phrase to define is 'things are getting low' by making a list of things that are needed. Having made the list, the problem now reads, 'We are low in A, B, C . . . Z. I certainly need to go shopping today.' Given her situation, the problem could be refined further. 'A, C, E and F are urgent because they are needed for breakfast and for cut-lunches tomorrow. The remainder can wait until the week-end.' The problem is now clearly defined and various alternative solutions can be generated.

The evidence on this aspect suggests that the more alternatives that can be generated the better the outcome. In the present case the possibilities are fairly limited. Some are listed below:

1. Walk and do all the shopping.
2. Walk and get the essentials, leaving the remainder until the weekend.
3. Change the breakfast and cut-lunch requirements and ask husband for use of the car the following day.
4. Ask children for help after school and get the lot.
5. Ask children to get the essentials after school.
6. Borrow essentials from neighbours.
7. Go to supermarket and ask them to deliver.
8. Hitch a ride with a neighbour.
9. Do total shopping and ask husband to pick it up on the way home.
10. Have a showdown with husband on the need for more help with the housework.
11. Buy a second car.
12. Say it is all too much and do nothing.
13. Any combinations of these, such as hitch a ride with a neighbour to demonstrate need for a second car.
14. Decide to go back to work and employ a housekeeper.
15. Decide to go back to part-time work to buy a second car in order to do the shopping.
16. Walk up, buy the lot, taxi back.

Without going any further, it is plain that many alternatives can be generated in the simplest of situations. Some of these are appropriate, some not. Decisions about these are the next step and we will return to this shortly.

Consider the plight of the woman who has recently returned home after treatment for her alcoholism. For her, the problem that upset her initially and precipitated her drinking is still there when she comes home. Her workaholic husband is still working eighteen hours a day, seven days a week. Her definition of the problem may go as follows: 'I feel depressed and lonely. The problem seems to be that my husband is always working. When he comes home he is too tired to do anything. He flops in front of TV, has a drink and goes to bed. When I get up in the morning, he has already left for work. He rarely sees the children because he brings work home at the week-end or goes to work. I want his support and companionship, life is boring and the children are getting out of hand. It is highly desirable that he spend less time on work and more with the children, or the family will disintegrate. The problem is to get him to see that our marriage is failing and that I am unhappy and so are the children. Now, what steps can I take?'

Her list of options was as follows:

1. Confront husband, demand more of his time, and threaten divorce.
2. Make a list of hours he has worked over last fortnight including week-ends. List the number of social outings during the last months. Document lack of communication with him and between him and children. Document financial position of family. Describe her own feelings of loneliness and feelings of being abandoned. Ask him what he thinks can be done to improve the situation and make specific requests for change.
3. Consult a marriage guidance counsellor.
4. Ask a friend for help.
5. Go home to mother.
6. Accept this as a woman's lot.
7. Ring his boss and demand that he does something.
8. Do nothing.
9. Ask him to change his job.
10. Offer to get a part-time job if he will work reasonable hours.
11. Get a full-time job to counter loneliness.
12. Get some tranquillisers.
13. Learn to play golf to keep busy.
14. Go to a solicitor and begin divorce proceedings.
15. Have a few brandies to calm down.
16. Pack a bag and go away to a seaside hotel for a week to think things over.
17. Jump off a bridge.

There are probably dozens of other options open, but at least careful thought has been given to generating a reasonable number of quite different ways of handling the situation without, at that stage, thinking very much about whether they are good or bad solutions.

This woman has ample time to think up this variety of solutions, but some problems require snap decisions. It is to one of these that we now turn. This is a pressure-to-drink situation that arises out of the blue for a male alcoholic. He is on an aeroplane, which has reached its cruising altitude. A friend whom he has not seen for years drops into the adjoining seat. After the usual remarks, the friend orders two whiskies from a passing flight attendant without consulting him and re-opens the conversation by telling him about his current activities. As the arrival of the drinks is imminent a quick solution to the problem has to be reached.

First, the problem has to be defined: 'This man, an old friend and drinking partner has suddenly appeared after three years and ordered me a drink. He does not know that I am an alcoholic. I don't want to hurt his feelings by refusing the drink, but I will hurt myself and my family more if I do drink. What can I do?'

Then the alternatives have to be considered:

1. Interrupt his conversation. Tell him that I don't want the drink because I am an alcoholic and must not drink.
2. Wait for the drinks to arrive and then do the same.
3. Interrupt and give another reason for not drinking.
4. Wait and give another reason for declining.
5. Apologise to flight attendant and ask her to change whisky for soft-drink and then offer explanation to friend.
6. Abuse friend for not having courtesy to ask you if I want a drink.
7. Say nothing, but don't drink whisky.
8. Say I am not feeling well and ask him to drink mine.
9. Drink whisky, but resolve to have only one.

We will use these three situations to illustrate the decision-making process, which is the next step.

Step 4: Selection of Best Option

In deciding what to do, we make a list of all the options that might work and put them in order from best to least likely. In doing this, it is essential to bear in mind the orientation discussed earlier. Any option that involves alcohol cannot be accepted: as the aim is to remain calm, the angry or aggressive options are also out. Any option that allows someone else to walk over the top of you, to hurt or to humiliate you or to make you feel small cannot be accepted, and all the other points have to be considered because all six sections of the problem-solving process are interrelated.

The shopping situation

The task here is to match the options with the problem and judge how likely each one is to solve the problem.

1. Walking up and doing all the shopping is rejected, because getting everything on the list will mean a package too heavy for her to carry. Decision — reject.
2. Getting the essentials is a possibility because it will solve the problem, but will mean two trips. Decision — a possibility.
3. This is rejected on two counts. There are no satisfactory substitutes for some of the items, and she knows it is important for husband to have the car the following day. Decision — reject.
4. Both children are studying for exams the following week, so she decides it isn't fair to ask them for help. Decision — reject.
5. Same as No. 4. Reject.
6. This is a possibility but her habit is to borrow from neighbours only in a real emergency. Decision — reject.
7. The supermarket requires orders to be in before noon. Decision — reject.
8. It is unclear whether any neighbour will be driving to the shop. Decision — reject.
9. She can ask husband to pick up all the goods on the way home, but he frequently works overtime. Decision — a possibility.
10. Having a showdown implies anger and aggression. Definitely out. It does however raise the possibility that she might need more help with the housework. This is another problem, to be solved later.
11. Buying another car is also another problem.
12. Doing nothing does not solve this problem and is likely to create more problems.
13. Another problem.
14. Another problem.
15. Another problem.
16. Walking up, buying the lot and getting a taxi back will solve problem and save a second trip. Decision — accept as best solution.

As a result of thinking through her problem calmly she has arrived at a decision that will almost certainly succeed. In the unlikely event of a taxi not being available, she decides to ring husband for help (a variant of option 9). While thinking this problem through it has become clear to her that the thought of going back to work on a part-time basis and using the money to buy a second car is very attractive, so she files this away as a separate problem, to be dealt with in the near future.

The workaholic husband

1. The first option involves a confrontation and a threat of divorce. In this form it is aggressive, and threats should not be made at all, because they back you into a corner. Decision — reject.
2. Describing the situation calmly, honestly and directly and asking for full communication about the problem is usually the best way. Accept as a good option.
3. Seeking marriage guidance is often desirable if the marriage looks like failing, but usually a face-to-face discussion between the partners is desirable first. Decision — a good option if number 2 does not work.
4. Any friend is likely to be biased and usually does not have the skills to settle marriage problems. Decision — reject.
5. Going home to mother does not solve the problem. Decision — reject.
6. Accepting situations that make you unhappy is asking for trouble. Women have rights in marriages and must assert them. Decision — reject.
7. Ringing his boss and demanding that he do something is likely to antagonise the husband, who has a right to keep his private affairs confidential. Decision — reject.
8. Doing nothing does not solve this problem. Reject.
9. Asking him to change his job might work. Decision — retain as a possibility.
10. Making an offer to work part-time in return for him working less might work. In this case it is not necessary, because there is plenty of money without the extra work he is doing. Reject.
11. Working to counter loneliness will not solve the children's problems. Reject.
12. Tranquillisers have only temporary effect. The problem would remain. Reject.
13. Learning to play golf might help, but the basic problem would still be there. Reject.
14. Seeking divorce might be necessary if he refuses to change, but this seems premature. Decision — keep this option open.
15. Having a few brandies is not possible for alcoholics. Avoid at all costs. Reject.
16. Going away for a week is not necessary. Once the options are

listed, it is better to decide and act at the first favourable opportunity. Reject.

17. Suicide would probably make the situation of the children worse, and their rights are very important. Reject.

The woman decides to face the husband (option 2), to seek marriage guidance if he will not change (option 3) and, if necessary, to seek divorce (option 14). In fact, as was reported earlier, she lost her nerve when he came home, failed to assert her rights, and said nothing. Her return to alcoholic drinking followed shortly after.

The aeroplane drink

1. This option sounds good because action is taken immediately after a lightning review of the options. It would solve the problem provided there is no reason why the friend should not be told of the alcohol problem. In this case there is no such reason. Decision — accept as the best option.
2. Waiting is not a good idea. The longer the time, the harder it is to justify delay. Reject.
3. A quick interruption with another reason for not drinking would be appropriate if there is a good reason for not telling the friend about the alcoholism. Decision — reject in this case.
4. This option involves delay and does not specify the reason to be given. Avoid lying at all times. Reject.
5. Equally as good as option 1 if she has disappeared and returns with the drink before option 1 can be implemented.
6. Abusing people is aggressive behaviour, which, in this case, would almost certainly lose him a friend who at the worst has been a little discourteous. Reject.
7. Saying nothing, but not drinking, leaves him with the new problem of disposing of the drink. Decision — reject.
8. Saying he is not feeling well is a lie. Alcoholics are often inveterate liars and this habit has to change during recovery. Reject.
9. Anything involving drinking is out for alcoholics. Reject.

The man put option 1 into operation and everything went off smoothly. The friend changed the order and the conversation flowed on.

These three cases serve to illustrate how the orientation and the generation of options usually leads to a sensible decision on what to do to solve the problem. Wherever possible, fall-back options should be generated in case the first does not work. For the woman with the workaholic husband, it would probably have been better if she had included in her decision a further clause. 'If he reacts badly, I'll drop it and allow a few days to pass before I return to the subject. This will give him time to think about what I have said and perhaps he will then be prepared to discuss the situation.'

Step 5: Putting the Decision into Action

This is assertion, to which the next chapter is given. It is useless working out what to do if, when the time comes, the person does nothing. That means he or she allows other people to trample on her or his rights without even letting them know what they are doing. This is actually showing a lack of respect for the rights of others, who have the right to know about conditions or circumstances that concern them.

People fail to act because they are afraid of getting hurt emotionally and sometimes physically. They also fail to act because they are afraid of upsetting others and for various other reasons. Even if the decision turns out to be wrong, it is better to act than to do nothing, because it gives them the chance to try again and at least lets others know where they stand and how you feel.

Step 6: Assessing the Success of your Action

Quite simply, this is just looking at the result of putting a decision into action. There are many possible outcomes, a few of which need special consideration.

Complete failure

If the action does not solve the problem, at least the person has done his or her best. The only thing to do is to accept the situation as a new problem to be solved and to start again. It is possible that she or he failed to take account of critical factors. For example, there is reason to suspect that the workaholic in question had ceased to love his alcoholic wife long ago and was remaining in the marriage because he was worried what his business partners might say. If she had acted, this fact may have emerged and divorce may have become the first option in the revision of the problem. As she did not act, she blamed herself and felt guilty about not doing anything. She had no chance to discover an important fact before she resumed drinking.

If you don't succeed, say 'stiff luck' and start again.

Complete success

No problems. This will increase your sense of self-esteem and make it more likely that you will handle that sort of situation well if it crops up again.

Partial success

Compromise solutions are frequently the best we can achieve. This may come about because, in the original sizing up of the situation, we overlooked an important element or failed to see that the rights of others were being infringed. Perfect solutions are rare, and too many people fail because they believe that perfect solutions can always be found. At any time where the rights of the individuals conflict to some degree, a perfect solution is unlikely.

Generation of new problems

Free and full discussion of a problem frequently generates new areas for discussion. In her assessment of the options in the shopping problem, the housewife came to realise that she wanted to go back to work and decided to use the money to buy a second car. Her husband pointed out that it would also be necessary to get some domestic help — a new problem to be solved.

Summary

Working out what to do or knowing what to do to solve a problem is an essential step in coping with life without alcohol. Most alcoholics have been failing in at least one significant area of life and each one needs to change his or her behaviour quite markedly in order to cope successfully. Good problem-solvers have a positive and specific orientation to life, have developed abilities to specify properly what the problem is and are not content with a vague and woolly definition. They also have learned not to act impulsively, but to generate a whole series of options about the way in which a given problem may be solved. In choosing between the options, they ensure that they protect their own rights and feelings, but also consider the rights and feelings of any others who may be involved.

Once an option has been selected, it should be put into operation without delay and without worrying about what others will think. In assessing the outcome, the most important aspect is to realise that no matter how carefully the problem was sized up, failure is always a possibility, and we have to learn to cope with failure. The best way is to say something like: 'Well, that certainly didn't work, but at least I gave it everything I had, so that's O.K. Stiff luck for me. I'd better go back and try again. I must have missed something important somewhere along the line.'

The three examples included one that was unrelated to alcohol. Most of the problems that result in alcoholics returning to drink arise in the family and have little or nothing to do with alcohol or drinking. It is the way alcoholics assess each situation as it occurs and the way they go about solving these everyday problems that have the potential for relapse drinking. Becoming a good, calm, problem-solver will increase the probability of remaining abstinent.

9
Being Assertive

In the previous chapter, a framework for working out what to do when faced with a problem, a choice, a demand, or an event was outlined. It was maintained that this rational appraisal of and sensible decisions about these day-to-day problems were essential for survival of alcoholics, many of whom tend to act impulsively on the first solution that comes to mind instead of carefully considering all the available options.

Working out what to do in any given situation is only part of the process. The next part is equally important in dealing with the problem. *We have to ACT and put the chosen option into effect. This action is called assertion.* If we fail to act, we may get angry, depressed or otherwise upset, and this can lead to a relapse. In this chapter it is argued that learning the skills of assertiveness enables alcoholics to regain control of their lives because they can replace two unadaptive ways of behaving. Thus angry, aggressive behaviour, which was shown to lead to trouble in Chapter 6, can be replaced by calm, assertive behaviour. Similarly, submissive, non-assertive behaviour, which allows others to dominate us, can also be replaced by assertive behaviour, which allows us to protect our rights and feelings from those who want to humiliate, manipulate and ride roughshod over us. It is with a list of rights that need to be protected that we begin.

The Basic Rights

Throughout this book emphasis has been placed on the fact that a recovered alcoholic is just as worthy as anyone else, and has a right to be treated as a normal member of society. Similarly, it has been stressed that living in the past is dangerous, and that once amends have been made for past misdeeds, the past should be forgotten and the alcoholic should concentrate on getting the present fixed, with some thought for the future. It is essential for alcoholics especially to learn from the mistakes they have made in the past and not repeat those mistakes. However, as we have already said, it is equally important that they do not feel guilty about their past or allow anyone close to make them feel guilty. In the chapter on self-esteem, the recovery process was seen as moving the poorly functioning, self-centred, dishonest, alcoholic Self towards an individually chosen, abstinent, fully functioning Ideal Self. Unless we become assertive and protect our rights and feelings by taking action, this movement will not be possible. In order to protect these basic rights, we have to know what they are. Fourteen rights are listed below. The first two, like the other twelve, are rights common to everyone, but are so critical for alcoholics that they head the list.

1. The right not to drink alcohol under any circunstances.
2. The right to be treated as a normal member of society and not as something strange or abnormal.

The remaining rights apply to everyone irrespective of their sex, age, occupation, race or religion.

3. The right to protect our feelings.
4. The right to be treated with respect.
5. The right to ask for something we want.
6. The right to make mistakes.
7. The right to say no and not feel guilty.
8. The right to ask for help.
9. The right to take time to think.
10. The right to be as happy as possible and to feel good about ourselves.
11. The right to refuse to do our best at all times.
12. The right to say 'I don't know'.
13. The right to be satisfied with less than a perfect solution.
14. The right to change our minds.

These rights belong to us. They are not rights we have to earn or win. They are not things that are given to us by other people who consider themselves as better in some ways than we are. When a baby is born it has these rights, even though it needs others to protect and help it for many years. Any alcoholic who is attempting to recover is entitled to a full restoration of these rights. While drinking excessively, alcoholics are without sense and are even insane at times. They do not protect their rights and feelings well and, what is worse, rarely show consideration for the rights and feelings of those with whom they live and work. Once we fail to grant others their rights, we forfeit our own. So any non-drinking alcoholic who is willing to be considerate of the rights and feelings of others is entitled to all the rights that others share.

Right 1

During the drinking years, alcoholics often accumulate a number of friends or acquaintances with whom they drink heavily. After treatment, some of these people exert pressure on the alcoholic to return to some form of drinking and often pour ridicule on the idea that it is essential for complete abstinence to be maintained. Remarks such as the following are common.

'One or two couldn't possibly hurt you!'

'What sort of a friend are you if you won't drink with me?'

'You mean you won't drink with me to celebrate my promotion?'

'The boys have missed you. Come over for a few drinks now to celebrate your recovery.'

Often this pressure to drink occurs because of the total ignorance about alcoholism, but sometimes it is because that person has a drinking problem himself or herself and reduces his or her own feelings of guilt by getting someone else to join in. *Because alcoholism cannot be cured, but merely arrested, all alcoholics have the right to refuse to drink no matter what the occasion, no matter how close the 'friend' and no matter how great the pressure.*

Right 2

Because of the lack of understanding in the community about alcoholism, because of the havoc that usually accompanies the drinking years, there is an understandable tendency for those who have been affected to treat the alcoholic as a second-class citizen who cannot be trusted, who is likely to go off the deep end at any moment, and as one who is different or abnormal. *A non-drinking, recovering alcoholic is not abnormal and has the right to be treated as a normal member of society.* Because the way others regard alcoholics is understandable, the process of getting others to accept this basic right will certainly depend on the maintenance of sobriety and on evidence of being worthy of trust, and this may take some time. The major thing is how the alcoholic views himself or herself. If the alcoholic has in his Self the ideas that he or she is O.K. so long as no drinking occurs, that he or she is normal and not some social outcast, then he or she will act in ways that tend to prove this. If, however, she or he accepts the notion of being hopeless and of being a failure unworthy of trust, then the chances of a return to drinking are high.

Rights 3 and 4

Everyone has the right to protect their feelings so that they don't become hurt, humiliated or upset by the words or actions of others. This right does not disappear because someone is an alcoholic, but people are more likely to say things that hurt alcoholics than they are likely to say hurtful things to others. These remarks include obvious ones like 'What would you know? You're just a drunkard' to more subtle ones like not being consulted by the family about important decisions. Outside the family, alcoholics are entitled to protect their feelings from doctors, lawyers, tradesmen and generally to be treated with respect by all with whom they come in contact.

Right 5

Everybody has wants and everybody has the right to express these wants clearly and directly. An important part of living is being able to communicate to one another so that we know exactly where others stand and they know how we stand. However, many people seem to expect others to read their minds or they express their wants and desires in such vague and indefinite ways that others cannot know with any certainty what the position really is. In the following remarks we can see the difference between a calm assertion of a want and an aggressive and a submissive version.

(1) 'I want you to stop raking up the past, because we cannot change what has happened, and talking about it only upsets us both. I want to concentrate on making our present lives happy.' This is an assertive statement, which says quite clearly what he or she wants and gives a reason for it. It is done calmly and lets the other person know what the problem is without attacking him or her.

(2) 'You really are a pain in the neck the way you are always throwing the past in my face. Why don't you shut up about it or I will leave.' This is an aggressive way of handling the situation, which may solve the problem of raking up the past, but which will almost certainly make the other person resentful and perhaps cause further problems because he or she might get angry and tell the speaker to leave.

(3) 'All this talking is upsetting me. I think I'll go to the library.' This is a non-assertive way of trying to cope. It leaves the other person in doubt about what actually is upsetting us. And with-

drawing from the situation by going to the library leaves no chance for the situation to be clarified.

When we want something, it is best to say it clearly, directly and honestly. Then we stand a good chance of getting it. Some examples are:

(1) 'It would be terrific if you would visit me more often.'

(2) 'I want you to stop telling people I am an alcoholic without my permission.'

(3) 'I would like it if you would come with me to a few meetings of Alcoholics Anonymous.'

(4) For an alcoholic with very strong non-drinking habits, 'I know you like to have a drink with your meals. Keeping alcohol in the house will not endanger me now, so I want you to feel free to keep bottles here and to drink when you wish.'

(5) 'I feel that I am not being consulted about managing our finances. I am not drinking now, so I want to take part in all financial decisions.'

Right 6

No matter how expert we become at coping with the problems that face us, we will make mistakes from time to time and *we have a right to make mistakes without being blamed, accused or being made to feel guilty*, because everyone makes mistakes. When some alcoholics make mistakes they are likely to associate the mistake with, and blame the error on, their alcoholism rather than accepting it as a normal mistake that anyone might make. Mistakes are not crimes. An appropriate response to making a mistake is to say, 'Stiff luck for me. I got it wrong. I'd better try again.'

Right 7

Many people believe that when a friend or member of the family asks them for help, they must say 'yes' because they have a right to be helped. Generally speaking, we try to help as often as possible, but we have a right to say no when it conflicts with other priorities. We have a limited amount of time and energy, and if we say 'yes' to everything and everyone, our lives become a mess. It is not selfish to say 'no' if it is not in our best interests when we look at all the demands being made upon us. If we say 'yes' consistently, we may find ourselves without the time or energy to cope with something really important.

Close friends may get hurt a little if we refuse a request, but it is in their interests as well as ours not to agree to do something we don't want to do, because we would resent it and them.

Right 8

Alcoholics are inclined to be over-cautious about asking other people for help. Generally we should try to become as self-sufficient as possible, but there are some situations and events with which we find it difficult to cope because we don't have enough experience or ability. In these situations, it is wise to ask for help from those who are more likely to be able to deal with it. Many people, in fact, feel flattered when asked to help in areas where they are competent. Of course, they have the right to say no, and if they do, we must accept this and seek help elsewhere without resenting the refusal.

Right 9

Many people want us to make instant decisions when there is really no overwhelming urgency. Insist upon your right to take time out to examine the options available to you, so that you are less likely to make the wrong decision. When someone says, 'I need an answer right now' it usually means 'fairly soon'. If you say, 'Look, I want to think this through. I'll get back to you today, as soon as I've reached a decision', this will usually be accepted. Agreeing to go on a holiday with someone when it would cut across other commitments or with whom you really wouldn't feel at ease is often done under such pressure. Agreeing to join an organisation or go to a party when you really don't want to can be avoided by taking a brief time out to think about whether you really do want to agree.

Right 10

Many alcoholics don't feel they have a right to feel happy or to say to themselves, 'I'm really a nice sort of person when I'm sober.' Everybody has this right, no matter how bad the past has been, provided a concentrated effort is being made to succeed in the present. They should not wallow in self-pity or feelings of guilt. They should make the present as happy as possible for themselves and make the lives of those close to them happy too.

Right 11

This is a variation of saying no without feeling guilty. While we may not say no to a request, we may say, 'Well, I can't help all day, but I'll come along and help clean up for two hours in the morning.'

Right 12

There is no reason in the world why we should know everything, so there is nothing to be ashamed of in saying, 'I don't know.' If you are really interested or curious, you may want to find out, but often the best thing is to suggest to the one asking the question where to go to find out the answer. If not, you just leave it at, 'Sorry, I don't know.'

Right 13

Because protecting our rights and feelings also involves consideration of the rights and feelings of others, it is often impossible to please everyone. Compromises on some issues will have to be reached. Despite this, some people feel that anything less than a perfect solution is a failure. This is irrational, because when we are trying to reconcile rights that are often conflicting, perfect solutions are just not on.

Right 14

This is really a variation of our right to make mistakes. If we made one decision about how to act and then find we have made a mistake, or if fresh evidence or other factors not previously considered become available, we have the right to change our mind. Many people become stubborn once they have made a decision, and stick to it even when there is clear evidence that they have made a mistake and that they should change their minds.

Protecting Our Rights

As we have already stated in earlier chapters, the most effective way to protect our rights is to become assertive. Assertion involves remaining calm, stating our wants and expressing our feelings honestly, directly and appropriately. It also involves taking into consideration the rights and feelings of others, and very importantly it includes the expression of positive feelings, such as kindness, gratitude, affection and love.

ASSERTION INVOLVES:

1. Putting our problem-solving choice of option into action.
2. Protecting our own rights and feelings.
3. Considering the rights and feelings of others.
4. Expressing positive emotions towards others.
5. Expressing wants and feelings honestly, directly and appropriately.
6. Being calm.

The motive for assertion is to communicate ideas, feelings and desires to others so that the problem can be clarified and solved through full and free discussion. Many people believe that the purpose of life is to get their own way at all times, to win every argument, and that the best way to achieve these aims is to be very aggressive. To gain their objectives they are prepared to hurt, to humiliate and to alienate others.

AGGRESSION INVOLVES:

1. Putting our case by raising our voices, yelling and demanding in an angry manner.
2. Ignoring the rights and feelings of others.
3. Trying to achieve our goals at the expense of others.
4. Closing off communication.
5. Alienating others.
6. Being angry.

The motive for aggression is to dominate, to hurt and to humiliate others to gain one's own ends. Aggression is aimed at stopping communication and preventing an examination of options that don't please the aggressor. The way of behaving that many others frequently adopt is to be non-assertive or submissive.

NON-ASSERTIVE OR SUBMISSIVE BEHAVIOUR INVOLVES

1. Being so overly concerned about what others think of us, about hurting their feelings, about pleasing them that we fail to act on what we have decided to do, or something that is unlikely to solve the problem well.
2. Failing to protect our rights and feelings.
3. Allowing others to hurt and humiliate us.
4. Ending up feeling miserable and depressed.
5. Being anxious.

The motive underlying non-assertion and submission is to please other people. It rarely works, as they end up losing respect for us, they become irritated, disgusted and feel pity for us. *Our wants and feelings are not communicated, so discussion is restricted.*

Factors in Being Assertive

The most important thing in being assertive is the *carrying out* of whatever it is we have decided to do after carefully considering all the available options. A case study of a female alcoholic is useful here. This woman married in the middle stages of her alcoholic life. She soon realised that she had made a mistake, because the marriage was making her unhappy. Had she analysed the situation then she might have listed her options in order as:

1. Putting up with things and hoping they will get better.
2. Speaking to husband about her wants and feelings. Asking for specific changes.
3. Seeking marriage guidance.
4. Obtaining divorce.

She did not analyse the situation but adopted a mixture of options 1 and 2 over the next eight years, usually putting up with the problems and trying to communicate her feelings to her husband from time to time. As it happened, she lacked assertive skills and backed off discussion because he became aggressive every time she raised the issue. This led to further drinking, hospitalisation and a return to the same situation. This situation continued for three cycles. After the third hospitalisation she sought marriage guidance from a counsellor experienced in dealing with alcoholics. The marriage was examined and the basic problems isolated. Both she and her husband agreed to make fundamental changes in the treatment of one another to give the marriage another trial. This failed because the husband did not really believe that women have any rights and soon reverted to type. Despite her financial dependence on him, this young woman started divorce proceedings. Despite her fragile hold on sobriety, she continued to assert her rights and is now divorced. She has now been sober for eighteen months and is obviously very happy, leading an interesting social life and doing well at her job in personnel work. Once she found the courage to seek help and began to assert her right to be treated with respect, her life began to improve. An earlier assertion of these rights probably would have led to the same end, and some years of alcoholic drinking may have been avoided.

Another alcoholic started a cycle of going into hospital for treatment, coming out and going straight back to drinking. This led to three hospitalisations. The problem here was massive anxiety about going back to work. The counsellor arranged for the man to ring his personnel officer from the hospital. The personnel officer was told that the alcoholic had voluntarily sought treatment and leave without pay was arranged.

After leaving hospital the third time, the man was advised by his counsellor to ring and thank the officer for his help. To his surprise and delight he was told that arrangements were being made for him to start work in a different department on his return. This lowered the anxiety level a great deal and a week later the man returned to work accompanied to the door by his wife. Since he was helped to assert himself to make the two telephone calls and helped to get into the front door without alcohol, he has gradually been coming to terms with his problems.

Aggressive and non-assertive behaviour are not concerned with clear communication and consideration of the rights of the other person. An example will clarify this difference. A male alcoholic, in his second year of sobriety, has decided to pluck up courage and tell his mother he is about to get engaged to a girl whom he has known for many years. As a first step he wants to invite the girl to his home for a meal with the aim of introducing her to his mother. The mother has always dominated him. She chose the school he went to, decided that he should become a mechanic and, in fact, has played a major role in every big decision he has made. He has come to realise that trying to please her has become the main motive in his behaviour. He has practised being assertive at work and with his friends and found that it paid off. In deciding what to say to his mother he considered three options, one assertive, one aggressive and one his customary submissive role.

Assertive option

'Mother, I have some good news. I have been going out with a lovely girl called Jean and I intend to marry her. I want to invite her home for dinner so that she can meet you and the immediate family. I have arranged for her to come next Saturday at seven. I assume that will be O.K. with you.'

Aggressive option

'In the past you have never allowed me to do anything without asking you first. I'm sick to death of that and the way you carry on about everything. I'm getting married to a girl called Jean whether you like her or not. She's coming to dinner next Saturday. If you're not nice to her, we will walk out and I won't be back.'

Non-assertive option

'I've met this girl called Jean and I was wondering if it would be O.K. if I invited her home sometime soon. I hope you like her, because I'm thinking of getting married. What do you think?'

The definition of the problem to be solved might be: 'I want to inform my mother that I have met a girl whom I intend to marry and that I want to bring her for dinner next Saturday. What is the best way to do that?' Quite clearly the non-assertive option will not solve the problem, because it does not specify how he feels about the girl, nor does it specify when he wants to bring her home, or why he wants to do this. It leaves the domineering mother with a lot of easy ways to refuse or delay. For example she might respond:

'Yes, that's nice. We'll have her over sometime soon.'

or

'Well, I'm pretty busy, but I'll see what can be arranged.'

or

'I think you're too young to be worrying about getting married. Wait until you are making more money.'

The aggressive option contains at least four remarks that are likely to make the mother angry, and are almost certain to make her resent and dislike the girl without even meeting her. Even if she did agree to the dinner, it would certainly be a most uncomfortable meal for everyone. The aggressive, angry tone gives the mother the chance to change the subject completely by accusing the son of not respecting her rights because she is being told quite rudely what will happen if she refuses to co-operate. This is the very form of emotional blackmail that the son resents in his mother.

The second part of asserting ourselves is to realise that if we insist on protecting our own rights and feelings, *we must grant others the right to protect their rights and feelings* unless they behave in ways which make them impossible to communicate with. In the example above, the mother certainly has the right to be consulted about someone being asked for dinner and the right at least to be informed about someone her son intends to marry. If she refuses to meet the girl or is discourteous to her when she comes, these rights would vanish and the son would be faced with a new problem about the best way to act from that point. An assertive response might be to take the mother aside and say, 'I understand your reaction about Jean because you are a very possessive woman. However, I want you to stop being rude and start being courteous to her. She has a right to be made welcome here. She really is a nice girl and you would like her if you would only give her a chance. I will not tolerate rudeness. I *am* going to marry her and I would like to remain on friendly terms with you, but that won't be possible unless you accept the decision and be pleasant.'

This statement begins by showing that he can understand her feelings and actions. However, it immediately goes on to describe her behaviour as *discourteous* and asks for an immediate change. The statement becomes even more assertive at the end with a calm statement that if she continues, their relationship will be endangered.

The final factor in being assertive is to learn how to *express positive emotions*. These are expressions of kindness, gratitude, warmth, consideration, affection and love. If we are kind to and considerate of others, they are likely to respond very positively towards us. If they help us, we should thank them in an appropriate way. Many alcoholics find it difficult even to say, 'Thank you.' With those we love, it is essential to speak and act in ways that make our love and affection quite clear to them. It is not sufficient for us to know that we love someone. Others cannot read our minds. We have to tell them how we feel and demonstrate our affection and love by touching them, putting our arms around them and saying, 'I think you're terrific. I love you.'

Alcoholics, and especially male alcoholics, seem to experience difficulties in doing these simple things, but they are essential aspects of recovery. People respond to these actions by liking the person more. Those who have these difficulties often maintain that they can't change because they were brought up in homes where there was never any open display of these emotions. While such a background undoubtedly makes it harder, everyone can change his or her habits once they become aware of the necessity for doing so.

Others, particularly males, believe that making a lot of money or taking a second job is a sufficient way to express the love and affection they feel. This is ridiculous, of course, because while making money might be essential, it has little or nothing to do with feeling emotionally secure and with being loved. The failure to display love and affection openly and directly is almost certainly the major cause of marriage breakdown. In summary, assertion involves:

1. Taking action once we have worked out how to solve a problem.
2. Protecting our own rights and feelings and considering the rights and feelings of others.
3. Displaying positive emotions openly and directly.

As assertion is concerned with establishing and maintaining communication, so that problems get solved with a minimum of fuss and distress, we need to know the basic ways of protecting our rights and feelings. In this section, part of a chapter of an excellent book on assertion by Jakubowski and Lange (1978) has been used in an adapted and abridged form.

Six Types of Assertive Communications

Type 1: I want statements

These statements begin in the following ways:

1. 'I want you to do this' or 'I want you not to do that.'
2. 'I'd appreciate it if you would do this.'
3. 'I'd like it if you do that' or 'I'd prefer you didn't do that.'

Want statements do not guarantee that we will get our way or have our wishes met, but they do inform the other person exactly what it is we want or don't want, or what it is we want them to do. If their wants conflict with ours, at least they know where we stand. If they express their wants, agreement may be reached on a solution. Alcoholics may need to make want statements like:

> 'I want to be treated as a normal person. I want you to stop being apprehensive about the possibility of me drinking again. At the moment I'm O.K. and intend to remain so. I am going back to my old job as a journalist. I know you don't like me working, but I'm bored out of my mind.'

'I know you psychiatrists are busy people, but I want you to be on time for our appointments. It upsets me to wait two hours nearly every time I come.'

'Yes, I would like to go out to dinner, but I'm working late so I prefer to go to a place where I don't have to get dressed up.'

'I am not drinking, nor do I intend to, so please stop searching through my cupboards while I'm out. I want you to trust me. Is that O.K. with you?'

Expressing wants is not the same as making a non-negotiable demand such as 'Be nice or I leave.'

In the earlier example of the man wanting to bring his girl home for dinner, the final remark in the aggressive approach was: 'If you're not nice to her, we will walk out and I won't be back.' This is a non-negotiable demand, not an assertive remark like, 'I assume that will be O.K. with you', which does leave open an option for the mother to state that she would prefer the following week, but really puts her on the spot if she wants to say no. The non-assertive option finished with, 'What do you think?', a question that left the situation open to any sort of manipulation by the domineering mother.

Type 2: I feel statements

In order to express our feelings clearly and directly, it is desirable not to use words like 'upset' or 'good' to cover all our feelings, but to specify quite clearly which emotion we are experiencing. So instead of saying 'I'm upset', we should state whether we feel angry, frustrated, annoyed, anxious, depressed, guilty, sorry for ourselves, or envious. Assertion of any one emotion can also be quantified to show the degree of our anger, for example. By saying 'I'm a bit angry', 'I'm very angry' or 'I'm extremely angry', we communicate our degree of upheaval more fully. Usually, a description of the behaviour that led to the emotional arousal accompanies 'I feel' statements.

'When you ignored me at the party, I felt unhappy and depressed. I would like you to pay more attention to me when we go out together.'

'I was extremely annoyed when you invited your friends to stay for the week-end without consulting me. I had made other arrangements, which I had to cancel. In future, I want you to discuss such things with me and not make unilateral decisions.'

'I felt very happy when you told me how much our life had improved since I stopped drinking. I'm glad our married life is improving.'

Type 3: mixed feelings statements

Sometimes we are happy about one aspect of a situation, but upset about another aspect. This is a conflict situation, which results in most people saying nothing, where it is desirable to get the unpleasant aspect fixed. Such a situation arose for a recovering alcoholic whose boss announced publicly that he was getting a rise and saying how glad he was to see an alcoholic coming good. The man was pleased about the rise and furious about the reference to his alcoholism. A good assertive way to handle this would be to get the boss alone and say, 'I'm delighted that you've found my work good enough to give me such a big raise in salary, and I appreciate your confidence in me. At the same time, I was a bit upset about the reference to my alcoholism in front of the others. They have fully accepted me as a worthwhile member of the team, and I don't want my past to be raked up. Would you mind dropping reference to that bad period in future? I'd certainly appreciate it if you would.'

Type 4: empathic assertion

Empathy is the capacity to put ourselves in another's shoes and imagine how he or she feels or thinks. Empathic assertion involves a two-part statement, where the want or feel statement is preceded by an empathic statement. For example:

'I know you are under a great deal of pressure right now, but I want you to help me with this urgent problem.'

'I know you don't like talking about my alcoholism, but I want to discuss my AA attendance with you.'

'I know that you think our social life is not so hot, but I want to explain how it will improve as my habits of non-drinking get stronger.'

Empathic statements usually soften down the want or feel statements, because they indicate we understand the wants or feelings of the other person, even if we don't agree with them. The importance of empathic statements is that they increase the close relationship with the person. With strangers, it is of less importance than with those for whom we feel affection and love.

Type 5: discrepancy assertion

This type of assertion is used where there is a discrepancy or conflict in what was promised and what was done, and we want it resolved. It is a three-part statement, where the promise is restated, the performance described, and a statement of our wants is put forward.

'You said that you would never throw the fact of my alcoholism in my face. During our discussion about whether to buy a car or not, you mentioned my enormous expenditure on alcohol three times. I want you to stop doing that because it irritates me and it serves no useful purpose.'

'You promised that I would be involved in all important family decisions now that I'm sober and rational. Yesterday while I was at work you and the children decided where we would go on our holidays. I want the discussion re-opened because I want to put forward where I think is a better place to go.'

There is nothing aggressive in the way discrepancy assertion takes place. The concentration is on pointing out that there is a discrepancy between what was promised and what actually occurred. There is no personal attack of the sort: 'You're not to be trusted and that gives me a pain. You promised.' A straightforward description allows the other person to bring out facts to show that he or she had not broken a promise. For example: 'Yes, I can see your point, but the children and I were having only a preliminary talk about where we would like to go. We intended to discuss the whole matter with you at the week-end and see what you wanted before a decision was made. Young Tom was so enthusiastic about going to the snow that he forgot that a decision had to involve you.'

Type 6: assertion of negative feelings

This is an extension of type 5, to cover all situations that upset us in some way. This type of assertion involves four parts:

1. Objectively describe what upsets us.
2. Describe how this affects our life.
3. Describe our feelings about this.
4. Describe what we want to happen.

Families of alcoholics find this technique very useful. For example, the wife of an alcoholic who has not had any alcohol for two years might say:

'[1] We were invited to dinner by Bill and Joan. You refused the invitation without consulting me. [2] I like Bill and Joan and I miss their company. I am getting very lonely because we never go out together now. [3] This isolation from other people and companionship is making me depressed. [4] I want you to consult me in future and to consider the importance of mixing with others as a factor in your full recovery. They know you are an alcoholic and won't put pressure on you to drink.'

Alcoholics, too, have the right to react negatively, and it is most important that these negative feelings are not bottled up, because this usually means that they are accepting things and submitting to situations that they do not like. Assertive action is essential to avoid the feelings of depression that result from bottling up intense anger. Consider the situations where the wife of an alcoholic always goes home to her mother whenever a difficult problem arises. He might deal assertively with his negative feelings by saying:

> '[1] Every time anything hard comes up, you run home to your mother for advice. [2] That makes me feel inadequate, and I get angry. [3] I don't want to get angry because I know that getting angry leads to trouble. [4] I want you to stop doing that. I am O.K. now I'm not drinking. Marriage is a partnership, and I have a right to be consulted. If we talk calmly about these problems, I'm sure we can solve most of them without outside help.'

Elements in Assertiveness

Alcoholics need to practise these various methods of being assertive as circumstances arise. While the examples above involve all the following elements, let us make it quite clear what the characteristics are that mark off assertive behaviour from non-assertive or aggressive behaviour. There are eight aspects of this.

1. *Show respect for ourselves and for others*

The aim here is to protect our basic rights and our feelings. We should never allow anyone to trample on these rights or to hurt our feelings so that we get angry, anxious or otherwise upset. At the same time we have to acknowledge that other people have rights and feelings, and we have to be careful to take account of these so that we don't hurt them.

Alcoholics often are in a difficult position here, because the profound difference between a practising and non-practising alcoholic is not understood. Once an alcoholic stops drinking and begins to make an effort to live without alcohol, he or she is as worthy as anyone else. Alcoholics begin to feel self-respect when they start to assert their rights to be treated in the same way as non-alcoholics. When they begin to become less self-centred and selfish and change towards showing consideration and respect for the rights of others, the recovery process is well under way. Respect for others should not be confused with deference to others because of their position, rank, status, high income or social standing. We do not show deference to anyone because of these factors. Some people in high positions are not worthy of respect, because they abuse their positions for personal gain. Respect for others is independent of status.

2. Be honest

During their drinking years alcoholics are usually dishonest, and lying becomes a part of their way of life. Lies are told about how much they drink, how often they drink and how much they spend on alcohol. The fact of their alcoholism is denied in order to conceal the extent of the problem from others. Lying about absences from work, about hidden supplies, about illnesses caused by the excessive intake and about personal life is the norm.

In order to be assertive they have to be honest with themselves and honest with those around them, because the purpose of being assertive is to help lead a successful life by solving problems and thereby raising the sense of self-esteem. Dishonesty cuts off effective communication, leads to failure and to a drop in self-esteem. Honesty involves assessing their wants and feelings accurately and expressing these wants, feelings, opinions and preferences so that they don't violate their own self-respect or put someone else down. Probably the most dishonest thing alcoholics can do is to continue to deny that they are alcoholics. Denial is usually a prelude to resumption of drinking.

The next four aspects are concerned with whether the assertive communication is APPROPRIATE. To be appropriate, the assertive behaviour has to occur in a favourable location, at the right time and be put forward with just the right degree of firmness. The nature of the relationship between the two parties will also need to be taken into account.

3. Select the right place

Some places are appropriate for a particular type of assertive behaviour and others are not. Generally speaking, private places are better than public ones, but other assertive behaviour has to occur at meetings, gatherings or parties. Public criticism also usually requires a public rebuttal if the criticism is unwarranted. Below are some examples of assertive behaviour that took place in wrong locations.

(1) At the annual Christmas party an alcoholic publicly asked her boss for a move to another department because she was being sexually harassed by a male member of staff who had tried to blackmail her into having intercourse with him or he would have her dismissed. She had every right to be assertive but she chose a public, social occasion, causing some embarrassment to her superior, who

was totally involved with running a successful party. Making an urgent appointment at work would have allowed the complaint to get a much more favourable response.

(2) A male alcoholic criticised his wife about her attitude to AA in front of three other alcoholics on the street outside the meeting place. The privacy of the home would seem to be the appropriate place for discussing this problem.

(3) The husband of a female alcoholic complained bitterly about her lack of sexual responsiveness during a dinner party, to her embarrassment and the disgust of the other guests. Clearly a dinner party is no place to discuss such private details. If he had a case at all, it should have been discussed calmly with her in private.

4. Choose the right time

The timing of an assertive statement or action often decides whether it will be effective or not. The following principles can be used to guide the decision on when to act.

(a) Generally speaking we should act assertively the moment anyone tries to hurt or humiliate us or to otherwise trample on your rights. Whenever such an event occurs, run quickly through the possible options and act immediately. For example, if we are criticised unfairly, it is wise to put the matter right as soon as possible, as seen in the following example.

Supervisor. 'Well, it looks like you're getting back to your old habits. You have been absent for nine days during the last month. I suppose you are hitting the booze again.'

Worker. 'No! I have not been hitting the booze again. If you had taken the trouble to check, you would have found that I had the flu and was off for seven working days with a doctor's certificate to prove it. The other two days were compassionate leave. My parents were killed in a car crash. Would you please stop making these unfounded accusations.'

(b) It is a waste of time acting assertively if the person with whom we are communicating does not have time to listen to us.

Man. 'I want to discuss our budget because I think we are getting into trouble with all these new household appliances you are buying.'

Woman. 'Yes, or course. But right now I have to get the children to school. I'm going straight to the college where I have a three-hour session on business administration. Can we leave this till later?'

(c) It is undesirable to introduce important issues if the other person is tired, irritated by something else or is not feeling well. We have to consider their rights not to be faced with important decisions when they are not at their best. Thus a discussion about a bad school report on one of the children would be better discussed after dinner rather than immediately one or both parties come home from work, when either may have had a particularly bad day. One problem here, of course, is the danger in putting things off and waiting for a 'perfect time', which never arrives. Being assertive means taking action and not putting things off.

(d) While the general rule is to act as quickly as possible, it is also essential to remain calm. Despite our best efforts not to get angry or upset in any way, sometimes a surge of anger may get out of control, and it is best to get this under control first, before acting assertively.

(e) Where the problem arises in a conversation between two people, it is usually better not to interrupt the other person. Listening carefully to the argument or point of view of the other person is an important part of being considerate of the rights of others. However, when the other person perceives our silence as an admission of weakness or guilt, or when he or she dominates the whole scene, it is necessary to interrupt the flow and assert ourselves immediately.

5. Be direct

Being direct means asserting yourself in such a way that our wants or feelings are conveyed to others clearly and unambiguously. Many people have developed habits that cause them to be indirect and to hint at their meaning rather than to state it in any way that will be understood.

Direct statement. 'I am going to an AA meeting tonight because I'm feeling a bit jittery.'

Indirect statement. 'I think I should go to an AA meeting soon because I've been feeling a bit jittery."

Direct statement. 'I want you to cook the dinner because I have to finish this dress for Julie to wear tonight.'

Indirect statement. 'I wish you would help me sometimes. I'm up to my ears in work.'

Unless you state clearly and unambiguously what it is you want or what it is that you feel, the other person simply doesn't know your requirements, unless he or she makes an inspired guess.

6. Adjust the degree of firmness

The intensity of assertive statements should vary to suit the occasion. The following conversation shows the intensity of assertion rising as a 'friend' applies more and more pressure to drink alcohol.

Friend. 'Here we are, Bill. Just one drink for old times' sake.'
Bill. 'No, thanks, Harry. You know I'm an alcoholic and can't drink. I'll have a glass of mineral water instead.'
Friend. 'Turn it up! Mineral water! You're O.K. now. One drink can't hurt you. Take it.'
Bill. 'If you were a real friend of mine you wouldn't try to make me do something that will hurt me. I want you to stop putting pressure on me.'
Friend. 'I've thought for a while that you are changing. A good friend wouldn't refuse to drink with me. Drink up.'
Bill. 'I do not want to drink with you. I want you to go away. Clearly our friendship has finished.'

7. *Adjust the degree of assertiveness according to the relationship with the other person*

Usually we adjust our behaviour a little, depending on whether we are at work, with loved ones or with friends. Being assertive is just another piece of behaviour, which we adjust to meet changing personal relationships, but the principles do not change. We have to protect our rights and feelings against violation in all situations. The way we assert these rights may vary slightly, as in the following situations, when someone wants to refuse a request because of a prior appointment at the dentist's.
Stranger. 'I'm conducting a survey about customer-reaction to our new product. Could you spare me five minutes or so to answer a brief questionnaire?'
Self. 'Sorry. I can't help. I'm running late for an appointment with the dentist. Some other time.'

Superior. 'This is urgent. I want you to do this. It will take only five minutes.'
Self. 'You also asked me to do this other job as a number 1 priority. I cannot do both because I'll be late for the dentist. You decide which is more important and I'll do that, but I can't do both. I'll do the other as soon as I get back.'

Spouse. 'Jean has just told me that she has been invited to spend a week-end at the beach with a family whom I don't know. Can we discuss this?'
Self. 'I can see that this is urgent, and I want to help, but the dentist has made a special appointment for me to fix this tooth which has kept me awake the last two nights. I am running late now. Can you stall a decision until I get back? I won't be longer than one hour.'

8. The appropriate frequency

There is a danger of people turning off if we are constantly saying 'I want' and 'I feel' because they see us as selfish and self-centred. In part, consideration of the rights and feelings of others and expressions of positive emotions will lower the level of these statements. However, we need to get our priorities right and be assertive only about the important things in life. Quite often we can go along with the foibles and eccentricities of others, put up with their irrational demands and be tolerant of their different life-styles. However, when these lead to a violation of our rights, assertiveness becomes necessary.

Assertiveness in Family Life

Situations that end in alcoholics reaching for alcohol because they are unable to cope usually occur in the family. Dyer (1977) asked a large number of people to list the five most common situations in which they were manipulated or victimised by others; 83 per cent of the situations were connected with family life. The list included being forced to visit relatives, to make phone calls, to chauffeur people around; to suffer nagging parents, children, in-laws, angry relatives; to pick up after everyone, to be a servant, not to be respected or appreciated by other family members, to have no privacy, and so on.

The ideal family is one where all the adult members are emotionally independent of one another, where there is respect for selves and for one another, where there is trust, consideration, kindness, gratitude, appreciation, love and affection. The ideal family may not exist, but at least we can strive towards that goal. If the members of the family are unaware of tensions, resentments and so on, they cannot deal rationally with one another. If everyone is calmly assertive at appropriate times, their problems will emerge and be solved with a minimum of fuss. As perfection is impossible, compromises will often be the best solution.

The Greatest Barrier to Being Assertive is Ourselves

People who have not being coping well with life usually lack assertion skills. Their non-assertive and aggressive habits have become very strong. These habits have to be unlearned and the new assertive habits learned. The factors that underlie aggressive and submissive behaviour and those that stop us being assertive form the content of the following chapter.

Summary

After working out what to do about a problem or situation, we have to put our solution into action. The best way to tackle most problems where our rights or feelings are in danger is to be assertive. Assertion involves:

1. Taking action.
2. Protecting our rights and feelings.
3. Considering the rights and feelings of others.
4. Displaying kindness, gratitude, appreciation, affection and love to those who help us or those who are close to us.

The rights that need protecting are:

1. The right not to drink alcohol under any circumstances.
2. The right to be treated as a normal member of society.
3. The right to protect our feelings.
4. The right to be treated with respect.
5. The right to ask for something we want.
6. The right to make mistakes.
7. The right to say no and not feel guilty.
8. The right to ask for help.
9. The right to take time to think.
10. The right to be as happy as possible and to feel good about ourselves.
11. The right to refuse to do our best at all times.
12. The right to say 'I don't know'.
13. The right to be satisfied with less than a perfect solution.
14. The right to change our minds.

The motive for assertion is to communicate our ideas, feelings and desires to others so problems can be clarified and solved by full and free discussion. By contrast, the motive for aggression is to dominate, to hurt and to humiliate others so as to gain our own ends. It is aimed at stopping communication and at preventing an examination of ideas and options that don't please the aggressor. The motive for non-assertion or submission is to please other people, which, as we shall see in the next chapter, is a sure recipe for disaster.

Six types of assertive messages were described:

1. I want statements.
2. I feel statements.
3. Mixed feelings statements.

4. Empathic assertion.
5. Discrepancy assertion.
6. Assertion of negative feelings.

In asserting these messages we need to:

1. Show respect for ourselves and for others.
2. Be honest.
3. Select the right place to deliver the message.
4. Choose the right time.
5. Be direct and say what we mean.
6. Adjust the degree of firmness to the situation.
7. Adjust the degree of assertiveness according to the relationship with the other person.
8. Not to overdo being assertive. We should use it with appropriate frequency, saving our strong assertion for times and situations that are important. We should be assertive if someone is attempting to violate our rights.

It is necessary to be assertive on the job, while shopping, in dealing with professionals, with government agencies and so on, but most importantly in the family circle, where the majority of manipulating and victimising takes place. Family members often expect and ask too much, and expect full and immediate attention to their needs and wishes without showing consideration for the rights and feelings of the alcoholic members of the family.

The chief source of lack of assertion, however, lies within each individual, because no one can be hurt or be manipulated by others unless he or she allows this to occur. The reasons underlying lack of assertiveness are the subject of the next chapter.

10
Factors That Stop Assertive Behaviour

Introduction

Our model of recovery suggests that it is essential to replace angry aggressive behaviour and anxious submissive behaviour with calm assertive forms of action. This implies that our aim in life has to change from trying to win or from trying to please other people, to looking at situations as they arise and *trying to do our best to cope with them*. It demands a change of attitude from one where we see ourselves as in some sort of competition with others to one where we try to use our own skill and potential to the full, to do the best we can without comparing our efforts with others.

If we are to stop being aggressive and to stop being anxious, we need to think about why we get angry and aggressive and why we feel anxious. Unfortunately, we acquire many ideas, beliefs and attitudes during our lives that are not in our interests, and these have to be changed if we are to cope. These are the ones that lead to anger and to anxiety.

Beliefs that Lead to Anger

If we perceive that things are getting out of control, we feel unsafe, insecure and powerless to cope. This is a threat to our sense of well-being, which is followed by a rise in the level of anger and to aggressive behaviour. The internal dialogue that leads to the anger and aggression is based upon a series of irrational, stupid beliefs, which are illustrated by the following:

1. *'I have to win, because losing will prove I'm a failure.'* There are two irrational statements here. We do not have to win all the time to

be successful. Everybody is bound to lose at one time or another. If we do lose, it does not prove we are failures. Also it is being claimed here that 'I have failed' is the same thing as 'I am a failure', and this is obviously ridiculous. Many people fail, but this doesn't prove that they are failures. They may just have gone about things the wrong way or omitted to take account of some important factor. Those who start off by saying 'I must win' or 'I have to win' are backing themselves into a corner where, if they don't succeed, they will feel terrible. If we start with a rational belief such as, 'It would be good to win here, so I'd better think carefully about what to do,' we stand a much better chance of getting the right solution, of being successful and increasing our sense of achievement or self-esteem. If we fail, we haven't backed ourselves into a corner because we have replaced 'I've got to win' by 'It would be good to win', which allows for the possibility of not winning.

2. *'I'm in charge here, so I must not make mistakes.'* Variations of this are: 'I'm a man, so I mustn't show any weakness or indecision' or 'I'm the father, so I must get my way', or 'I'm the boss, so I mustn't let these guys see that I don't know everything about the job' or 'I should be able to do this cooking because I'm a woman'.

These are all irrational statements. *Just because a person is in charge, or because a person is a man or woman or the boss, does not mean that he or she has to be, must be or should be able to do everything connected with that status or position.* Quite clearly *it is desirable* for a boss to know a lot about the job. Quite clearly, for a woman who agrees to do the cooking as part of a partnership contract, *it is desirable* for her to be able to cook. If the man doesn't know important things about the job, he has the options of learning them quickly or giving up the job. There is no sense in saying 'I must be good at this' when there is at least one option that makes nonsense of the statement. A person in this situation might rationally say: 'If I want to remain in this position, it would be desirable to learn about A,B,C and D, because they are important in carrying out the job. How can I get this information and learn these skills as quickly as possible?'

That is, the lack of certain knowledge and skills is seen clearly as the problem to be solved. Saying 'I have to win or be good at this' doesn't help. In fact, if people don't have the ideas or skill, they may look upon themselves as failures or try to bluff it out with aggressive behaviour to those under their direction.

3. *'The world should be fair to me. If it is not, I can't stand it.'* There is a magical, Alice-in-Wonderland, irrational quality about this. There is no reason why the world or anyone in it *must*, *should* or *ought* to be fair to anyone. The only way to ensure that people are

not unfair to us is to calmly insist on our right to be treated fairly in a particular situation or on a particular occasion. Saying we can't stand it when something upsetting occurs is also without sense because, in fact, we can stand just about anything that happens to us. The world may be a pretty rough place where nasty things happen to us. We may be overlooked for promotion, robbed of our belongings, be let down by a close friend or deceived by a wife, husband or lover, but complaining that the world shouldn't treat us like that is a waste of time. These are just situations to be handled like any others. If we can do something about the situation to fix it or make it better, we do so. If not, we need to give up saying 'It's terrible' or 'It's awful' or 'It's horrible that this happened', and replace it with 'Tough luck, bad luck or stiff cheese that that happened, but I can stand it.'

4. *'What right have you to say to me? You should be more tolerant.'* The problem here is that instead of focusing on our own rights and working out a way to protect them, we are challenging a right that the other person has, to express her rights and opinions. Instead of this angry response, it is better to assert our own wants and feelings by saying: 'Last week you promised that you would stop being aggressive. A moment ago you attacked me because I wanted to discuss our lack of social life. I want you to stop being aggressive, because that makes me feel insecure. Instead, I want you to say calmly what your position is, then we can discuss it.'

Basically people become aggressive and try to deny other people their rights because they think they will lose if they are not aggressive. All of the situations above contain at least one irrational element built around the concept of NEED.

1. 'I *have to win*, because losing will prove I'm a failure.'

   EQUALS

   'I *need* to win, because if I don't that will prove I'm a failure.'
2. 'I'm in charge here, so I *must* not make mistakes.'

   EQUALS

   'I *need* to show them I know my work, because I'm in charge, so I *need* to get everything right.'
3. 'The world *should* be fair to me.'

   EQUALS

   'I *need* the world to reward me for my efforts.'
4. 'What right have you to say that to me?'

   EQUALS

   'I *need* your love and affection, so you *must* not say hurtful things to me.'

All of these internal dialogues contain expressions such as should, must, have to, ought to, and need. When we examine them closely, we see that there is no valid reason why people should, must, have to, ought to or need to do what we want them to. It might be preferable if they do, but it doesn't make sense to say they 'have to' love us, be fair to us, or help us. These phrases are signs of emotional dependency and emotional dependency is a sign of immaturity. Young children may *need* to be loved and cherished, but adults can only *want* to be loved and cherished and take steps to achieve these ends. Similarly, there is no valid reason why we should, must, have to, ought to or need to do anything because someone wants us to or because we feel we must. Internal dialogues that contain messages such as these get us into trouble, because coping successfully needs independent thought and action, and these phrases are the ones used by dependent people.

Submission or Non-assertion

The causes of submissive, non-assertive behaviour are:

1. *Trying to please or fear of displeasing other people*

Many people make the mistake of believing that success depends upon pleasing husbands, wives, children, employers and employees, and they run their lives accordingly. They are constantly on guard against doing something that will displease the other person. This is a seductive position because it can be claimed that it is an unselfish way of behaving, which always considers the rights of other people. This is not true, of course, because in denying our own rights while making a decision, we never give the other person any idea of where we stand or what we feel or want. Thus we effectively stifle free and full communication about many issues.

The response of others to submissive people is to feel sorry for them, to despise them for their weakness, and to become irritated with them because they never come clean and say how they feel or what they want out of life. Submissive behaviour may avoid unpleasant situations, such as outright confrontations and conflict, but it rarely, if ever, solves an important problem satisfactorily. One of the main aims in life is to preserve or build up our self-respect and our self-esteem. This aim will not be achieved by submissive behaviour.

Fear of displeasing others is also based on irrational needs for safety and security. The use of words like should, have to, must, ought to, and need to is common, as illustrated in the following sentences.

1. I *must* get high marks in the exam or my parents will be upset.
2. I *need* her to like me, so I won't complain about her always being late.
3. I *should* go over now because she's my mother.
4. I *have to* make a good speech to prove I'm good enough to hold down this job.
5. Maybe I *ought* to go to the doctor with my wife, though it will be most inconvenient.

To change submissive statements into assertive ones, change the musts, shoulds and so on into wants and desires, as below:

(1) I want to get high marks in this exam because that will keep my occupational aspirations open. How can I do this? Studying regularly and revising my work often, keeping calm and planning my work, and keeping healthy with exercise, proper diet and sleep will ensure success, because I know I have the ability to do well.

(2) She is always late for our appointments. This means she is not considerate of the rights of others. I'll describe her behaviour, tell her what effect it has on me and ask her to change. If she objects, then maybe I'm better off without her.

(3) My mother does need help with the garden, but I can't go today because of these other arrangements. I'll ring her and tell her I'll be over tomorrow.

(4) A speech is called for. I'll make a list of the important things I want to cover and think carefully about how other people feel when a new manager is appointed. I don't want to hurt anyone, but I want to make my policy clear.

(5) My wife is very ill. Even though it's going to be difficult, I want to be with her because she is very apprehensive. I'll cancel my other appointments.

Note that the outcome is the same in this last example. The man goes to the doctor with his wife not because he feels an obligation or need but because it is the sensible thing to do. He is considerate of her rights, but not because of some irrational compulsion that might make him feel resentful about cancelling the other appointments. The following example is centred on a wife trying to cope with a relapse by her husband.

Wife. 'I'd better not speak up about his drinking again or he'll get angry with me. I need his love and affection so I won't run the risk of upsetting him.'

A distinction has been made between NEEDS and WANTS. When we say we *need* someone, we put ourselves in an emotional strait-jacket, which will prevent us acting at all or make us take an action that will not solve the problem. In this case the woman is concerned about her alcoholic husband drinking again. Her emotional dependency or need prevents her from taking action that may halt him in his tracks.

Needs should be translated into wants. If she had started with the rational position, 'I want his love and affection', she could then take positive action to get this, possibly without provoking him to anger and aggression. She might have used the technique of empathic assertion. 'I understand that you are under a great deal of strain because you are having trouble at work but I want to discuss with you the problems you are causing for yourself and for me by attempting to cope with difficulties by drinking alcohol.' While this attempt to stop him drinking might not work, at least she is beginning to assert herself and make her position clear. It is certainly more likely to work than doing nothing. If he returns to excessive drinking because she said nothing, the chances of him displaying the love and affection she wants would be minimal.

2. *Fear of rejection or retaliation*

The most common place where fear of rejection is the motive underlying submissive behaviour is within the family or in some other close relationships. Wives and husbands fail to assert themselves because they want to please their partners and because they are afraid that if they really speak up and say quite honestly and openly what it is that they want, and state quite frankly how they feel, then they lay themselves open to being rejected or open themselves up to some form of punishment. This is seen in the following statements:

'If I do that, she will get annoyed and make my life hell, so I'd better keep quiet.'

'The boss will think me a fool if I tell him that there is an easy way to do this job. After all, he's been in the job for years. I'll just go on doing it his way.'

'He is not loving and kind to me, but I'd better shut up or he'll get angry.'

'If I tell her that she made a mistake, she will bring up my alcoholic past to prove that I'm in no position to criticise.'

'Our relationship is in a mess because of my alcoholism. If I speak up I'll get the silent treatment. I couldn't stand that.'

'If I ask her to go out with me, she will tell me she doesn't mix with alcoholics. That would be awful.'

'I know I should tell her I can't stand her sister, but she gets so moody if I criticise her family I'll pretend to be enthusiastic about the visit.'

The common element in all of these is deciding to do nothing when something should be done, or deciding to do something other than what needs to be done, because someone else might reject us or retaliate by becoming aggressive, angry, moody or giving us the silent treatment. In the chapter on assertion, the need to consider other people's rights and feelings was stressed as being of vital importance. This is not to be confused with these situations, where something is done or not done because we are afraid of being abandoned, rejected or attacked if we do what we know should be done.

The result of submissive behaviour of this sort is to stifle any remote chance of free and open discussion. Quite often, we make mistakes about how the other person might react to us if we do assert ourselves. For example, the wife of an alcoholic who had been sober for many years, and who was making a huge success of his accountancy business, declared that she wanted a divorce because it was clear that he no longer cared for her. It turned out that while he was very assertive at work, he believed that he had to make up for his alcoholic years by trying to please her. As a result, at no time did he ever tell her what he wanted out of life or how he felt about the way their income was being ploughed into housing and the comforts that went with it. She thought he was doing it because of an obsession with security. He thought that security was what she wanted, whereas both really wanted to spend a significant portion on travel and entertainment. His desire to please her, and her reluctance to tell him what she wanted, led to a situation where each was guessing at the other's wishes and feelings. Once the problem was realised and the benefits of being assertive were explained, the marriage problem vanished.

3. *Mistaken sense of responsibility*

The problem here is mistakenly believing that if we do something, the other person will feel hurt and that would be our fault. 'She would obviously get upset if I said that I wanted her to stop talking about how much money has been wasted on alcohol. That would be my fault. I won't say anything.' Raking up the alcoholic past serves no useful purpose and reference to it should stop. This man was going to act positively by asking for this, but stopped because he thought that she might feel hurt and saw this as his fault whereas it would have been hers.

4. *Feelings of guilt*

Feelings of guilt about the alcoholic past serve to prevent assertive behaviour and lead to submissive actions.

'I'm just an alcoholic, so I have no right to say anything here.'

'They know I've recently been hospitalised for alcoholism, and they would laugh at any suggestions I might make.'

'I made a mess of helping the children while I was drinking, so I'd better leave it to her.'

'It's dreadful for a woman to be an alcoholic. I think he's wrong, but I won't say anything, because I've forfeited my rights to take part in making decisions.'

'If only I hadn't been so aggressive while I was drinking, I could have said something about his disgraceful behaviour. He shouldn't have shouted at me like that.'

Feeling guilty about the past inhibits effective action in the present. It is vital that alcoholics do not feel guilty, so that they can act assertively to protect their rights and feelings in their non-drinking present. As we saw in Chapter 9, rights are not given, but belong to us provided we are not drinking. Failing to act or taking the wrong action because of guilt at being an alcoholic is a sure recipe for disaster.' Other people consciously or unconsciously manipulate us by making us feel guilty. In various ways they say: 'If you really cared for me then you would do this or wouldn't do that.' Thus a child might say 'Why won't you take me to the circus? All the other kids' fathers do.' Others might say:

'Don't worry about my back. I'll get the chair myself.'

'That's O.K. Don't worry about my cold. I'll do the cooking.'

'It's good to have a brother. You can always be relied upon for a loan.'

The brother is made to feel it would be wrong to refuse a loan. The cooking is done and the chair brought by someone making someone else feel guilty. The child tries to manipulate his father into taking him to the circus through guilt. Guilt feelings have to be resisted or assertiveness becomes impossible.

5. Mistaken beliefs in perfect solutions

The belief is common that there are usually perfect solutions where nobody feels hurt or upset in any way, and that if they do it is our fault. Perfect solutions are not all that common, and provided we have given careful thought to the problem, considered all its aspects and given thought to the rights of others as well as to our own rights, then we have done the best we can. If in the process we say no to a request for help, or stop someone from doing what they want, we have done our best. If that someone feels hurt, it may be because they were asking too much of us, presuming on our relationship or otherwise expecting too much. If you say no and give reasons for your refusal, you have no reason to feel bad if they get upset. This may be less than a perfect solution, but it may well be the only one that takes all the factors into consideration.

The desire for perfect solutions sometimes leads people to trample on the rights of those they are trying to protect. Such an example occurred when a male alcoholic took his wife to a dance. During the evening a stranger, somewhat the worse for drink, asked her to dance. She declined to dance with him. Shortly after, the stranger came back and became insistent that the wife dance with him. Now the husband firmly believed that he had to protect his wife and became quite aggressive, threatening to punch this man unless he left his wife alone.

Fortunately, the wife knew her rights, and she quietly asked her husband to keep quiet and to leave her to deal with the problem in her own way, which she did without any fuss. Discussing the incident with her husband later, she asked him not to assume, just because he was a man and a husband, that he had to protect her. As she pointed out, she had had years of experience dealing with men and had learned techniques of getting rid of pests like that one. By taking charge of the situation unasked, the husband was actually trampling on her rights, because he wrongly believed that this was his obligation and his right. She had actually considered her options and decided that if her usual techniques did not work, she would ask the management to remove the other man, an option her aggressive husband had not even considered.

6. *Wanting to keep the hidden benefits of submission*

The pay-off for people who are submissive is that submissive people do not make decisions. If we don't make decisions, we can't be blamed for any unfortunate or unforeseen outcome, so we can always blame someone else. Being assertive carries other hidden dangers, which can be avoided by being submissive.

(a) If we are assertive we will often come up against someone else who is equally assertive of a different viewpoint. Usually the honest, direct and calm approach of the two can be resolved by a compromise, or by one seeing that the other has a stronger case. If we are submissive, the point of view of the other will prevail, even if it is in fact wrong. But it does avoid conflict.

(b) If we are submissive, we can avoid the danger faced by assertive people who put forward views or opinions that in fact can be shown to be wrong. If someone criticises us, and we believe him or her to be wrong, we lay ourselves open to be proved wrong if we assert ourselves. This, of course, is just a genuine mistake in judgement and should be treated like all mistakes. 'Stiff luck for me! I really thought I was right, but anyone can make an error.'

7. Manipulating others to make decisions so we hide our true feelings about the situation

Wife. 'We haven't been out together for months. Bill and Joan have asked us to their party. Let's go.'
Husband. 'You would get tired if we went, and you do have to start work early tomorrow.'

INSTEAD OF REAL FEELINGS

Husband. 'I am frightened of that situation. People will notice I'm not drinking and laugh at me. That would annoy me and I might drink.'

The effect of the husband's first remark is to try to get her to decide not to go, without him revealing his true feelings about the issue. Of course, if he does drink at the party when she has insisted on going, he could blame her for deciding to go against his advice. This, of course, is quite irrational, but such situations do occur.

8. Fooling ourselves about our feelings

Submissive people often work out that something is wrong and that they should do something about it, and then talk themselves out of it by saying 'Well, I'm probably wrong, so I'll say nothing.'

Recently, a female alcoholic was convinced by a lot of circumstantial evidence that her husband was having an affair with another woman. She decided to assert herself and find out what the situation was, but then convinced herself that she was imagining things. The husband, who in fact was having a mild flirtation, came to believe that his wife didn't care about him and the flirtation became a major sexual encounter. Almost certainly this would have been avoided by a calm assertion of her rights as a wife.

Dependency and need for approval

Lack of assertion reflects a state of dependency. Submissive people are dependent on others for praise, for gratitude and for rewards, and are frightened of losing love and affection. They are EXTERNALLY directed instead of INTERNALLY directed. Assertive people, on the other hand, work out what to do, taking the right of others into account, and then proceed to act on their decision without trying to please others and without worrying about how others will react. They are INTERNALLY DIRECTED or EMOTIONALLY INDEPENDENT.

Their reward comes from knowing that they have done their best. If someone else says they have done a good job, this external reward is a bonus. We all like these bonuses and we all *want* them, and the more we get the better, but internally directed, *emotionally independent people do not* NEED *external reinforcements.*

The Effect of High Need For Approval

1. The more we try to please others, the less we succeed

The paradox of trying to please other people is that the harder we try, the less it works. On the other hand, if we concentrate on the problem, think through the various options that are available, and protect our rights and feelings by being assertive, the chances of dealing with the problem effectively increase enormously. If we succeed, our self-esteem rises, and so does our confidence about handling this sort of problem. These positive feelings and this confident outlook are transmitted in various ways to others, who begin to look at us in a new and favourable light. Someone who has seen an alcoholic making a mess of things for many years is almost always impressed by this new, confident person who handles day-to-day affairs efficiently. As assertion and problem-solving involve consideration of the rights of others, there is no way it can validly be shown to be a selfish, self-centred approach.

2. Need for approval is based on and leads to uncritical acceptance of the 'rules' of society, and this leads to problems

In Chapter 3 a theory of self-esteem was outlined, which was not based upon what 'society' had decided was right and proper for men and for women, for young and old, for employed and unemployed, and for heterosexuals and for homosexuals. It was argued that much of the trouble in society can be traced to the uncritical acceptance of these rules, and that many of the problems that face alcoholics during the recovery period are based upon accepting these 'rules', which are laid down for various groups.

The example of the alcoholic male who mistakenly believed that he had to protect his wife from the unwelcome demand to dance is an illustration of this problem. This man had consciously or unconsciously accepted the unwritten rules that a man must be strong, independent, aggressive and in all circumstances must protect his wife and children from harm. The assumption that a man is better able to do this than a woman is clearly ridiculous, and ignores the rights of women to protect themselves. As we saw, the man had no rights or responsibilities in this affair, until such a time as his wife asked for help.

As we shall see in the chapter on recovery from alcoholism by women, they are often subjected to enormous social pressure to conform to the roles prescribed by society. Alcoholism in women is regarded as being far worse than it is for men. Why is this? Because society says so. Actually, it is a dreadful state of affairs being a practising alcoholic, but it is equally bad for both sexes. During the recovery process, women can often go to absurd lengths to please their husbands and their families and those with whom they work, because they are aware of the great stigma attached to being a female alcoholic. Trying to please others doesn't work. It is unadaptive and therefore these social pressures have to be strenuously resisted.

Some men, on the other hand, uncritically accept the notion that they must be the breadwinner in the family. If they find it hard to earn a living, they become depressed because they are not living up to their image of what a man is. Few ever seriously contemplate or accept the fact that their wives may be better equipped to earn money while they cope with the domestic chores.

Many male alcoholics have sexual problems after hospitalisation. The chief one is impotence, the greater proportion being psychologically based rather than medically based. The image fostered by society is that a male should be virile, sexually aggressive and powerful. The incidence of sexual problems in non-alcoholics is very high, but male alcoholics who accept society's views are often profoundly disturbed by their poor sexual performance. Instead of going to a specialist sex therapist, they withdraw from sexual encounters, thereby denying their partners their sexual rights. They are often ashamed to seek treatment because men are supposed to be virile, and to admit their difficulty openly is too disturbing.

3. Others begin to feel sorry for, to resent and to depise those who are showing signs of dependency

Take the case of a woman in middle-level management who is always doing things to please her superiors, but who also bends to the wishes and demands of her subordinates. In time both her superiors and subordinates will come to see her as a vacillating, indecisive executive. Even though she may think some of the practices of her superiors could be improved, she never volunteers suggestions for improvement. Even though she can see that certain foremen are failing to control their teams, she says nothing directly and honestly about it, because of her desire to please everyone. Consequently, feelings of pity, irritation and disgust may arise, and statements such as the following will begin to occur more and more frequently. 'For heaven's sake, say what you mean. How can we carry out the management's policy if we don't know what it is?'

Within families, alcoholics who feel they have lost the right to be assertive, effectively stifle communication by trying to please, and resentment about this may grow. The temptation by both the family members and the alcoholic will be to blame the problems on the alcoholism whereas this is a common problem in many families, where someone is non-assertive.

The Growth of Different Types of Dependency

Blane, who has worked for years with alcoholics, maintains that conflict arising from failure to resolve dependency needs causes the anger and depression that leads some to begin abusing alcohol. Undoubtedly infants are completely dependent on parents and other adults from birth for physical needs such as food, liquids, shelter and warmth. Apart from this physical dependency, there is clear evidence that there is also a psychological dependency, which shows itself from birth. Children brought up in institutions where there is an absence of handling, of bodily contact and psychological warmth may fail to develop physically, emotionally and mentally.

Children brought up in normal circumstances require trust, love, warmth and affection in a fairly stable environment to develop emotionally and to become mature, independent people. The search for identity that characterises the adolescent phase is where the stable, new independent young adult emerges. The presence of a dependable, warm and loving environment aids this process of striking out on one's own, tentatively at first but with ever-increasing confidence, by providing the stable dependable base for these explorations in growth. As these tentative moves, often punctuated by hasty retreats, meet with success, confidence grows and the feelings of independence from parents gradually become stronger, until finally the mature independent young adult emerges.

Unfortunately, not everyone has this secure parental base from which to explore the new world of adulthood. Probably the most devastating event for the teenage explorer is the sudden withdrawal of this warmth, affection and support and its replacement with anger and hostility. Take the case of a young girl who fell in love with a young man, decided to marry him, and became pregnant. On finding this out, the man took off for distant parts. The girl's parents could handle the situation while marriage was in sight, but when the man left they turned on her, castigated her for her 'loose morality' and insisted that she put the child in an institution after a discreet birth. The girl was determined to keep the child, met another man who adored her, and married him. Now this young lady was effectively abandoned and deserted by her parents at the time of intense need for support and dependency. She was made to feel guilty for having the child, guilty for keeping it, and on top of this she felt guilty about hating her parents for not meeting her expression of dependency needs with support.

This patient presented for treatment at age 42, when she had had three other children and was still in love with her husband, whom she thought was a most tremendous person. She had been feeling guilty and depressed for all twenty-four years of their married life. Her interest in sex had been sporadic, and her relationship with her husband was on the point of collapse. One of her many problems was that she could not bear him to leave each Sunday for the four days' absence required by his unusual job. This was traced back to fear of abandonment in the same way that her parents had abandoned her. Only when this was explained to her, and the relationship to the adolescent trauma made clear, was she able to see the stupidity of punishing herself for something she was not guilty of in the first place, and the folly of making her husband and children suffer as well. With some extra counselling, this woman was cured of a problem based on dependency, anger and depression that had suffused her entire adult life.

Now the main point of introducing this story is to show how subtle can be the dependency needs that lead to our anger and depression. It may well be that many alcoholics need individual therapy sessions to discover the basic causes of their emotional upsets. Quite clearly, dependency needs are a major factor, and these need to be explored, so the growth of emotional stability and maturity can be resumed.

Blane sees alcoholic dependent males as belonging to a number of types. The first type is the one who openly relies on others for care and support. These men lack initiative, often remain in the home environment, maintaining a child-like relationship with parents or sisters. Paradoxically, some become drifters closely attached to a dominant female who cares for them. When faced with adult male responsibilities they react with extreme anxiety and turn increasingly to alcohol. Others marry a very dominant female and enter a dependency relationship with her.

The second group of dependent males Blane distinguishes is those who are usually found in public drinking places, with lots of male associates acting in a very masculine and often aggressive manner. Blane maintains that these heavy drinkers have very high dependency needs, but are fearful of expressing them openly because of the sanctions against males being dependent and the stress on self-reliance, independence and strength. This conflict is said to generate the anxiety that leads to the drinking. This group he calls counter-dependent.

The third group includes those who are part dependent and part counter-dependent. These men fluctuate between the two, but their lives are marked by sporadic attempts at practising the sorts of solutions found in adolescent behaviour. This implies some flexibility and a desire to overcome the immature dependency, and the outlook for these men in terms of emotional growth is good indeed, provided they get the sort of guidance they need.

Dependency and Confidence

The relationship between dependency and the confidence to work out solutions to problems and to put them into effect is quite clear. Only when dependency relationships are worked through in the way that is characteristic of adolescents will a firm emotional base be built on which future action can be based with confidence. Alcoholics are generally reported as being very high in dependency, and this, as Blane points out, leads to conflict states and to a rise in anxiety level. The problem for some alcoholics is to resume their emotional growth, so that control over the emotions is achieved. This may entail a close examination of their lives to see which category, if any, of dependency best fits them and to take steps to become emotionally independent of that source. This is not to say in any way that the supply of support, warmth, friendship and affection is to be cut off. These attributes are the very stuff of which lasting, fruitful and strong relationships are built. All families and close-knit groups need a firm base of trust and support from which to operate. An adolescent-like *dependence* on such relationships is what causes the trouble. All members of a fully-functioning group have to contribute to the group strength, and adults should have achieved a fairly high level of emotional strength, so that they can play their part in providing the secure base for the younger members to operate with confidence.

Confidence includes the capacity to be able to handle criticism without getting angry, resentful or depressed. This implies that we should also be able to handle failure, and we will all inevitably fail sooner or later. Some will fail more often than others but, provided we are not psychologically dependent on others, we will cope with failure and have the confidence to try things out, even where negative assessment by others is possible or even probable. Emotional immaturity that involves dependency leads to definitional positions like: 'I must succeed in pleasing my wife, to prove that I'm a man. If I don't, then that will prove I'm a failure and a hopeless character.' These dependency feelings lead to emotional arousal, usually anxiety, and result finally in a low level of coping with the problems life throws up to us.

For men, then, emotional dependency causes a conflict between their socially learned role of being independent, strong and assertive and the child-adolescent habits of dependence. Conflict states cause emotional upheavals and vacillating behaviour. These unpleasant feelings are often alleviated by recourse to alcohol. Most people drink, many drink a lot, a fair number drink to excess and become alcoholic. The problem for some alcoholic men is to recognise that they may be emotionally immature and depend heavily on others for their very existence.

Women, on the other hand, usually do not get into conflict about expressing dependency feelings, because it is acceptable in most Western societies for a woman to be dependent. This is a firmly established part of the female 'role'. Of course, this is slowly changing, and women are increasingly coming into conflict situations because of the demands on them to be independent. The problem for women is to see a need to become emotionally independent and to learn and practise the techniques of assertiveness without worrying about what is 'right and proper' for females.

As we saw in the example of the dependent young girl who became pregnant, pulling out the supportive rug from under her feet had a long-term devastating outcome. In effect, her emotional growth stopped or even regressed at that point and her 'adult' life had been a mess ever since.

Now, in an ideal world, all adolescents grow emotionally and become mature adults. This clearly does not always happen, and in fact the majority of adolescents have some emotional problems. When these are severe, emotional illness or alcoholism follows. Women have a further dependence, which is, in part, of a different kind. This is the financial dependency brought about by the way our society is structured, with men being seen as the breadwinners and women being seen as the housewives and child-rearers. The point of view consistently taken in this book is that apart from the biologically imposed differences men and women alcoholics face, similar problems face them in recovery. This is the case with emotional dependency. Both men and women need to resume their emotional growth, to learn to control their emotions and to outgrow dependency needs. Physical growth to adulthood is often not accompanied by this necessary emotional growth, which is part and parcel of the total growth to adulthood and maturity.

Let us return now to the full model of rational thinking that enables us to cope with any problem that might arise in our lives. Dependent people are emotionally immature, lack the confidence to carry out solutions to problems, even when it is quite clear what to do to solve the problem, and are not, therefore, likely to assert their rights and feelings. They will assess a problem as a threat, will become emotionally agitated, and finally will fail to cope. Those who are not dependent, and who are emotionally mature, will confidently assert their rights by trying out the solution they have decided on.

While dependency needs are unfulfilled, frustration will lead to anger, hostility, resentment, anxiety and depression. The thing to do is to recognise any dependent status and take action to become emotionally independent. Blane's description of men's drinking-groups is clearly correct for alcoholic men who depend on these gatherings for support and for emotional succour. In a sense they are like adolescent peer-groups, which rather than encouraging growth tend to perpetuate emotional immaturity by reinforcing dependency, indirectly and covertly, often by maudlin expressions of friendship and praise for acts of physical and sexual prowess, combined with superficial relationships and mutual dependency on alcohol. This is not to say that all drinking-groups are like this. Some come together for brief, genuine social encounters, but the alcoholic is most unlikely to belong to such a group. He will be found in a group of very heavy drinkers, where the ability to drink a great deal and 'hold his grog like a man' is highly praised. The advice given to alcoholics to avoid such groups is sound.

How to Stop Being Dependent

To stop being dependent, five steps are necessary:

Step 1. Concentrate on the problem that faces us instead of worrying about how awful it is, how unfair it is or how upsetting it is.

Step 2. Stop trying to please other people and stop worrying about how they will react to our solution to the problem. Say, 'To hell with what they think.'

Step 3. When we have worked out the best way we can think of to solve the problem, ACT.

Step 4. If we fail to solve the problem say: 'Stiff luck. That didn't work. I'll try something else.'

Step 5. Protect our rights and feelings from harm.

Summary

In this chapter it has been suggested that strong but irrational beliefs connected with aggression or submission interfere with becoming assertive.

The irrational beliefs that lead to anger and aggression, and which are contained in socially inspired remarks or internal dialogues like:

1. I have to win, because losing will prove I'm a failure.
2. I'm a man, so I mustn't show any weakness.
3. I'm the boss, therefore I must not make a single mistake.
4. I'm the father, so I have to get my way.
5. The world should be fair to me. If it is not, I can't stand it.
6. What right have you to say that to me? You should be more tolerant.

Each of these statements contains at least one irrational element. Where is the evidence that the world should be fair and where is the evidence fathers and bosses shouldn't make mistakes? People do have the right to say things to us that we may not like, and failing does not prove someone is a failure. All of these statements are based upon a view of the world that is unreal.

The causes of non-assertion (submission) include:

1. Trying to please or fear of displeasing other people.
2. Fear of rejection or retaliation.
3. Mistaken sense of responsibility.
4. Feelings of guilt.
5. Mistaken beliefs in perfect solutions.
6. Wanting to keep the hidden benefits of submission.
   (a) Not making decisions means we are not to blame if things go wrong.
   (b) Not having to argue with assertive people.
   (c) Being proved wrong if we are assertive.
7. Manipulating others to make decisions so that we can hide our true feelings.
8. Fooling ourselves about our feelings.

The effects of high need for approval or dependency

1. The more we try to please others, the less we succeed.
2. Uncritical acceptance of the 'rules' of society.
3. Being despised, resented and being felt sorry for.

Different types of dependency

Three different dependent types were isolated.

1. The indecisive, clinging person, who is obviously dependent. These people often marry dominant partners, who can be relied on to make decisions.
2. The outwardly aggressive male found in male drinking-groups, where capacity to hold liquor and so-called 'male characteristics' are highly valued.
3. A type that swings between the two first types.

Dependency is seen as leading to inner conflict leading to anxiety and to drinking to allay these anxieties.

Dependency and confidence

Those who are high in need for approval or dependency will lack confidence and have difficulty asserting themselves to protect their rights and feelings, and often will not do what they know has to be done because they lack this confidence in themselves. Dependency or needing the approval of others is a sign of immaturity, because when dependency needs are unfulfilled, anger, anxiety and depression appear.

The five steps to stop being dependent

Step 1. Concentrate on the problem that faces us instead of worrying about how awful it is, how upsetting it is or how unfair it appears.

Step 2. Stop trying to please other people and stop worrying about their reactions to us.

Step 3. When we have worked out what to do, simply do it.

Step 4. If we fail, say, 'Stiff cheese. I'll try again.'

Step 5. Protect our rights and feelings every time they are endangered.

11

Is Recovery Really More Difficult for Women?

In this chapter the main focus is on the recovery of female alcoholics following treatment. Not only are treatment programmes devised for males, but the assessment of recovery rates for females is usually based on the same criteria used for males. It will be argued that this practice introduces a cultural bias concerning the results to such an extent that we cannot accept with any confidence the rather consistent statements that women have a lower recovery rate than men.

An analysis will be made of those factors that seem to show that the recovery process for women is likely to be more difficult. Once again it will be seen that most of these factors are concerned with whether or not we accept the imposition of beliefs about what are 'appropriate' roles and personality characteristics for women in a male-dominated society. It is concluded that despite some real, practical difficulties associated with being a woman in such a society, women have at least one major advantage over men, and that most of the so-called disadvantages can be overcome. Furthermore, the evidence from follow-up studies shows that the proportion of women alcoholics who recover is equal to if not greater than that of male alcoholics.

The Incidence of Alcoholism Among Women

Until recent years alcohol abuse has commonly been considered to be a predominantly male activity. Excessive and harmful drinking by women has received scant attention, and the majority of studies where women's drinking problems were examined were poorly designed. Tamerin *et al.* (1974) and Browne-Mayers *et al.*(1976) reported that the proportion of alcoholic women to men had risen from 1 in 5 in the 1940-50 period to about 1 to 3. The difficulty of getting accurate figures because of the frequency of 'hidden drinking' among women was commented on by Johnson and Garzon (1978).

In 1980 Plant pointed to a steady increase in female alcoholism in Britain over the past twenty years. He stated that while the number of men admitted to psychiatric wards since 1964 with a diagnosis of alcoholism has doubled, the corresponding number of women had trebled. He noted also the disproportionate increase in the rate of convictions for drunkenness, deaths from liver cirrhosis and drunk-driving charges. Reports by councils and agencies dealing with alcoholism in the UK all show a dramatic rise in the percentage of women among their patients, especially in women under 30 years of age.

In another recent review, Homiller (1980) quotes the USA Department of Health and Welfare conclusion that the number of alcoholic women is increasing at twice the rate as that for men. She also quoted people such as the medical director of the National Council on Alcoholism who estimated a 50/50 ratio.

The reasons for the increased incidence of alcoholism in women are unclear. Women are certainly drinking more, in line with the increased consumption of alcoholic beverages in Western countries since the end of World War II. Part of the reasons may be because of the change in the retail outlets for alcohol, where women can buy alcohol with the rest of the shopping at the local supermarket or at the drive-in bottle shop. Coupled with the less restricted life-style for women and adolescent girls, they may just have become 'more visible' and more likely to seek formal treatment, instead of being treated discreetly by the family doctor. The women's rights groups may also have produced an unexpected and unwelcome result. Fraser (1973) concluded, 'by entering the male-dominated battleground which has yielded such ironic spoils as heavier alcoholism and earlier mortality, the liberated woman may well be subject to the pressure to conform to the same code of behaviour as her brother'.

Part of the reason may be bound up with changes in packaging of alcoholic beverages and the availablity of cheap, large containers. In Australia there was a slight drop in beer consumption, but a 300 per cent increase in the sale of table wines between 1970 and 1978. Much of this wine was sold in four-litre casks at low prices. Two-litre flagons have also been sold at low prices. It does not seem unreasonable to suggest that some of this becomes the staple diet for the army of women 'hidden drinkers' and of those not so hidden.

Treatment for Women Alcoholics

In 1971 Curlee noted that treatment for women alcoholics was usually the same as that advised for males. There appears to have been little change since then, and more often than not men and women are treated identically in mixed groups. While this may have some beneficial effects, little research has been done on patient attitudes and responses to various forms of therapy and treatment, where sex differences may be important. For example, research into the teaching of social skills and of assertion-training indicates that for males, active participation in groups seems to yield the best results. Curlee's study, however, suggested that men and women showed a different reaction to group situations. The male patients gave high preference and importance ratings to group therapy, where informal contact with fellow patients was possible, but women patients rated contact with the counsellor, psychologist interview, reading and time to think higher than did the men.

Schultz (1975) noted the predominance of male therapists in the treatment of alcoholism and suggested that perhaps women therapists are more appropriate as role-models for female patients, while her other evidence suggests that women progress better in all-female therapy groups. Sokolow *et al.* (1981) have reported that women do better in terms of remaining abstinent if they are treated in groups that are predominantly female.

Outcome of Treatment for Women

Most of the studies that attempt to assess how alcoholics fare after treatment do not report separate results for men and women. In the studies that do, the measures of recovery or success rate used vary enormously, the common ones being indices of:

1. Mental and physical health.
2. Occupational functioning.
3. Social functioning.
4. Family relationships.
5. Legal and criminal activities.
6. Alcohol consumption.
7. Abstinence.

In assessing mental health, various measures are used. Some of these are sex-related in normal society, and by definition will show women making less progress. A healthy adult in our society is said to be one who possesses characteristics such as independence, adventurousness, dominance and calmness and objectivity. These are the attributes taught to males as desirable male objectives. The socialisation of females on the other hand has been towards compliance, dependence, warmth and similar 'feminine virtues'. When we set up scales and norms for mental adjustment, they are made up of the masculine attributes. Not surprisingly, females come out as less well-adjusted.

In some studies, occupational data are presented on length of employment, job stability, promotion and income, without reference to the fact that many alcoholic women are not even in the workforce. Measures of social functioning fail to take into account the extra difficulties faced by women because their husbands are far more likely to have left them than are the wives of male alcoholics. This simple fact alone makes most of the social functioning data suspect. The same problems arise with the family functioning, where we even get absurd reports of a greater incidence of divorce-separation among women at, say, one year after treatment as indicating 'a poor response to treatment'. The fact that these separations occurred before or during treatment is often ignored.

Undoubtedly, the social sanctions against women drinking heavily let alone becoming alcoholic, the sex biases in psychological measures of adjustment, and the differential reactions of husbands and wives of alcoholics may make it more difficult for women to recover, but they do not prove that women alcoholics will not recover as well as men, providing part of their treatment is specifically aimed at their peculiar difficulties, and providing the sex-bias is removed from the assessment.

Recovery Rates

Twenty-six studies give separate success rates for both men and women. Of these, sixteen showed no significant differences between male and female recovery rates, seven provided evidence of higher improvement rates among female alcoholics, while three supported the popular view that men will find it easier to recover from alcoholism than women.

These twenty-six studies were conducted in the USA, Canada, Scotland, Ireland, New Zealand, Australia and England. The institutions represent a fair cross-section of the varying facilities offered by treatment centres. Although many of the individual studies can be criticised, it seems reasonable to conclude that, contrary to 'expert belief', women have recovery rates that are the equal of, if not better than, those of men. To this list it would be safe to add Corrigan's (1980) study of 150 women drawn from three different types of treatment centres and from a wide cross-section of the community. A huge 71 per cent of the women had not been drinking in the month prior to the follow-up interview, which was thirteen months after treatment; 41 per cent had been abstinent for the entire period and a further 12 per cent had had a drink only on a rare occasion. Few studies of males reach such high success rates.

Table 2. Percentage of Males and Females Productively Functioning and Socially Stable and Abstinent

	MONTHS		
SEX	6	12	24
Female	68	61	65
Male	33	30	33

The measure of success in most studies was abstinence, but some included family adjustment and occupational functioning. For example, Alford (1980) assessed employment-productivity, family-social functioning and drinking behaviour in his study. The following table shows that the females did twice as well as the males when the criterion was productively functioning and socially stable and abstinent. The ratio of success for females over males dropped slightly when the criterion of success was abstinence or light-moderate drinking, but was still heavily in favour of females. The women in this study attended AA much more regularly than the men. Alford notes that 'even light-moderate drinking in this alcoholic population was associated with a relatively higher amount of socially disruptive behaviour', so it seems reasonable to look at the three-part criterion as the better indicator of recovery. Discussing this finding of a 2:1 success rate for females over males, a result quite unexpected to the author, Alford suggests that, 'acceptance of AA philosophy with its emphasis on *surrendering* to the belief that one is "powerless over alcohol", that one's life has become unmanageable, that one cannot control some aspect of his behaviour may be more difficult for males in a contemporary society which continues to value a strong, independent, self-reliant if not self-disciplined model'. Whether this is a male chauvinist response to an unexpected result or a rational acceptance of the differential pressure from society on men and women is unknown. What is clear is that the overall results clearly indicate that women throughout the world have demonstrated that their recovery rate is at least equal to that of men.

Sex-related Factors in Recovery

1. *Social attitudes*

In the previous section reference was made to social sanctions against female drinking. In Western society, generally, the consumption of alcohol by males is regarded as normal and even desirable. The non-drinking male is often seen as deviant, and extreme pressure to drink is frequently brought to bear on him. Even very heavy drinking is acceptable, and in some circles the man who can drink vast quantities of liquor is admired. Only when the harm he is doing to himself and to others becomes blatantly obvious and where his alcoholism can no longer be tolerated does this attitude change to one of non-acceptance and rejection.

For women, on the other hand, anything beyond light social drinking is taboo. In our society, women's roles have clearly been defined to include bringing up children, cooking, sewing, housekeeping, overseeing the education of the children, entertaining the husband's friends and providing sex, but these roles do not include heavy drinking. Alcohol abuse, tolerated in men, in women is treated with scorn, derision, general avoidance and ostracism.

A recent study indicates also that a double standard of mental health is applied to men and women. Clinicians — 46 male and 33 female psychiatrists, psychologists and social workers — were asked to indicate the characteristics of a healthy male, a healthy female and a healthy adult. The characteristics attributed to a healthy adult were similar to those for the healthy male, but not to the healthy female. Women were described by the clinicians as differing from men by being more emotional, more easily hurt, less competitive, less independent, more submissive, less objective and more easily influenced.

If this evidence is coupled with recent research that shows that medical practitioners dislike treating alcoholics generally, then the chances of female alcoholics receiving sympathetic helpful advice from clinicians seem very remote.

While social attitudes to a whole variety of women's activities are slowly changing, it seems unlikely that attitudes to drinking, drunkenness and alcoholism in women will change dramatically in the short-term. This has to be accepted. However, the social rules that define a woman's role as housewife, cook, child-rearer and so on bear some thought, because there is evidence that failure at these tasks, the emotional response to failure and the loneliness and boredom felt by some women result in the resumption of heavy drinking.

In terms of our model the sequence here would be something like this.

Trigger	*Evaluation*	*Consequences*
Women should be good housekeepers, cooks, child-rearers. This means they should stay at home rather than work.	I *need* to be a good housekeeper, etc. I am not good. I have failed. I'm hopeless. This is awful. I can't stand it.	Anxiety, guilt, shame, depression. Drinking. Less capacity to cope. Alcoholic drinking.

Now it is not what society in general says that causes the emotional responses that in turn lead to alcohol abuse. It is the interpretation of these values that is important. Change the individual's belief system and the problem disappears. That is, it is important to understand that to a large extent what society currently says is the right way for women to behave is irrelevant to how we run our lives. If a woman is not a good housekeeper or cook, then all she should do is to change her belief system to another, and the unpleasant emotional reaction will disappear. To break the circle, she should use rational processes to examine the situation. The first thing is to think through the evidence.

(1) 'Where is the evidence that I need to be a good housekeeper, cook, etc. This is a whole load of rubbish made by males. There is no need at all. I could go to work instead and use the money to pay others to do the housework and mind the children. Others do it successfully. There is no evidence that women must be good cooks and so on. In fact, if there is any evidence, it suggests that men are better cooks. Perhaps the rule should be that men stay at home and women go to work. Only if I decide to stay at home does it become desirable that I be competent at these tasks. Then it may be a good idea to take cooking lessons, to buy recipe books or take courses in child-rearing. If I still don't succeed, then I definitely can stand it. Stiff luck for me. This would not prove I'm hopeless. There are ways to compensate. I'll examine all the possibilities.'

Concerning the attitude that it is worse to be a female alcoholic than a male alcoholic, there are several possible responses, one of which we might examine.

(2) 'This is another lot of rubbish. Anyone who abuses alcohol loses control of his or her life. My problem is to remain abstinent so that I can run my life and become fully functioning within the constraints of my ability and circumstances. I will remain calm and

accept the fact that there are people who say this, but I cannot readily change their attitude. Stiff luck for them.'

The only rational attitude to alcohol consumption is for society to accept light social drinking for those who can handle it, but to frown on heavy drinking and alcohol abuse by both men and women. For alcoholics, the evidence is so strong that alcoholics cannot drink at all without grave danger of relapse, that the only rational decision is abstinence.

2. *Self-esteem*

Reports and anecdotal evidence about the lower self-esteem of women alcoholics abound in the literature on alcoholism. We have already seen how Beckman *et al.* (1980) gave a self-esteem questionnaire to male and female alcoholics and to female social drinkers and how the average scores were 2.83 for female alcoholics, 3.26 for the males and 4.80 for the female social drinkers, where the range was from 0 to 6. That is, the female drinkers were found to be significantly lower in self-esteem than the female social drinkers and the male alcoholics.

Blane (1968) wrote 'The central, perhaps inevitable, feature in women with alcoholic problems is a concern, even a preoccupation, about being inadequate and inept, surrounded by an aura of futility that bespeaks her utter helplessness to change herself.' Kinsey (1966) found that many of the 46 alcoholic women he studied believed they were not the kind of person they would like to be, thought themselves to be unattractive, experienced feelings of guilt and loneliness and were dissatisfied with the impression they made on others.

Wood and Duffey (1966) observed that as women alcoholics grew up, 'every one developed feelings of worthlessness and inadequacy'. Curlee (1968) concluded that heavy drinking destroyed the fundamental source of a woman's self-esteem based on her female roles of wife and mother. This in turn led to more excessive drinking and to destruction of self-confidence.

In the chapter about self-esteem it was argued that Rogers's method, in which overlap between the Self, as it is currently perceived, and the Ideal Self is the best measure of self-esteem. *A recent experiment, (Clarke, 1974) actually used this method and found no differences between women and men alcoholics in self-esteem.*

This study reinforces the argument in favour of closely examining social pressures to conform to the norms of society and being prepared to reject them. The evidence on self-esteem scores, as usually measured, is quite clear. Both men and women alcoholics have lower scores than 'normal' people, and women alcoholics are significantly lower than male alcoholics. In terms of treatment and of recovery it seems clear that part of the treatment for alcoholism must be directed at raising self-esteem for both men and women. In order to do this, it is important to understand how self-esteem is measured, and how changes in self-esteem, both up and down, come about.

Most of these evaluations directly or indirectly measure how we think about ourselves in terms of descriptive words such as strong v. weak, happy v. sad, assertive v. compliant, calm v. anxious, thoughtful v. impulsive, orderly v. disorderly, dominant v. submissive, aggressive v. timid, and confident v. shy. High scores are given to those who describe themselves as strong, assertive, dominant, orderly, aggressive and confident. These are the traits that, in our culture, men are taught from childhood as being appropriate male characteristics. Low scores are given to those who describe themselves as weak, compliant, anxious, disorderly, submissive, timid, shy, loving, affectionate and considerate.

Some of these traits are those that have been deemed to be appropriate characteristics for women, and much of their life-experience has been spent in accepting and internalising such roles. When asked to respond to such questionnaires, it is hardly surprising that women get lower scores than men. This is part of the same cultural conditioning we examined earlier, and we can treat it the same way.

Trigger	*Evaluation*	*Consequences*
Women alcoholics are lower in self-esteem than men alcoholics.	This is true only to the extent that I accept that the display of characteristics deemed to be masculine define adjustment and self-esteem.	I need to change my view of women's roles to include assertiveness, strength and confidence, and behave accordingly.

This is not to deny the fact that both men and women alcoholics have a poor opinion of themselves and have low self-esteem. The question is how low self-esteem comes about. The best evidence we have about this strongly suggests that experiences of success or failure determine our view of ourselves. In summing up the work on self-esteem and other self-report measures we can do no better than to quote Homiller (1980).

> As has been noted, addiction for women is less acceptable than it is for men. It may be that women report themselves as deviant, in so far as they

> are told they are deviant. Deviance from norms is 'deviant' but not necessarily 'sickness'. Hence, to interpret the elevation on self-report scales as sickness alone without considering cultural and ethnic norms, is to overlook the probable impact of labelling. Such interpretation can become part of an insidious tautology. Female alcoholics score higher on scales purporting to measure psychopathology, therefore they are judged to be 'sicker', are treated as if they are 'sicker' and therefore score higher on scales measuring psychopathology. (pp. 7-8).

The message is clear. Low self-esteem scores need not be a cause for concern. They may simply reflect acceptance of feminine roles. Probably, alcoholic women would benefit from courses in women's rights, and it is desirable for many to adopt some of the 'masculine' roles such as assertiveness in order to protect their own rights and feelings in their return to a sober existence. The solution is to say that it is the people around us who are wrong in their attitudes to women, and it is time they stopped treating women as second-class citizens. It is clearly undesirable to be an alcoholic, but this is no worse for women than men.

Fortunately, our society is slowly changing, and women are asserting their rights to protect themselves and their feelings and aspirations from attacks by society. New occupations and better conditions for women are opening up. The demand for equal treatment in all areas is slowly being met. Alcoholic women have to cope with their inequality in the first place by realising that different social sanctions are irrational and that they can be on the same footing as men emotionally. Both have to cope with the fact that they are alcoholic.

A recent study by Joan Volpe (1979) of 40 alcoholic women in a halfway house indicates that recovery is associated with re-definition of the Self. She sees the alcoholic as having to learn to cope with an identity as a stigmatised person. Among the tasks that help in restoring a sense of identity, of self-worth, are resuming or gaining employment, becoming honest with oneself and others, overcoming rationalisation in favour of realistic assessments of life's events, being content with small achievements and successes, and coming to terms with the role to be played as a member of the female sex. In her study Volpe found that marital status was unimportant, since family disintegration was seen as an almost inevitable consequence of alcoholic drinking. The overall picture was one of re-definition of the Self in relation to the external world, an aim that is central to AA, the topic of the following chapter.

In summary, it has been argued that the commonly held view that women alcoholics are lower in self-esteem than men alcoholics is wrong, because it is based upon socially imposed values on what constitutes 'proper feminine roles and characteristics'. There is no doubt that female alcoholics are low in self-esteem, but so are male alcoholics. Both have to build up their sense of self-esteem by achieving little successes.

3. Telescoped drinking history

It is well documented that, on the average, women begin drinking at a later age than men, drink less during their alcoholic progression and present earlier for treatment. This telescoped drinking history is commented on by Beckman, who quotes seven studies supporting this finding.

Travers and Hendtlass (1978) present Australian data on 370 persons presenting for treatment at a number of centres in Victoria, Australia, over a three-month period in 1977. 75 per cent were male and the average age of the total group was 42 years 6 months. As with studies in other countries the reported drinking histories for men and women were markedly different. The average age of beginning to drink for males was 19.1 years. For females it was 29.4 years. The distribution of scores for males was markedly skewed, with about 60 per cent beginning to drink between 16-20. The distribution of scores for females was more like a normal distribution, with a few starting very early or very late in life with a peak in the 21-30 age-group.

The average drinking-life for men at time of admission was twenty-five years, compared with seventeen years for women, in spite of the fact that the men were younger at time of admission. The reported average daily consumption was 262 grams of alcohol for men and 186 grams for women, which is only 71 per cent of the male average.

While this factor is often commented on by writers on alcoholism, the implications are rarely discussed. The one exception has been to link this sudden onset of drinking at a later age than men to frequent reports that women begin drinking to alleviate the emotional reactions to specific life situations, such as divorce, separation, bereavement or an obstetric or gynaecological problem. Wilsnack (1973) reported that 81 per cent of alcoholic women had obstetric-gynaecological problems compared with 35 per cent of non-alcoholic women.

No reference is ever made to the fact that this telescoped drinking history may have some advantages for the women over their male counterparts, who drink much more heavily for longer periods. On the surface, at least, *a case might be made that this different history will result in less physical damage, less emotional damage and less damage to the capacity for rational thinking.*

As far as physical damage is concerned, we need to be cautious, because it is possible that the physical reaction to alcohol is different for men and women in many areas. For example, it has been shown that increasing doses of alcohol may lead to acute alcoholic hepatitis and to cirrhosis of the liver. Most patients who react this way have been drinking excessively for over ten years, but this period is less for females who appear to be more susceptible to liver damage than men and have a worse prognosis. No such evidence has been forthcoming on other physical symptoms, such as atrophy of brain cells. There are insufficient data on cognitive functioning to suggest that alcoholic women are better or worse off than men in terms of reasoning capacity, memory and motor skills. In the absence of such data, the safest assumption would be of less damage in these areas, putting women in a better position to control their recovery than men.

The report of females beginning drinking in response to quite specific life situations does not necessarily lead to a better or a worse outlook. What it does mean is that women may need specific counselling in ways of coping with such events during the general learning of coping skills. That is, treatment for women alcoholics may need to be different.

4. Marital status

As mentioned earlier, women alcoholics lose their husbands through divorce, separation or death in larger proportions than the men alcoholics lose their wives. In all probability the divorce or separation is caused by the social stigma attached to female drinking and because of the social conditioning that leads females to accept the proposition that it is their duty to love and support their husbands who have slipped beyond the normally accepted male drinking-pattern. Males on the other hand are not taught such supportive behaviour as being a part of the male role and fail to cope with the social stigma surrounding their wives' drinking and opt for divorce or separation. The divorce/separation rate for alcoholics is shown by Travers and Hendtlass as 26.5 per cent for males and 27.7 per cent for females, which they compare with the state figures of 2.9 per cent and 3.5 per cent. That is, the divorce rate for alcoholics was very high indeed, but not very different for men and women. On the other hand the alcoholic women were widowed at three times the rate for alcoholic men.

In an English study the divorce rate is quoted as 10.5 per cent for alcoholic males as against 23.5 per cent for females. Of the originally married men, the majority was still living with their wives, but of the originally married women, two-thirds had lost their husband by death, divorce or separation (Glatt, 1961).

Female alcoholics, more often than male alcoholics, are found to have alcoholic spouses. In a Swedish study 51 per cent of alcoholic women had an alcoholic spouse as against 13 per cent of alcoholic men. Heavy drinking by the husbands of women alcoholics has also been commented on by Mulford (1977). For male alcoholics, being married did seem to increase their recovery chances because they had someone with whom to discuss their problems (48 per cent for single men, 66 per cent for married men); for women, however, being married has no such effect. Whereas 38 per cent of the married men listed their wife as the person with whom they discussed their problems, only 18 per cent of the women listed their husband. Mulford attributes this difference to the fact that some 88 per cent of the husbands were drinkers, as opposed to 57 per cent of the wives of alcoholics. This is additional evidence that the marital relationship may be relatively unrewarding, if not disturbing, for female alcoholics, especially as 49 per cent of their husbands were classified as 'heavy drinkers'.

At Montclair it has become obvious that women who are living with heavy-drinking men who live off the female alcoholic financially, spiritually, emotionally and sexually, and who frequently engage in physical assault, have a very low chance of recovery. These women, many of professional status, seem to have lost all sense of identity and cling desperately to the one remaining person whom they think is the last one who may offer them the love and affection they seek. A quick return to alcoholic drinking almost inevitably accompanies a return to such a relationship.

If we accept that women without husbands are worse off than those who have them, then alcoholic women are at a decided disadvantage because of the disappearing habits of their husbands. The problem then becomes one of how best to manage without one, or even of how to acquire another. Many women, especially those without children, may in fact be better off without husbands as this leaves them free to construct a new life, to try to enter an occupation that suits their interests and aspirations without reference to the preferences of husbands. For some, the inability to fulfil the sexual and domestic expectations of the former husband will have been the precipitating factor that led to the alcohol abuse. For these, the absence of the former husband may indeed be a benefit. Altogether, this marital difference may not be the disaster it is assumed to be.

Consider the case of a 42-year-old woman married to an immature, sexually hung-up man of similar age who acts like a rebellious teenager and who constantly manipulates situations and conversations to make her angry. After seventeen years of this she finally blows up when he takes a mistress quite overtly and provokes her so much that she begins to drink heavily and finally ends up in hospital being treated for alcoholism. This woman has children aged 12 and 10, but has a permanent job to which she can return.

It seems quite likely that she may well be better off without such a husband, whose emotional demands conflict with the necessity to remain calm during the post-hospital phase and for that matter for the remainder of her life. So a divorce may be to her advantage rather than to her disadvantage. The alternative would be to solve the problem by getting the husband to change his behaviour in order to salvage the marriage. Probably the best way to do this would be to enlist the service of an expert marriage guidance counsellor, one who understands women's rights and the difficulties of recovery from alcoholism.

One problem connected with divorce in such circumstances comes for those women with little or no occupational skills who have children to support. Because society is structured in such a way that men are those who are trained to earn a living, it may be difficult for divorced women with no occupational skills. Nevertheless, depending on the level of social security and services, women may survive quite well without a husband, may learn an occupational skill and get a job. Many, of course, will have worked after marriage and may return to the same field. The greater the entry of married women into the work-force, the greater the possibility of return after treatment for alcoholism. As the proportion of women in full and part-time occupations seems to be rising, this looks promising.

A study carried out in 1960 of the husbands of female alcoholics showed three distinct groups of husbands who had stuck to their alcoholic wives. Those who had married when their wives were already drinkers usually had marked personality difficulties, being neurotics, psychopaths, heavy drinkers themselves, and had physical difficulties or sex problems. Among the husbands whose wives later became alcoholic, there were two main groups. Some were older than their wives and dominated them. These were often successful business men who were basically insecure and anxious and who often treated their alcoholic wives as though they were children. The second group consisted of intelligent, rigid and obsessional men who were dominated by their alcoholic wives (Flintoff, 1975). None of these groups of husbands seems to fit the description of ideal husband. This study clearly casts doubt on the assumption that alcoholic women will have difficulty with recovery if they are divorced or separated. The problem seems to be with those who continue to try to live with these immature men.

5. Initial reason for drinking

Alcoholism in women appears more likely to be precipitated by a specific event or situation than for men. One study found that twice as many women as men referred to an unhappy love affair, divorce, the death of a child, parent or spouse or some other specific reason when describing the point when they started drinking heavily. This ties in with Mulford's (1977) study, where woman alcoholics indicated a greater tendency than men to drink for psychological reasons and in response to stress. 'They more frequently (a) experienced personal crises; (b) reported a heavy drinking, unsupportive spouse; (c) used other sedatives in addition to alcohol; (d) drank spirits as their usual beverage; and (e) reported more suicide attempts.'

Mulford maintains that this heavy drinking by women in response to stress and specific crises is heavily frowned upon. Heavy drinking is seen as 'manly' but 'unladylike'. Young men are rewarded by their peers for demonstrating capacity to drink vast amounts of liquor, but society makes it clear to women that they should not behave in this way. Thus men, who may be reacting to the same crises and the same stress, can drink without strong social reaction. In other words, female heavy drinkers are held to be more sick than males, and this is seen as a factor that will make recovery more difficult for females.

The factor that is overlooked here is what exactly is being learned. During recovery, drinking in response to crises and to emotional upheavals is not possible, and alternative ways of handling these situations have to be learned. As women have started their drinking careers later than men, they have previously had an opportunity to learn and practise alternative ways of handling these situations early in adulthood, whereas men are almost encouraged to drink to solve these problems. As Mulford puts it, 'Hence, a positive force in the recovery process, and an advantage women alcoholics have over men, is that they have experienced an alternative lifestyle.'

Clearly, women who have been practising ineffective methods of coping in response to situational crises and stress need to learn new and effective ways of coping. In particular, they need to learn that resort to alcohol only makes these situations worse, and that calm, rational problem-solving followed by assertive behaviour is a method likely to be effective. The point is that male alcoholics need to learn this as well.

Another reason given for drinking is that alcoholics have a repressed but unresolved craving for maternal care. It is said by those who favour this theory that alcoholism is more prevalent among men because women have greater opportunities to be dependent, while men cannot openly express their dependency needs, as this does not fit the view of men as strong and independent. It could be agreed that this is another factor working in favour of alcoholic women. Presumably they are less restricted in openly being dependent, so generally their dependency needs are more likely to be satisfied and consequently they should be less strongly motivated to seek artificial gratification through the use of alcohol.

6. *The belief that women alcoholics are sicker than men alcoholics*

There is still a widespread belief among those who work with alcoholics that the women are sicker than the men. Many factors are quoted to substantiate this view. These include:

(a) *Dependency on drugs*. Alcoholic women have sought medical help for their emotional problems more often than alcoholic men, and women have consumed far more prescription drugs. This may result in additional medical complications and a more difficult detoxification process. Women may also have developed some dependence on drugs as a means of coping with everyday problems and anxieties. It has been estimated that about 70 per cent of psychotropic drugs are prescribed for women, mainly for anxiety and depression.

Throughout this book it has been emphasised that the control of our emotions is the critical factor in recovery after treatment for alcoholism. In the same way that alcohol prevents us from thinking clearly and rationally, so do intense emotional states. A third potential source of interference with rational, clear thinking is the use of the drugs commonly prescribed for the management of anxiety and depression. If it is at all possible, the use of these drugs after treatment for alcoholism has finished should be avoided.

This factor may indeed weigh against recovery in females unless the treatment procedures take this into account. Every effort should be made to ensure that, as far as possible, women alcoholics are alerted to the dangers of cross-addiction, and are weaned off prescribed drugs during in-patient care. The relatives should be advised not to encourage the use of mind and mood-altering drugs, especially early in the recovery period, unless they are prescribed by a doctor familiar with the problems of alcoholism.

(b) *High levels of negative emotional states*. Every time groups of men and women are measured on anxiety, depression and neuroticism, the women get higher scores than men. This applies to all groups, regardless of whether they drink or not, whether they work or not, whether they are alcoholic or not, or whether they are high school or university students. This applies to questionnaires in which questions such as, 'Do you feel nervous, anxious, concerned?' are asked. Women respond by indicating that yes, they are more nervous, anxious and concerned than men.

Whether or not they actually are, or whether the higher scores merely reflect social conditioning, in that it is regarded as 'normal' for a woman to be that way so she is prepared to admit it, is debatable. On the other hand, men are expected to be strong and dependable, so admission of anxiety states is in one sense an admission of failure. This difference in social expectations may be sufficient to account for the findings. Clinicians find females suffer more than males from debilitating neurotic illnesses. This again is possibly traced to the same social source. As we saw earlier, women are encouraged more than males to seek help for their emotional illnesses. This does not prove in any way that the men are any less anxious or depressed, but merely that it is more psychologically difficult for males to seek help for emotional conditions.

When we consider alcoholics, the same problems of interpretation occur. Attempts to isolate a female alcoholic personality have failed dismally, and the numerous attempts to determine personality traits that characterise women alcoholics have produced conflicting and ambiguous findings. Much of this research is centred on measures of anxiety, neuroticism and introversion-extroversion, so the area of negative emotions has been well covered.

The strong possibility of the circular argument quoted in the section on self-esteem being applicable here must be considered. Train women to accept that they are deviant, and they will report themselves as deviant, they will be judged as deviant, and they will accept that they are deviant. This does not necessarily mean they are 'sicker', except in the psychological sense that the acceptance of deviance from norms not recognised as being applicable only to males is seen as sickness and becomes sickness.

(c) *Drinking history*. The telescoped drinking history of female alcoholics has been seen by some as an indication of a greater degree of illness. The argument is that if women present for treatment after a shorter period of alcoholic drinking than men then they 'must be sicker'. It would seem that there are other possible explanations of this phenomenon. One might centre on the high level of susceptibility to liver damage found in women.

(d) *Marital instability*. The high incidence of divorce and separation in women alcoholics is seen as evidence of this instability. The rival explanation connected with different social pressures on men and women has already been discussed.

(e) *Suicide attempts*. Statements are made that women alcoholics are more likely to suicide or to attempt suicide than males. Eight studies support this contention, but Glatt (1961) found no significant difference between males and females in suicide attempts. Beckman (1977) also notes that suicide is *generally* more frequent in women than in men, and quotes three further studies, where it is argued that suicide by alcoholic women is restricted to those with serious mental disorders. In these studies, the suicide attempts precede hospitalisation quite frequently, and can be seen as a symptom of the disease that frequently occurs while alcoholic drinking is in full flight.

Balance sheet

Over all, the evidence that women alcoholics are sicker than their male counterparts is unconvincing. Much of the evidence can be put down to social conditioning, and most of the remainder is based on inadequate evidence. Many of the factors commonly assumed to place barriers in the way of the recovery of women alcoholics are really in the nature of self-fulfilling prophecies.

If we let women know that they are expected to be more passive, less adventurous and more emotional than men, they come to believe that they are and to behave as if they are. The prophecy is fulfilled. A thorough knowledge of the socialisation processes commonly found in Western society and a rational examination of them may help women alcoholics to realise that many of the factors said to weigh against their recovery have little or no substance. On the other hand, because of a lifetime of acceptance of women's roles the recovery process may actually be more difficult unless immediate steps are taken to acquire some of the so-called masculine traits, including assertiveness.

There are two factors that may actually be in favour of women. Firstly, there is the possibility of less intellectual impairment because of the different drinking history. Provided that any possible emotional behaviour can be controlled in the ways outlined, this factor may well outweigh some of the other disadvantages. Secondly, there is now some evidence that the outcome of treatment that is AA orientated is better for women than men (Alford,1980). It may be regular attendances at AA or it may be the better cognitive functioning or even some other factor or factors. The point is that, contrary to almost universal prediction, the women showed a higher recovery rate than the men.

12
Alcoholics Anonymous

Does AA Work?

The very anonymous nature of AA membership makes it difficult to answer this question with rock hard data. In part this is due to the reluctance of AA to submit its members to scrutiny and experimental manipulation. AA claims, and quite rightly claims, that any attempt to measure in a rigorous way the relationship between AA attendance and success rate could well be resisted by AA members, who have been guaranteed anonymity. More importantly, the act of measurement could well disturb the recovery process, which appears to be working successfully within AA.

What can be said with confidence is that, prior to the formation of AA, few alcoholics recovered. Alcoholism was a mystery to the well-meaning general practitioners, psychiatrists, psychologists and religious workers who tried to help these suffering people. The second statement that can be made is that since AA was formed, countless thousands of AA members have stopped drinking and have become fully functioning members of society. This can be and is attributed to their participation in AA as, generally speaking, alcoholism is still a mystery to most in the helping professions.

There are some studies available that do provide evidence of a connection between AA attendance and recovery from alcoholism. The first real follow-up study was carried out by Bill C— (1965). Bill attempted to follow up 393 members of an AA group who had attended at least ten meetings during the period 1955-60. Of these, 38 per cent could not be contacted, 50 per cent had remained sober until 1963, and of those who had relapsed, 20 per cent had been sober for more than a year.

In a four-year follow-up, Polich, Armor and Braiker (1980a) found that when they separated 'regular' AA attenders from the others, their success rate was three times as great as those who were going 'occasionally'. The authors suggest that AA attendance may be the most effective treatment in promoting abstinence.

In the Mississippi study described by Alford (1980), there was evidence of a strong connection between AA attendance and recovery. Table 3 below is adapted from the text and Table 1 of Alford (1980) to show how AA attendance was different for males and females, and how this difference was reflected in the recovery rates for the two sexes. The females attended AA in much higher proportions than the males, and had almost double the success rate after two years. When success was defined in terms of being abstinent *and* productively functioning *and* socially stable, the figures were about 6 per cent lower, but the success rate for females remained double that of males. In this Mississippi study the programme at the hospital was very heavily AA orientated. One cannot be certain that the greater AA attendance caused the high success rate, but the massive difference between the outcome for the two sexes strongly suggests this as the most likely explanation. This explanation becomes even more likely when the bulk of evidence suggests that there should only be a slight bias predicting a better female recovery rate.

Table 3. Relationship between AA Attendance and Recovery

	AA attendance in months		
SEX	6	12	24
FEMALE	50	46	46
MALE	41	22	19
	Percentage employed, socially stable and abstinent		
FEMALE	68	61	65
MALE	33	30	35

In Vaillant's (1983) study 200 Harvard graduates and 400 'blue collar' workers were followed up for forty years. This study sheds some interesting light on the relationship between personal adjustment at the time of entry for treatment, subsequent AA attendance and success rates. The results show first that being married, employed, never having been in gaol and having a stable psychosocial adjustment are factors associated with successful recovery. Table 4 shows how success was related to an additive combination of these favourable prognostic signs with frequent AA attendance over a

Table 4. Favourable Prognostic Signs. AA Attendance and Recovery

AA Attendance 1972-9 and prognosis score	Clinical status 1979		
	Stable remission (29 men)	Intermittent alcoholism (24 men)	Chronic alcoholism (47 men)
299 or less visits to AA and 2 or less favourable signs.	24%	67%	91%
300 or more visits to AA and 3 or more favourable signs.	76%	33%	9%

period of eight years for a group of 100 men. Of the 29 men who achieved 'stable remission', 76 per cent had been to AA more than 300 times, as opposed to 24 per cent who had been to AA less than 300 times. Of the 47 men who returned to chronic alcoholism, 91 per cent were poor AA attenders and only 9 per cent had been going regularly. While these results may not fully convince the sceptics, there is no doubt in the author's mind that AA plays a central role in recovery from alcoholism. How AA works and the reasons why it works are far from clear, but it is to this area that our attention now turns.

Alcoholics Anonymous

AA is best described in its own words:

> Alcoholics Anonymous is a fellowship of men and women who share their experience, strength and hope with each other that they may solve their common problem and help others to recover from alcoholism.
>
> The only requirement for membership is a desire to stop drinking. There are no dues or fees for AA membership; we are self-supporting through our own contributions. AA is not allied with any sect, denomination, politics, organisation or institution; does not wish to engage in any controversy, neither endorses nor opposes any causes. Our primary purpose is to stay sober and help other alcoholics to achieve sobriety. (The Preamble, reprinted with permission of AA Grapevine.)

AA's programme is embodied in the Twelve Steps, a group of principles that, if practised as a way of life, can be expected to lead an alcoholic to rid himself or herself of the obsession to drink and become a whole and useful member of society. AA's fellowship is outlined in the Twelve Traditions, which outline the means by which

AA maintains its unity and relates to the world about it, the way it lives and grows.

The basic principles in which alcoholism is treated as having physical, mental and spiritual components were derived from medicine and religion and from the knowledge and insight the founding alcoholics had into the disease with which they were afflicted. The fellowship was named after the book *Alcoholics Anonymous* published in 1939. 'In it alcoholism was described from the alcoholic's point of view, the spiritual ideas of the society were codified for the first time in the Twelve Steps, and the application of these steps to the alcoholics dilemma was made clear' (*Twelve Steps and Twelve Traditions* p. 16).

AA Meetings

From its beginning the telling of life histories has been the keystone of AA practice. In a typical AA meeting, about six alcoholics will speak. Most describe the ways in which their lives had or have become unmanageable and out of control because of their obsession with alcohol. They may describe their feelings of hopelessness and despair during this time. While discussing their present lives, some stress the doubtful state of their sobriety, the temptations facing them, the pressures they are under, and the difficulties they are having in coping. Many describe emotional states, such as resentment, fear, anger, frustration and anxiety, which are causing problems. Some describe the successes they are having and contrast the new-found control with the previous chaotic lack of control.

There is no formal discussion or questioning, but frequently members use the 'tea and biscuits' time that follows to seek advice, to discuss issues raised by the speakers, and to start an acquaintance with another member who seems to need help or who may give aid. These meetings are not run on convential 'group therapy' lines, where discussion and argument are common. At AA complete support and acceptance are the rule. Many who attend have stopped drinking, but others come in search of a way to stop. The life story has proved to be the most effective way of transmitting AA values and beliefs.

Each AA group is autonomous, except in matters affecting other groups or AA as a whole. Some groups run discussion sessions where topics such as the disease concept are elaborated, the meaning of 'a higher power' is clarified or emotions such as resentment are discussed. Sometimes these discussions are given over to a discussion of one of the Twelve Steps. Any AA member may be called upon to speak, but the right to decline is always open.

How Does AA Work?

Any attempt to answer this question in a few pages is doomed to failure. Apart from reading the various AA publications, the best analysis of this question can be found in an article by Ernest Kurtz entitled 'Why AA Works: the Intellectual Significance of AA' or a book published in 1979 by the same author entitled *Not God*. The latter is available through some AA outlets. What can be done is list some things AA does and leave it to the reader to judge why these practices work.

1. AA treats alcoholism as a disease

AA was really the first organisation to see alcoholism as a disease rather than a moral weakness or lack of will-power. AA sees alcoholics as finding themselves in a hopeless position where they are compulsively and obsessively addicted to alcohol. They are so limited in their control that they are being ruled by alcohol. The first and fundamental message of AA, according to Kurtz, is that alcoholics 'are not infinite, not absolute, *not God*'.

The first step of AA is a statement and admission of this essential limitation. 'We admitted that we were powerless over alcohol — that our lives had become unmanageable.' For AA members, acceptance of this first step is codified in the opening words used by each speaker at a meeting: 'My name is —— I am an alcoholic.' These last four words, if honestly spoken, indicate that the speaker accepts that he or she has the disease of alcoholism. For the author it seems that it may be the quality of acceptance that lays the foundation for a stable recovery. The higher the quality, the greater the chance of recovery. Included in this quality will be the following.

(a) *Acceptance is an all-or-none affair*. Anyone who has doubts about being an alcoholic is in peril. 100 per cent acceptance of being an alcoholic is essential. For those who resent being an alcoholic, who are angry because life has handed them a raw deal, who resent being unable to join in gatherings, dinner parties and so on by drinking alcohol, who want to be 'normal', who want 'to be like other people' and drink alcohol, there is danger. For those who believe it is not possible to join in these activities or to enjoy oneself without drinking alcohol, the chances of a relapse increase. For those who do not like the words alcoholic or alcoholism, the chances of recovery are diminished. Strong, durable foundations for recovery appear to depend on complete acceptance of being down and out, of being beaten by alcohol and of being unable to fight any longer. Ohlms (1983) defines alcoholism as 'a chronic, progressive, incurable disease, characterised by loss of control over alcohol and other sedatives'. Alcoholics have to accept without reservation that they have this disease.

(b) *There is stigma attached to the words alcoholic and alcoholism.* Evidence presented earlier in this book makes it clear that there is still a great deal of stigma associated with being an alcoholic or even with being the relative of an alcoholic. Many people know little or nothing about alcoholism. They have not had the benefit of exposure to education about the disease or are too close-minded to change attitudes that may have formed over many years. That is their problem. Why should we get upset because others have a problem? The only thing alcoholics can do is to accept that currently there is stigma and shrug it off.

With any luck the recent biochemical discovery of THIQ will help in countering this stigma. Certainly it has helped relatives of patients at Montclair to accept that alcoholism is indeed a disease. It has provided something tangible to grasp and this should help overcome the stigma.

(c) *The responsibility for recovery rests with the alcoholics.* During their alcoholic years alcoholics frequently find excuses for their drinking and shift the blame for their excessive drinking onto others. Alcoholic husbands blame their wives, their children, their jobs and even their pets for their drinking. High levels of pressure are used as excuses as are medical conditions and tiredness. The list is endless. AA insists on the alcoholic facing up to the fact that this transfer of responsibility to others is part of the disease, and that part of the recovery process lies in facing up to and dealing with the problems that life throws up and accepting responsibility for his or her own life.

(d) *Feelings of shame or guilt hinder the recovery process.* Many alcoholics feel ashamed because they have 'wasted their lives' or have failed to realise their potential. Many feel guilty about the harm they have done to others, especially those who are close to them. Kurtz is one who believes that alcoholics use the drug to hide from themselves and must deny this problem to maintain any sort of existence. He sees AA's insistence that alcoholics need one another as a mechanism for breaking down this denial of weaknesses in the basic self. For this reason he sees guilt-orientated therapies, which exhort the alcoholic 'to mend his ways' or 'to grow up', as doomed to failure, because the practising alcoholic has to drink 'to conceal his unendurable shame from himself'. AA teaches alcoholics not to feel ashamed.

The highest quality of acceptance may then lie with those alcoholics who 100 per cent believe and accept that they are alcoholics, who do not worry about the stigma attached to alcoholism, who accept total responsibility and get rid of the shame and guilt. Some even reach the highest level of acceptance by coming to accept that finding out that they are alcoholics was the greatest event in their lives. Such people say things such as: 'The day I found out and accepted that I was an alcoholic I felt marvellous. Here at last is a reason for my bizarre behaviour over all these years, and here is a programme that tells me what to do to stop drinking and begin to act rationally. I am back in control.'

2. AA helps to rebuild the self concept

After admission and acceptance, AA seems to guide the alcoholic to take a hard look at his or her past behaviour by identifying similar unadaptive behaviour in the life stories of other members. This identification process may not just be with one other person, but arise from a synthesis derived from a whole series of life stories. It is often helped along by an AA member's sponsor, part of whose task may be to suggest that the task is 'to look for the similarities'. The member comes to identify her or his own 'defects of character'. By observing others with lengthy sobriety he or she has role models on which to fashion her or his search for a new identity.

While it may be said that the whole programme is a prescription for building a new identity, it is at Step 4 that the pace quickens very markedly. In Step 4 each alcoholic is asked to 'make a searching and fearless moral inventory of ourselves'. AA sees the alcoholic's problem as having allowed instincts such as the desire for material and emotional security to get out of hand to such an extent that, 'Powerfully, blindly, many times subtly, they drive us, dominate us and insist on ruling our lives' (*Twelve Steps and Twelve Traditions* p. 43). These character defects are seen as the primary cause of drinking and failure in life.

Each alcoholic is asked to take a long hard look at himself or herself and at how these instincts have damaged relationships with others and how her or his reactions to others led to fear, greed, possessiveness, pride, worry, anger, self-pity, depression, anxiety and frustration. In Step 5 he or she is required to admit 'to God, to ourselves and to another human being the exact nature of our wrongs'. This vital step is seen as necessary to rid alcoholics of their terrible feeling of isolation as a necessary step in the process of being forgiven and to lead to 'straight thinking, solid honesty and genuine humility' (*Twelve Steps and Twelve Traditions* p.60).

By the time an alcoholic has reached Step Twelve, where he or she might try helping others suffering from the disease, the Self will have been reconstructed. In the terms spoken of earlier the Self will be congruent with the Ideal Self, and there will be no feelings of shame to cause harm. Drinking alcohol to hide from the Self will no longer be necessary.

3. AA teaches the value of living in the present

A favourite AA exhortation is to 'live one day at a time'. This is advice to the alcoholic to live in the present and to deal with things as they occur. Living one day at a time is directed first at alcohol intake. Each member is told not to think about remaining abstinent for the whole of a lifetime, but to concentrate on not having a drink today. This has been found to be easier for members to accept. When the next day arrives, she or he is not to have a drink for that day. Gradually the days mount up into weeks, months and years, but always one day at a time.

It is also associated with the advice to put the past behind oneself, because stirring around in the alcoholic pond may cause the alcoholic to drown. Similarly, it is part of the advice about 'not projecting' into the future. One of the unadaptive forms of behaviour typical of many recovering alcoholics is an impatient desire to solve all their problems in a few weeks or days, especially early in sobriety. If they are in financial difficulties, they may take more than one job. Others want to solve their personal and family problems in one day, when in actuality it may take months or even years to win back the trust and confidence of a spouse or of children who have been badly scarred by the alcoholic behaviour. Learning to keep cool and to tackle problems one by one is part of living one day at a time.

AA has produced two pocket-sized cards for members on this theme. The first is called 'Just for Today'. It contains nine pieces of advice. The first is: 'Just for today I will try to live through this day only and not tackle my whole life problem at once. I can do something for twelve hours that would appal me if I felt I had to keep it up for a lifetime.' The second is 'Yesterday, Today and Tomorrow', which concludes with: 'It is not the experience of TODAY that drives men mad — it is remorse or bitterness for something that happened YESTERDAY and the dread of what TOMORROW may bring.'

4. AA attacks self-centredness

In AA's understanding, self-centredness underlies all the alcoholic's problems. The programme and the fellowship are designed to cut through this 'centre of the universe' theory, by teaching that being honest with the self and being honest with others are mutually interdependent and both are essential for recovery. 'AA's very existence . . . continually testifies that progressive discovery of self-- continuing honesty with self requires others with whom one can be honest.'

Not infrequently members question other members' statements and actions privately. For example, a sponsor may think his protégé is on an 'ego trip' and gently query the state of his sobriety. Grandiose claims about progress may be regarded with scepticism, and discussion about these claims may follow. Alcoholics become only too aware of the dangers of deluding themselves about the state of their recovery.

5. AA provides a warm, supportive group of peers

Members of AA introduce themselves by their given names. Wealth, titles or occupation are of no consequence. There is no professional class in AA and, with the exception of a few necessary paid members who handle the day-to-day affairs, no paid officials. Tradition Nine states: 'AA, as such, ought never to be organised; but we may create special service boards or committees directly responsible to those they serve.' These boards or committees cannot issue directives to groups — AA cannot be dictated to individually or collectively.

This lack of structure and formal organisation is unique, and results in a truly egalitarian organisation, where any alcoholic who wishes to stop drinking can find himself or herself accepted without query. Speakers often tell quite horrifying and degrading tales about their past lives, tales that are accepted 'without value judgement' as part of the normal progress of the disease. Support and acceptance are the norm. Subordination of personal aims, preferences and desires for the common good is the goal.

6. AA sees a spiritual awakening as essential to recovery

AA's programme is described as 'spiritual rather than religious', and members rigidly enforce this distinction. In many ways this emphasis on the spiritual arose from an insight that led AA in its earliest days to separate from the Oxford Group, a non-denominational but specifically Christian group. Religion had been tried and found wanting, and moreover many alcoholics were atheists or agnostics. The result was a break from organised religion, but a retention of a spiritual core.

AA sees a member achieving a spiritual awakening when he or she practises the Twelve Steps. The meaning of this is contained in the discussion of Step Twelve:

> When a man or woman has a spiritual awakening, the most important meaning of it is that he has now become able to do, feel and believe that which he could not do before on his unaided strength and resources alone. He has been granted a gift which amounts to a new state of consciousness and being. He has been set on a path which tells him he is really going somewhere, that life is not a dead end, not something to be endured or mastered. In a very real sense he has been transformed because he has laid hold of a source of strength which in one way or another, he had hitherto denied himself. He finds himself in possession of a degree of honesty, tolerance, unselfishness, peace of mind and love of which he has thought himself incapable. (From *Twelve Steps and Twelve Traditions*, reprinted with permission of Alcoholics Anonymous World Services Inc.)

7. AA support is available day and night in most parts of the world

A remarkable feature of AA is that members will go to extreme lengths to assist another member who asks for help or who is in need. The AA prescription is: 'I am responsible when anyone, anywhere, reaches out for help. I want the hand of AA always to be there. For that I am responsible.'

Of course, AA is there in scores of countries throughout the world. A traveller in New York, Akron, London, Bombay, Sydney or Christchurch can find AA meetings and AA members. Central organisations in large cities man twenty-four-hour telephone services for AA members in trouble, or for alcoholics or friends and relatives of alcoholics seeking help.

Alcoholics who have cars pick up less affluent members and take them to meetings. Others try to encourage members who have had a relapse to stop drinking or to return to AA or they get them back to a treatment centre. Help in finding lodgings, in finding jobs, help with matrimonial problems are all there for the asking, with no thought of return.

8. AA is a way of life

AA provides a programme and a fellowship for recovery. It also provides a forum in which members learn new skills and find that these skills help them handle all aspects of their lives. Members learn to live a life in which being an alcoholic is accepted as an integral part. Being an alcoholic, the AA way becomes a way of life.

Participation in the formal AA programme often leads to the forming of friendships and relationships and to social activities. The connections established during the early years of recovery tend to be maintained. The final part of the Twelfth Step is: 'we tried to carry this message to alcoholics and to practise these principles in all our affairs'. Thus AA becomes a way of life in that the alcoholic who has achieved lengthy sobriety and some degree of mastery of the Twelve Steps is advised to try to carry the message to other alcoholics, and incidentally maintain his or her AA connection. Additionally, the member is advised to carry the new confidence, tolerance, love and AA spirit into the world at large on a 'give and take basis'. With whatever degree of serenity, with a new outlook on personal importance, power and ambition, with false pride dissipated and with a new self-image, each alcoholic may have the 'right principles and attitudes' for good living.

9. AA provides hope

None of us can live in any degree of happiness without hope that the future will at least be bearable and even enjoyable. Drinking alcoholics reach such a level of despair and distress that there seems to be no way out and frequently alcoholics contemplate and attempt suicide. AA offers hope by providing a programme and a fellowship that promise a way out of these depths. As usual, most of this is conveyed by the life histories of the speakers, some of whom will have been in AA and abstinent for many years. Some of these may become role models for others. Here is living proof that what seems impossible is, in fact, attainable. Few, if any, non-alcoholics can understand the depths of despair that alcoholics reach, the futility and the hopelessness of the condition. AA offers hope of a way out.

Over all, we can say that whatever the reasons for the success of AA, it can and does lead to the following changes, all of which are essential for recovery:

1. The capacity to stop drinking and to remain stopped.
2. Improved emotional control.
3. Improved ability to function comfortably in personal, marital, family, social, occupational and spiritual areas.

13

Common Questions Asked By Those Involved in Recovery

No one who has been through it needs to be told that living with a drinking alcoholic varies from very unpleasant to sheer hell. On the other hand, few know what to expect in the short-term and the long-term when abstinence following treatment begins. Will he or she be fundamentally the same, or will there appear to be a major personality change? Will the family functioning get back to some degree of normality? Will he or she be able to resume full time occupation? Will there be permanent brain damage, and will interest in and capacity for sexual activity be fully restored? What am I to make of him when, for the first time since marriage, he begins to express warmth and affection and to show consideration? Is this a sign of impending return to drinking? The answers to some of these questions are contained in this book, and the wives, husbands and families of alcoholics are advised to read the whole of it to gain an understanding of the causes of alcoholism, the causes of a return to drinking and the major problems facing alcoholics during recovery.

It should rapidly become clear that alcoholics are very little different from non-alcoholics. Most people fail to cope with their lives very effectively, and the incidence of emotional illness or instability in the general community is very high indeed. It will become clear that where people get emotionally aroused, they are likely to fail to cope. When some people fail to cope, they become aggressive, others assert that there really was no problem there at all, others take to tranquillisers or sedatives, most drink, many drink heavily, and a fair number drink to excess and some become alcoholic.

Those who have read this book carefully will have discovered that the unpleasant truth is that the alcoholism is a pervasive and recurrent condition, and that the chances of a return to heavy, abusive drinking are fairly high. The central theme of this book is that the alcoholic, like everyone else, has to learn to control the arousal of negative emotions. He or she has to learn not to be angry and aggressive, anxious and withdrawn, depressed and hopeless.

This does not mean that close relatives should regard an alcoholic as a bomb who might explode at any moment, and so tip-toe around fearful of upsetting things. The alcoholic has to resume normal life and to cope with the normal stresses of everyday living. However, everyone needs help, support and trust. This support and trust is more likely where those close to the alcoholic fully understand what is involved in recovery, and have an opportunity to discuss the recovery process with someone familiar with the problems. In an attempt to do this, some of the questions regularly asked by relatives are listed below:

Will Communication Improve?

One of the major problems in any relationship, whether it be between husband and wife, or between either of them and their children, between *de facto* couples and between young people contemplating life together is the maintenance of full and fruitful communication. Where alcoholism is a factor, the chances are very high that easy and frank communication has broken down and may even have been replaced by suspicion, resentment and even fear where aggressive behaviour has been commonplace. This breakdown in communication affects most marriages and is a major factor in marriage breakdown. Women require warmth, affection, and support from their husbands, but they don't assert their rights to these until the marriage is about to collapse or until she is hospitalised with extreme depression. Women put up with their workaholic husbands until similar ends are reached. Husbands take on extra work to meet the assumed needs of their wives, when one question would rapidly show that money is no substitute for warmth and companionship.

Children often get out of control because of lack of communication between husband and wife. Communication is necessary to evolve common policies about child-rearing, and on how to cope with the demands of adolescents so that discord is not caused by the children playing one parent off against another. Similarly, frank and open discussion between the alcoholic and the partner is necessary to clear the air, so that unfounded suspicions and resentments are cleared away before they cause trouble. Questions about anything connected with the illness should be asked and the answers clarified without living in the past. Both must accept the fact of the breakdown without resentment.

When you read the chapter on alcohol and aggression you will have discovered that alcohol prevents the drinker from thinking clearly, and emotional reactions such as anger, resentment, hostility and aggression in various forms take over. When abstinent, the likelihood of such anti-social, destructive behaviour occurring is dramatically reduced for most people, particularly if those around them play their part and behave sensibly too. One of the benefits you can get from reading this book is to learn to control your own emotions, and this is the greatest help that you can give to someone close to you who is recovering form the abuse of alcohol. There is clear evidence that a return to a stable, well-organised, calm and relaxed environment leads to a better outcome by providing an environment in which the practice of emotional control can occur in a fully supportive situation.

The more the wives and families of alcoholics remain calm and relaxed, the more the lines of communication between all the members are kept open and the more supportive everyone is, the greater the possibility of success. Now the alcoholic has to accept that he or she is an alcoholic without blaming anyone or anything. Nothing can be done to change that fact. It has occurred and it has to be accepted. Similarly, close relatives have to accept the member's alcoholism as a fact, without resentment or abuse or hostility, if they wish to help.

Fruitful communication seems to depend upon both the alcoholic and his or her relatives accepting that alcoholism is a disease, and understanding that this disease has a specific set of symptoms, like any other disease. By far the most damaging is the loss of contact with reality, which was described fully in Chapter 2. During this time alcoholics blame other people, often those who are emotionally involved with them, for their drinking and for the accompanying health, occupational, family and social problems that have arisen. Wives, husbands and others on the receiving end of this onslaught are often so bewildered that they begin to wonder whether they might actually be responsible for the massive drinking. The memory lapses associated with blackouts will have caused further confusion.

It is quite understandable and indeed predictable that those who have had to endure the unpredictable drunken behaviour for long periods, who have seen enormous amounts of money spent on alcohol over long periods will be resentful and find it difficult to trust the newly sober alcoholic. Only a full acceptance of alcoholism as a disease will enable forgiveness to occur. The best of the institutions treating alcoholics recognise this fact and, acknowledging that alcoholism is a family disease, offer services that include extensive family counselling while the alcoholic is an in-patient. This takes the form of education about the disease and how best to help the recovering alcoholic. The other half centres on marriage guidance and helping children to come to terms with the difficulties arising from the abusive drinking. Frequently after-care includes ongoing counselling in these areas.

Should the Fact of Alcoholism be made Public?

Another aspect that is a source of concern for families is the stigma that is still attached to alcoholism. There is still undoubtedly a great deal of stigma directed at alcoholics, but husbands and wives of alcoholics bear some negative judgement as well. The advice given to alcoholics to counter this is not to go around advertising that they are alcoholics. Because so few people know anything about alcoholism, the fewer who know the better. Some alcoholics get so carried away with the idea that they have to become honest that they believe that this means that they have to tell all and sundry that they are alcoholics. This, of course, is ridiculous. There is nothing dishonest in not telling others about being an alcoholic. In fact, broadcasting the fact can harm relatives. Similarly, families, relatives and close friends of alcoholics are advised that they have no right at all to publicise these private facts, because it may hurt the recovering drinker. Usually the relatives' motive is to try to protect the alcoholic but, splendid as the motive might be, it is a dangerous practice, often having an unfortunate result for the alcoholic, the relatives or both.

A common form of this practice is where the relatives warn friends before or during a visit. The problem is that this assumes that the non-practising alcoholic cannot handle these situations. One thing that is certain to be discussed during treatment is how to refuse drinks. If the hosts have been warned beforehand, they are likely to behave in a strange, non-relaxed way, which will affect everyone. The worst possible thing for all is to have the alcoholic feeling tense and unrelaxed. Feeling resentful about having decisions made for him or her on top of this is likely to produce a response like, 'Well, stuff it. If they all believe I can't handle this, I might as well prove them right.' Quite clearly the best thing to do is to discuss the whole business of making the alcoholism public. Very few people go around broadcasting that they have had pneumonia, venereal disease, mumps or cancer, so why change for the disease of alcoholism.

The necessity for alcoholics and their relatives to discuss this aspect becomes clear when it is realised that there is stigma attached to some close relatives of alcoholics. Quite recently an alcoholic who worked as a consultant psychiatrist in an alcoholic hospital was asked to talk about alcoholism by the principal of the school his two daughters attended. During his talk he spoke freely about his own alcoholism. Despite the fact that he spoke anonymously, the word quickly got around that this alcoholic was the father of the two girls. They became the subject of some teasing and abuse, which upset them very much. So in the reverse way, although the motive might have been good, the outcome was quite serious.

Like anything else, the decision about whether to let other people know about having had difficulties with alcohol abuse should be treated as just another problem to be solved. In most circumstances there may be very good reasons to keep quiet about this. For example, when convinced that maintenance of sobriety no longer presents a problem, a decision may be made to apply for a new job where knowledge of the alcoholic episode can be easily suppressed and where awareness of it may prevent a successful application. In this case, to overtly proclaim the previous problem would certainly harm the applicant, and the best course is to omit any reference to it. On the other hand, some people quite readily accept that a sober, industrious person may have had a problem in the past and be upset if they discover it after the appointment has been made.

This decision is a purely personal one. Quite clearly, as is shown by an example in this book about refusing to drink when an old friend is met by chance, it is sometimes simpler if the alcoholism is simply stated as the reason for not drinking. Resorting to outright lies is not recommended, as they can cause further problems. There is usually nothing wrong with failure to disclose this old problem and often nothing to gain by flaunting it openly. However, in the closed circles in which many alcoholics move, the former heavy obsessive drinking will be well known as will be the fact of having received treatment for alcoholism. Nothing is to be gained by trying to hide this and a lot is to be gained by simply stating the previous problem as the reason for staying off the booze. As stated earlier, the decision to make the alcoholism public will depend upon the person and the circumstances. About the only firm advice that can be given is that it is foolish to acknowledge it if it is going to cause harm in any way to any person.

What Professional Services May Be Helpful?

Very few people use the variety of skilled people in the community to help with their problems, and alcoholics and their close relatives are no exception, even though they have a greater need to do so. While obvious resources connected with social security and medical health may be used, the important ones, which deal with interpersonal relationships and pychological health, are rarely approached.

If a marriage has survived the alcoholic episode at all, it is almost certainly in an unstable, shaky condition, especially if the alcoholic is female.

In the chapter about the difficulties that face women alcoholics, it was shown that female alcoholism is regarded as being far worse than male alcoholism, and that the husbands of female alcoholics divorce them in droves. For one that has survived, individual counselling by a psychologist or marriage guidance officer knowledgeable about alcoholism and sympathetic about women's rights can be very beneficial. Working through marriage problems with a skilled person, particularly if the marriage partner can be persuaded to participate, should help enormously in sorting out the problems that indeed may have precipitated the alcohol abuse or which may have developed during the alcoholic phase.

The main advantage such a person has is that he or she is a stranger and will not be emotionally involved. Consequently, the counsellor is able to assess the problems rationally and to offer helpful ways of solving marital problems. These may range from showing how to change the ways of bringing up children, how to deal with adolescents, to an examination of the way to deal with extra-marital relationships that have occurred or developed during the alcoholic phase, and which pose problems for the future of the marriage. As is made clear in various places in this book, many alcoholics have unresolved dependency relationships, which lie at the root of their emotional problems. These may range from a clear-cut dependence on a mother having been transferred to a wife, to far more subtle forms of dependence, which will affect other areas of the couple's lives, and which really are no substitute for the mature partnership relationships that characterise secure, adult ones. Men who are dependent on their drinking-mates for reassurance and for support have to become self-reliant and strong and realise the hollowness of the maudlin expressions of friendship expressed by the others in these mutually supportive dependent collections of immature people. Unless emotional growth to full adulthood is achieved, these irrational childish needs for support and praise will eventually lead to further problems.

Can Psychologists and Psychiatrists Help?

Psychologists work in a wide variety of fields. Some design landing-systems for commercial aircraft, some are interested in the design of road signs and signals, some help children who are having difficulties with school, some work on behaviour problems of children, and some are concerned with industrial matters. The psychologists who are most likely to be of help to alcoholics and their relatives are those clinical and consulting psychologists who are concerned with the emotional illnesses and with the allied field of marriage guidance. Psychiatrists, who are medical practitioners concerned with psychological problems, do some of the same work as psychologists, and can prescribe drugs and perform operations as well.

There are a few psychologists and psychiatrists who specialise in alcoholism and the problems that accompany alcoholism. They will therefore have skills in treating people for emotional problems, they will have skills in marriage guidance, and they will have skills in interpersonal relationships. These will be supplemented by other specialisations, which vary from one to another. These people are the ones to seek out for help to sort out the marriage, emotional and other psychological problems of alcoholics and their families. These professionals may help sort out dependency relationships, so that the alcoholic can see the origin of his continuing problems with alcohol. These people can give guidance about the problems of adolescence, of the importance of open lines of communication, and of the necessity for the assertion of positive feelings, of warmth and affection, of consideration, and of care and love. For those who attend AA meetings, these helping agencies serve to reinforce the work of AA and can actively assist alcoholics in the mastery of the AA programme.

Can Anything Be Done To Help a Shaky Marriage?

Given the nature of the alcoholic disease, it is not surprising that marriages fail or become very shaky when one or both partners are alcoholic. The difficulty for those who are involved in such a relationship is to decide whether the relationship has irretrievably broken down and, if not, whether the heavy damage can be repaired. In the better hospitals, counselling on marriage problems will be begun during treatment. Alcoholic relationships and marriages are just like any others. To succeed there must be at least:

1. Communication between the partners.

2. Mutual trust.
3. Love and affection.
4. Consideration for the rights and feelings of each other.

During the alcoholic years often all four of these conditions are badly damaged because the alcoholic is sometimes insane. It is very difficult for those who don't understand about alcoholism to envisage that communication can be restored, that they can come to trust their partner, that the little love they may have left can grow and that their alcoholic partner will come to display kindness and consideration for their rights and feelings. Yet this does happen, because non-practising alcoholics who are really on the road to recovery may be quite dissimilar to their alcoholic selves. If there is still some love and affection left on both sides, it is worth working at it to restore the relationship to one where these four elements flourish. Where the bitterness and hate are overwhelming, it is probably better to end the partnership as soon as possible.

One reason why some such marriages are kept going is the false argument that separation or divorce will hurt the children. The evidence is that children are better off with a clean break instead of being torn apart in a stormy, emotional relationship which can never succeed. The thing to do with all marriages or relationships that have been badly damaged during alcoholic drinking is to fix them or finish them. This is where professional help is vital. If possible, get it at the treatment facility, because these professionals will understand the role of alcoholism in the breakdown, but will also be aware of the possibilities of saving the relationship once drinking has ceased and a serious attempt at abstinence is under way. Many marriage guidance counsellors know little or nothing about recovery and regard all alcoholics as hopeless derelicts. Such people can finish marriages that have good chances of recovery.

How Do We Deal With The Past?

The main issue here for those close to an alcoholic is what attitude can be taken about the past, where quite commonly the alcoholic period has caused a great deal of havoc in interpersonal relations, in marital affairs, in social areas and, of course, in financial matters. For the alcoholic himself or herself, the advice is quite categorical: she or he cannot blame the spouse or anyone else for the abusive drinking or try to make him or her feel guilty about it, because that is irrational. No-one can make anyone else drink to excess, for the drinking is the final act in a long chain of events. Some pretend that the problem that started the chain was of no importance, others resort to tranquillisers and anti-depressants, and some of these finish up seriously ill in hospital. Some even resort to self-destruction. Now, like alcohol abuse, none of these coping attempts solves the original problem, and some, like alcohol abuse, cause a great deal of harm to others. Alcoholics can usually recover quite well if they remain abstinent, but they will have a very poor chance of recovery if their past behaviour is continually thrown up at them and they are made to feel guilty about the damage they caused.

The only reasonable attitude is to accept the fact of the alcoholism and to find out how best to help the recovery process. It is quite clear that constant reference to the uncontrolled behaviour that went with the alcoholism may evoke guilt, anger and depression. The arousal of these emotions will very markedly increase the probability of a return to drinking. Guilt is one of the most destructive feelings that besets man. Being an alcoholic is not a crime, although many criminal acts may be associated with alcohol abuse. Therefore, it is irrational to treat the alcoholic as a criminal and make her or him feel guilty for crimes that were not committed. Everybody makes mistakes.

Will She or He Become More Decisive?

Emotional dependency is stressed as a central feature in abusive drinking. Those who feel that they must prove that they are big, strong and capable men, those who constantly need the affection of others or who have to be constantly reassured of their worth by others are emotionally immature people whose recovery programme should include a full analysis of their dependency-based behaviour. It is pointed out earlier in this book that dependency can range from quite overt reliance on others for support to subtle forms of dependency, such as is seen in the following example of a male alcoholic who had minor breakdowns for five years after his initial hospitalisation. His behaviour included buying a very large ostentatious car, working extremely long hours to amass large sums of money, being seen in expensive night clubs and buying drinks for the band after dancing with the partner in an attention-seeking manner. Basically this man was still emotionally dependent on his wife and constantly felt the need to prove his manliness to counter the deep-down dependency needs.

The scheme outlined in this book for coping with life's problems shows that those who are basically dependent on others lack the confidence to do what they know should be done in interpersonal situations. They do this because they fear that negative assessment of their words or actions will lead to the loss of support, appreciation and affection of those on whom they are emotionally dependent. It is pointed out over and over that expressions such as 'I must succeed because I need him to like me' are irrational and back us into corners where failure and feelings of hopelessness and of unworthiness follow inevitably. Emotional independence is the aim and the attainment of that goal is vital to freedom from alcohol addiction.

What about Alcohol in the House?

Whether it is safe to keep alcohol readily available in the home will depend on just how fully the recovering alcoholic has mastered the control of his or her emotions. There is firm evidence that some do this very quickly and can go into public drinking places, mix with former drinking acquaintances, keep liquor in the house for the social use of their families and friends and prepare drinks for others without the slightest temptation to drink. Others, indeed the majority, take much longer, and their emotional strength is fragile for quite a long period. The advice frequently given to alcoholics to avoid the situations where the original abusive drinking took place is appropriate for this group, who need a long period to practise non-drinking, to practise refusing drinks and more generally to learn how to cope with life without alcohol before they will have the confidence to handle alcohol without drinking it.

The best advice is to be guided by the recovering drinker and, when there is any doubt in her or his mind, to err on the side of safety, because the consequences of a mistake are too serious for risk-taking. On the other hand, consideration must be given to the rights of the others who are involved. They have rights to continue their civilised, social drinking, and the alcoholic has to consider these rights.

What to Do if a Relapse Occurs?

If a relapse should occur, help is needed. If the drinker is a member of AA, contact someone there immediately. If not, summon professional help. Doctors rarely know how to help alcoholics, so a call to the hospital where the initial treatment took place is probably the best choice. The objective again is to accept the fact of the relapse and to try to stop the drinking in the shortest possible time before unnecessary damage is done. If a period of re-hospitalisation is recommended, accept this advice and try to isolate the reason for the failure to cope.

When Is the Cure Complete?

The traditional answer to this question is 'never'. AA members are reasonably confident when, and if, the Twelve Steps of AA are mastered to a reasonable level. Certainly relapses after twenty and thirty years of abstinence have been recorded, and this reinforces the notion that alcoholism is an incurable disease, which can be contained only by continued abstinence. In terms of theory advanced in this book, complete control over alcohol entails continued abstinence and the development of full control over emotional arousal. If these conditions are met, other factors, such as assertion of positive emotions and of personal rights and feelings, will decide the issue. Theoretically, at least, the drinking behaviour will then not recur, even if the disease remains, ready for reactivation by even minimal social drinking in the first instance.

Abstinence can lead to the alcoholic becoming a 'dry drunk' or, with an accompanying emotional growth, to him or her becoming a fully functioning, happy person. The latter occurs for both sexes and for all ages, as is attested by the thousands of people who have discovered that there is no need to drink liquor to participate in the countless activities that make for a happy existence.

Will the Denial Disappear?

Not everyone who is admitted to hospital for treatment for alcohol abuse will admit to being an alcoholic, even after treatment, and instances of seriously ill alcoholics denying that their problems are liquor-based are common. The problem may be that it is extremely difficult for anyone to admit to themselves or to others that they are dominated by alcohol and that they are out of control. Attempts to cut down the intake, long periods of abstinence, repeated use of 'will-power', changes from spirits to beer and changes of environment are common ways of trying to demonstrate that the control is in the hands of the drinker and not with the alcohol. These attempts almost always fail, because this is the very nature of addiction. In many ways, heavy smokers are the same, constantly inventing excuses for returning to tobacco, finding reasons why it can't be harmful and blaming others for their return to the habit. Denial in various forms seems to be a universal human characteristic.

Denial of the problem for someone not yet admitted to treatment is bad enough, but denial after that is far worse. For the former, this usually results in a lengthened period of illness and heightened anxiety. There is continued apprehension that the concealed bottles will be found, that the shaking hands will be observable by others (a fact long since quite clear to most), that the morning drinking will be discovered and all this will be complicated by inability to remember what happened the night before and even where the bottles are hidden.

The problem is worse after treatment if denial still occurs, because this is completely irrational. It should be clear that failure to cope with life has occurred and that this was caused by addiction to alcohol. It should also be crystal-clear that the chances of returning to social drinking are so low that no sensible person would try it. Yet many still deny that they are alcoholic, ignore the devastation caused by the first episode and return to the old ways, because they see life without alcohol as unthinkable and insupportable.

What Is a Dry Drunk?

A particularly difficult condition that afflicts some non-drinking alcoholics, and one which is very distressing for their relatives, is known as the 'dry drunk' syndrome. Basically this occurs when the alcoholic stops drinking, often becomes very involved in AA, states that he or she is an alcoholic, but where the acceptance of being an alcoholic has not really occurred. The changes in behaviour and attitude that the relatives might reasonably expect to occur do not eventuate and, with the exception of actual drinking, the crazy thinking and behaviour characteristic of practising alcoholics continue. A lack of insight marked by an incapacity for realistic self-appraisal and marked over-reaction to trivial incidents mark this condition very clearly.

How to Recognise a Dry Drunk

1. *The discrepancy between word and deed*

The recognition of a dry drunk is made difficult because these alcoholics usually are heavily involved in recovery programmes such as AA, appear to have a vast knowledge about alcoholism, talk impressively about their character defects and give other indications of insight into their problems. However, they never seem to be able to translate the words into deeds. In some sense it appears that these people are very submissive. Their apparent acceptance of the AA programme, their constant talk about and apparent compliance with the principles of AA seem to take the place of any need to actually put the principles into practice. This is clearly a defence mechanism, designed to avoid recognition that the problems still exist. At the same time he or she stands a chance of being accepted by other AA members as someone who is making progress. More experienced members are adept at picking these dry drunks and, on occasions, are useful allies of the family in coping with the problem.

2. Over-reaction

A distinctive symptom of the dry drunk is to react violently to the simplest situations. The most innocuous remark can be taken as nasty criticism and blown up into a violent confrontation. A missed train, a meal being late, a broken or missing belonging, a missed phone call or someone arriving late becomes the excuse for a major eruption. An alcoholic playing Scrabble or Bridge may sweep the tiles or cards to the floor when losing a hand or when frustrated in a move. Anger and aggression are common, and this extraordinary violence will always be out of proportion to the trivial nature of the event.

3. Continuation of rationalisation and projection

Non-practising alcoholics who are making progress with their recovery are aware of the major role that rationalisation played during their alcoholic years. In order to protect their self-esteem, others, frequently close relatives, were blamed for their drinking. The dry drunk who is not making progress continues to rationalise to protect his self-esteem. This often takes the form of being highly critical of the behaviour and attitudes of family, friends and employers. By putting others down, he is able to bolster self-esteem by claiming that she or he is no better or worse or different.

If she or he stops going to AA, spurious reasons are concocted. These are often centred on the necessity to make more money in the interests of the family or on the need to spend more time with the family. These rationalisations are designed to overcome the deep-down knowledge that things aren't improving, and that AA attendance may be dangerous, because someone might confront him or her with the claim that progress is not being made.

This lack of insight is also shown by the continued use of projection. While an alcoholic is being super-critical of others, he or she may begin to claim that others are too critical. This is an attempt to rid the self of intolerable feelings and motives by recognising them in others, and pointing them out to others. A very dangerous form of projection is seen where others are accused of trying to force him or her back to drinking where these feelings and thoughts still exist within the self. This claim is often a prelude to a drinking bout.

4. Childish behaviour

This is shown by the dry drunk being easily bored, distracted, lacking the ability to concentrate and by rapid changes of mood. She or he is very likely to 'fly into a rage, pick up his ball and go home'. Most alcoholics during recovery begin to enjoy adult forms of relaxation again. They take up reading, participate in games, go to the movies and, not being pre-occupied with their alcohol supplies, begin to enjoy conversation. Not so the dry drunk, who has only a short attention span, who seems dissatisfied with everyone and everything. His or her behaviour is more like that of a child, and she or he still displays a deeply inadequate and immature approach to life.

5. Impatient attitude

While most alcoholics are impatient in the sense that they want to put right all the things that have gone wrong, to get a job, to regain the love and affection they may have lost, dry drunks carry this to extremes. They seem to require immediate rewards and satisfaction, and if the pay-off is not immediate, they tend to become agitated, depressed or resentful.

6. Passing judgement

Dry drunks seem to be very prone to pass judgement on others. Relatives, employers and friends are assessed harshly for their actions. Thus an employer or business associate may be judged as dishonest because the alcoholic is applying a rigid, unrealistic system to them. Wives and husbands are assessed as self-centred. There are no greys for the dry drunk; everything is black or white and most others are black.

7 Feelings of self-importance

While others are seen as dishonest, moronic, liars and cheats, the dry drunk tends to exaggerate his own importance, seeing the self as very intelligent, charming and witty. He or she, given the opportunity, will often live beyond the available means. The self-centred approach of drinking alcoholics remains unaltered, and the rights and feelings of others are ignored.

Family Reaction to the Dry Drunk

Naturally enough, families expect changes for the better when an alcoholic stops drinking. With dry drunks, things frequently get worse. Confusion, discouragement, bewilderment and resentment flourish in the face of this behaviour, and disastrous consequences may follow. The best thing for families to do is to ask for help from the original treatment centre, an AA sponsor or a counsellor familiar with the problem. The denial and lack of insight being displayed are usually too difficult to handle alone.

Is Social Drinking a Possibility?

The answer is NO! All the evidence reviewed here leads to the compelling answer that alcoholism is a persistent and recurring disease. Not one person in the world knows why some people become alcoholic while other heavy drinkers do not. However, once an alcoholic, the dangers of a return to abusive drinking once abstinence is abandoned are so high that drinking must be ruled out. Gambling with our own lives and with the welfare and happiness of those close to us is too high a stake for anyone. Certainly, there are reports of short-term and mid-term maintenance of social drinking. These are more than matched by the steadily increasing numbers of alcoholics attempting to return to acceptable levels of intake who fall by the wayside one by one. While whole-life reports of abstinence are common, whole-life reports of secure social drinking among alcoholics are unknown.

Why do alcoholics think they can become social drinkers? For some, the problem lies with their relatives who, seeing them physically fit again and not having the slightest idea of what alcoholism is all about, actually try hard to persuade the alcoholic to drink again. 'You can handle it provided you take it easy. It is just a matter of will-power.' For many others, it is the feeling of well-being that accompanies the return of physical health, the feeling that they are missing out on 'the good life' and resentment about others who seem to be able to drink without harm. Above all, it is centred on forgetting, or even repressing, just how dreadful their alcoholic life had become and how unmanageable their lives had become.

For all these would-be social drinkers the fundamental problem seems to be a less than 100 per cent acceptance of being alcoholic and a less than 100 per cent conviction that alcoholics can't drink. In the nine years that Montclair has been treating alcoholics, of the many who have elected social drinking, there is not one known case of long-term success. Most last less than a few weeks before being hospitalised again.

A big factor in relapses is undoubtedly the phenomenon known as 'euphoric recall', which is part and parcel of the alcoholic disease. Alcoholics tend to remember all the good things that happened during their drinking career and to forget the misery, degradation and ruin that accompanied the excessive drinking. Perhaps one reason why AA works is because of the constant reminder about these unpleasant facts. The reports of lengthy periods of abstinence lasting for the remainder of someone's life come from AA. Members who gain control over alcohol through abstinence and membership of AA stay on, helping others battling their way to this ultimate objective, and it is to this factor of mutual help that AA owes its effectiveness. It is to a brief description of AA that we now turn.

What about Alcoholics Anonymous?

All the evidence about alcoholism points to the fact that AA is the one organisation that has been and still is able to help those with drinking problems to remain abstinent and to become fully functioning citizens again. Medical, psychiatric and psychological practitioners may help, but the only organisation that has consistently shown how to conquer the disease labelled alcoholism is Alcoholics Anonymous.

This book is devised as an adjunct to AA, as serving a complementary role, and is not seen in any way as a substitute for membership of AA. There is nothing in this book that contradicts AA procedures, practices and philosophy. Indeed the prominence given here to prevention of arousal of negative emotions is seen as consonant with AA and the ways of doing this are in harmony with AA practices. Evidence regarding the success of AA-orientated programmes strongly suggests that patients who go through them and who regularly attend AA meetings have a very high chance of recovery in whatever way that recovery is measured.

Alcoholics come from all walks of life. Alcoholic doctors, lawyers, psychologists, dentists and judges have the same basic problem as truck drivers, salesmen, shop assistants, labourers and the unemployed in recovery from alcoholism. AA provides an international fellowship for them all, to help themselves and to help one another. Go to a strange town of any size in your own country or visit a city in another country and AA meetings and support are available. For the alcoholic who feels a desire to drink again or has related problems, a telephone call brings immediate assistance. It is argued in this book that AA is like an extended family, a family that has numerous aunts, uncles, grandparents, cousins and so on. This family provides a secure, safe environment for discussion of the numerous problems that face alcoholics and which enables the emotional growth talked about in this book to occur.

This may well be one of the main reasons for it being the only organisation that works. Doctors, psychiatrists, marriage counsellors and psychologists may help with certain problems but, for most if not all alcoholics, this guaranteed 100 per cent stable, supportive base is essential. It is there that, among other activities, emotional problems can be worked through and emotional growth achieved.

The time spent on AA activities sometimes causes resentment among close relatives. There are two things that can be done about this. The first is for them to accept that AA attendance is in the best interests of everyone concerned, because it alone has the proven track record of securing and maintaining abstinence and of helping alcoholics to achieve full maturity. The second is to try to provide the similar calm acceptance of the fact of the alcoholism, to provide the same blame-free atmosphere, to help with the numerous problems that may have to be solved and more generally to offer this same stable fully-guaranteed support. Membership of AL-ANON and ALATEEN may be very useful as well.

Al-Anon and Alateen

Recognising that those close to alcoholics also suffer from the effects of excessive drinking, Al-Anon was set up to help them. It is an organisation similar to AA in many respects, but the membership is made up of the relatives, friends and employers of alcoholics. The aims of Al-Anon are:

1. To help solve problems caused by alcoholic drinking and to help formulate a practical guide for living with alcoholics, whether practising or recovering.
2. To help one another to gain insight into common problems created by alcoholism by sharing experiences, strength and hope.
3. To provide a calm, relaxed atmosphere for the whole family unit, including the alcoholic, whether drinking or sober.

Al-Anon is therefore concerned with education about alcoholism as a family disease that impairs the mental and physical health of the family as well as that of the alcoholic. Alateen is a parallel organisation for the children of alcoholics.

Will there be a Marked Personality Change in the Non-practising Alcoholic?

Let us suppose that drinking ceases to be a problem, maintenance of sobriety presents little or no difficulty, and the emotional control advocated in this book has been achieved in so far as it is possible to achieve such a state. Probably all of us will allow anger or anxiety to get under our guard from time to time, especially if we allow ourselves to get extremely tired or exhausted. If emotional control has been mastered, these feelings will be recognised in a short space of time, the irrational thinking that led to it will then be analysed, and a rational approach will be adopted. Anger or anxiety will be replaced by appropriate problem-solving behaviour in a cool, calm frame of mind.

If he or she is coping with life successfully, if the desire to drink alcohol has disappeared, if there is more honesty, more tolerance, more unselfishness, more peace of mind and some degree of serenity, this could be described as a major change in personality. Indeed, it frequently is. However, in no case does the person become unrecognisable. The basic person is still there. The recovery process allows these good characteristics to emerge or become more regular and predictable, while the undesirable personality characteristics disappear or appear at less and less frequent intervals.

Will a Sense of Identity Return?

A major problem for alcoholics is their low level of self-esteem. Relatives can help them if they understand that alcoholism does not mean that alcoholics are derelicts, or that they are weak-willed, irresponsible or inferior to other people. In fact, many non-alcoholics have worse problems. Many find it difficult to communicate with others, are dishonest and lie and thieve. One in three non-alcoholic marriages is in chaos, children are being abused and matrimonial disharmony is rife. Many can't cope with their jobs, and others are beset with loneliness, boredom and despair.

The self-esteem of many alcoholics is kept low because they think it is necessary to drink to lead a full and happy life. Relatives can help by pointing out that large numbers of people don't drink, and that it is very rarely that anyone else is really interested in what others are drinking or why they are not drinking alcohol. Sobriety in fact appeals to other people and helps with social or occupational success. Salesmen who have long periods of abstinence report their success with clients going up and not down. Social pressure to drink, however, is used as an excuse for a return to alcoholic drinking. If drinking recurs, self-esteem takes a plunge.

How Long Does Recovery Take?

Many alcoholics can't wait to leave hospital to set everything right, to fix their marriages, to start working again. Both alcoholics and relatives need to remember that the damage caused by alcoholic drinking took place over years. Not only does the alcoholic have to make profound changes in his or her behaviour and attitudes, but the attitudes of family members, of friends and of those in the work place have to change to readjust to a new and sober man or woman. Recently, at Montclair, family counselling was in progress for the husband and seven daughters of an alcoholic. Not one of the children had ever seen the mother sober. When she went home on a week-end visit they all commented on 'how quiet mum is'. This family is now functioning well after about a year of sobriety, but it took and is still taking time to break down the old attitudes of mistrust, shame and apprehension. One daughter, who received the brunt of some aggressive behaviour, was slow to respond and was very wary and vigilant. She is now much more relaxed and accepting, but initially this caused the mother some concern. Families as well as alcoholics have to learn to appreciate small gains, little improvements. All the problems can't and won't be fixed in a day, and indeed the process usually takes years.

A related problem is that of overwork. Many alcoholics, perhaps feeling guilty about the enormous amount of money spent on alcohol, plunge back into work or take two jobs to try to get their financial situation under control. Others try to catch up on the neglected pile of jobs around the house. The motives for this overwork are fine, but actually this can be very dangerous for alcoholics, as physical and emotional exhaustion leads to irritability and lower resistance to alcohol. Recovering alcoholics in fact should initially try to avoid all extremes, including forming new and intense personal relationships, until recovery is well under way.

It is not infrequent for male alcoholics who may never have married or for females who have been divorced to form close relationships, often with other alcoholics, early in recovery. Relatives can help by gently suggesting that the first priority is to concentrate on achieving sobriety and that there is plenty of time to make up for losses. Certainly becoming involved emotionally with other alcoholics is very dangerous, especially early in sobriety.

What About Prescribed Drugs?

The drugs to be avoided are the psychotropic or mood-altering drugs used as an aid to sleeping and to relieve anxiety, tension and depression. Up to 1978-9 these were the most prescribed group of drugs in Australia, but they have slipped to second behind analgesics, which accounted to 12.3 per cent of all Benefit prescriptions. This was followed by the psychotropic group with 11.3 per cent or 10.5 million prescriptions costing over $30 million. About 70 per cent of these are written by general practitioners, mostly male and usually for females. Australian surveys indicated that 4-7 per cent of men and 7-18 per cent women use one or more psychotropic drugs daily, or on most days, with another study yielding figures of 7 per cent for males and 13-18 per cent for females. The highest consumption for both groups was in the 46-65 years group.

Now it seems that it is quite likely that people have an unfounded belief in 'miracle cures' and take these drugs when the real problem is non-medical. It seems highly unlikely that tranquillisers will cure a marriage failing because of the cruelty of one of the partners. It seems unlikely that it will prevent a marriage falling apart because of infidelity or alcoholism. Anti-depressants may relieve unpleasant feelings of self-pity temporarily, but they will not cure the problem of a workaholic husband, no social life, no companionship and a complete lack of love and affection. Sleeping tablets may bring some rest to the angry, resentful man who is not being promoted, but they will not change his lack of ability to get on with his superiors, which really underlies his failure to gain advancement.

Addiction to prescribed drugs can work in two ways. The partner of the alcoholic may take them to help remain calm during the recovery phase, or the alcoholic may take them to 'help' in his or her recovery. Neither of these coping devices is recommended, as, generally speaking, people are better off without them. These drugs vary in their effects, but all are 'mood-altering'. What this really means is that they affect the way we think. Some people react quite strongly and become fuzzy and confused. The consistent theme of this book is that we must think clearly to *stop* negative emotions from occurring at all. The partner has to think clearly to help the alcoholic, and he or she has to think clearly so that the goal of a full and rewarding life without alcohol will be reached. Drugs may stop this clear thinking, and are to be avoided if at all possible.

What Chances Are There of a Full Recovery?

Three areas of great concern to both alcoholics and to those close to them are:

1. The chances of a successful recovery, where success includes giving up alcohol, being able to function productively, to adapt socially and to integrate into the family setting.
2. The chances of resuming a full sexual life.
3. The chances of being able to think clearly and to behave rationally.

Whole books can be written about the research in each of these areas, but a brief summary will have to suffice.

Recovery rates

Recovery rates, no matter how they are defined, vary dramatically from facility to facility with a range from 0 to about 70 per cent. A recent review put the average success rate at about 31 per cent, testifying to the difficulty of treating the disease successfully. Others claim that 80 per cent of *treated* alcoholics *eventually* recover. These differences show how important it is to choose the best hospital for someone close to you. When selecting an institution for treatment, the following are some questions to ask:

1. Does the institution have an abstinence orientation? If they say they can train alcoholics to drink socially, go elsewhere.
2. Is it AA orientated? AA does work, and the period while treatment is ongoing is an ideal time for an introduction.
3. Does the programme have a large segment of instruction

about the disease of alcoholism and its treatment? Essential.

4. Does the programme make different provision for males and females? Essential.
5. Is there a programme for relatives and those emotionally close to alcoholics? Essential.
6. Is there an after-care programme for both the alcoholic and his or her relatives? Essential.
7. Is relaxation therapy included? Essential.
8. Are professionals — such as psychiatrists, psychologists and doctors — employed? Essential.
9. Are any of the therapists alcoholics? Alcoholic males and females find it easy to communicate with non-practising alcohol role-models who are engaged in therapy.
10. What provision is made for social work? In every facility dealing with alcoholics, there is a wealth of work surrounding legal, occupational and family situations. Separations have to be organised, bail found, lawyers contacted, sickness benefits clarified, leave of absence organised, personnel officers contacted and so on.
11. What experience does the facility have with alcoholism? There is no substitute for experience.
12. What is the general atmosphere in the hospital like? A cheerful, optimistic, caring one is the best. Ensure that alcohol cannot be obtained.

In one study by Polich *et al.* (1980b) of success rates, 474 alcoholics were followed up for four years. At the end of that period only 7 per cent were totally abstinent, 7 per cent were classified as social drinkers, 5 per cent were switching between abstinence and social drinking, while 81 per cent had a major abusive drinking problem during the period. One out of five is the most optimistic result one can claim for this study.

In a study by Finney and Moos (1981) 131 alcoholics were followed up for twenty-four months. For the group who had been totally abstinent for the first six months, 29 per cent relapsed during the next eighteen months; of the group who had drunk during the first six months but who had been totally abstinent between the fifth and sixth month 47 per cent relapsed. Of those who attempted social drinking during the first six months, 86 per cent relapsed. Of those who had major relapses in the first six months, 76 per cent were still having drinking problems.

The extremely high relapse rate for those attempting social drinking in the first six months after treatment is alarming, especially as their intake symptoms were less severe than the others. In fact, the authors speculate that this less advanced state of alcoholism may have led to over-confidence in their ability to handle alcohol. There was evidence that this group tended to return to 'more negative work environments — lower in involvement, peer cohesion and staff support, and higher in work pressure and control — than the abstainers'.

It seems likely that the members of this group may have been so confident of their ability to cope that they failed to realise the importance of learning new methods of coping with difficult situations and almost immediately reverted to the old coping methods, including alcohol intake. This is irrational behaviour because it completely ignores the evidence that this form of behaviour has led to disastrous consequences in the past. There is every reason why it should lead to relapse. The 86 per cent relapse rate within eighteen months is evidence enough that they could not handle social drinking, especially when compared with a relapse rate of 29 per cent for the abstinent group.

Freedberg and Johnston (1981) report the results of a Canadian study designed to compare a group of alcoholics who were abstinent after twelve months with a second group from the same intake who had returned to heavy drinking. All subjects in this study were employed full-time, and 80 per cent had been referred for treatment by their employers under threat of job loss if they did not attempt to deal with their drinking and improve work performance.

The first result of importance is that the success rate in terms of abstinence at twelve months was 39.4 per cent. Abstinence was defined as being without drink for the 90 days period prior to the twelve months point. The second result was that 'there is a fairly high probability that a return to social drinking will ultimately lead to relapse to destructive drinking patterns' (page 32).

For the first six months of the observed period both the abstainers and those classified at twelve months as heavy drinkers showed improvement in productivity, absenteeism and lateness. Individuals in the drinking group usually began to drink heavily in the second six-month period. At twelve months the abstainers generally maintained this improvement, whereas the drinkers deteriorated on all thirteen measures used. Not only were the employment indices of productivity, absenteeism and lateness down, but there were significant differences on communication skills, interpersonal relationships, relations with children, depression, marital relations and sexuality. This study also showed females tending to be more successful in maintaining sobriety if there were more women than men in their therapy groups, rather than more males than females. The reverse was true for males.

One of the better results comes from the Mississippi study described by Alford (1980). The results for complete abstinence, satisfactory productivity, good family functioning are shown in Table 5. The bottom line, which shows that 49 per cent of the intake were abstinent AND productively employed AND functioning well in the family setting after two years, is quite a good result when compared with the general run of reports, but it does underline just how difficult recovery from alcoholism can be when success in three areas has to be reached in order to count as a success.

Table 5. Percentage Abstinent, Productively Employed and Functioning Satisfactorily in Family at Three Time Intervals

	Months		
Area	6	12	24
Abstinent (%)	58	45	51
Employment (%)	64	64	66
Family functioning (%)	57	53	58
Satisfactory in all three (%)	51	45	49

The importance of relatives understanding alcoholism and understanding how best to help an alcoholic is clear. Most relapses are precipitated by events related to the family. Both the alcoholic and the family of the alcoholic need support in the early stages of recovery in most cases.

The overall picture is clear. The recovery rates reported by various institutions vary enormously. In part this is due to differences between the patients who enter, to differences in how success is defined and to the other factors built into the research design. Over and above this, however, some facilities are much better than others in the treatment and after-care provided. The result from most facilities is not encouraging, and they reinforce the notion that alcoholism is a difficult disease to treat successfully. Yet some of the results are very encouraging, producing success rates well above the average. Any hospital reporting a success rate in excess of 45 per cent is clearly in the upper bracket, while those in the 50-70 per cent range, while rare, are obviously to be sought out.

Will Sexual Activity Return To Normal?

Females

Literature about female alcoholics frequently mentions 'wild bouts of promiscuity' as being characteristic behaviour. More recent reports suggest that frigidity is more likely to be typical. In fact, there is little published research into female sexual activity worthy of note. By far the most common response given by female patients at Montclair in response to queries about the effect of alcohol on sexual activity is: 'I became much more active with my partner. My motive was to get *reassurance* that, despite my drinking, I was still loved.'

The one fact that is now beyond dispute is the connection between drinking during pregnancy and the birth of children with physical and intellectual deficits and deformities.

It has been known for nearly a hundred years that women who drink alcoholically are likely to have deformed children. The latest fact to emerge in this area is that even light, social drinking can have very damaging effects on the unborn child. Recognising this, the medical profession is now advising pregnant women not to drink at all. For alcoholic women of child-bearing age, the danger to foetuses is one more good reason for complete abstinence.

Males

Because of the greater ease of measuring male sexual performance and because of the generally greater emphasis on research into male alcoholism, a great deal is known about the effects of alcoholic drinking on male sexual desires and performance. The first fact is that the more men drink in any one session, the less likely they are to be able to gain an erection. Controlled studies of male social drinkers show that this is the case after as few as five or six drinks.

The second fact is that male alcoholics have a permanent impotence rate of about 8 per cent while the incidence of impotence that lasts for months after hospitalisation is very high indeed. The problem with impotence is that most of those who are impotent are not suffering from any physical damage, but from anxiety about having an erection. This anxiety, which surges during sexual encounters, actually prevents the erection occurring. Fortunately, this problem can be cured by sex therapists who specialise in such problems.

The third problem is connected with extensive abusive drinking over a long period. The alcohol causes physiological changes that lead to marked physical changes. Pubic and body hair disappears, and breasts and other female characteristcs appear. This feminisation process can be directly attributed to alcohol.

The fourth and final fact is the most disturbing of all for males of child-bearing age. There is evidence that alcohol abuse by males may result in the birth of deformed children. The evidence for this is as follows:

(1) Alcohol intake to a level of about 0.07 per cent results in damage to male sperm. In one study the mid-sections of the sperm were swollen and the heads and tails of sperm fell off.

(2) It seems possible that damaged sperm can fertilise eggs. To test this possibility, two groups of mice were used. One group was fed alcohol for twenty-six days, taken off the booze for two days and then mated with non-drinking females. The offspring were compared with the offspring of non-alcoholic males. While the rate of conception was the same, the litters of the alcoholic mice were smaller in number, most were stillborn or died shortly after birth, and generally these animals were in poor shape.

(3) Alcohol has shown to be a poison that directly attacks the testicles, causing damage.

It would seem that there is a possibility that human sperm damaged by alcohol can fertilise eggs and produce less viable offspring. This is another reason for abstinence, particularly when it is realised that male sperm has an active lifespan of well over one month.

To sum up. Alcoholics who are in the early to middle stages of the disease usually recover their normal sexual drives and performance as soon as the alcohol withdrawal phase is ended or shortly thereafter. Provided abstinence is maintained, there seems to be no permanent damage.

Will Intellectual Functioning Get Back To Normal?

There is no doubt that prolonged alcoholic drinking causes brain damage. In severe cases the damage is so great that normal functioning becomes impossible. Some become affected by the Korsakoff Syndrome, in which memory for recent events is so badly impaired that patients cannot find their way back to a room if they are taken out, and cannot remember names or faces of those they have just met.

Fortunately, most alcoholics stop drinking before they get to this stage. For these there is a rapid recovery, especially after the first two weeks, depending on the age at hospitalisation. Even those over 50 years of age show this recovery, although it does take longer than for younger men and women. This recovery of mental skills can continue over months, and even years, and eventually most alcoholics function better than during most of their drinking lives. There is one area where the damage can be seen to be lasting. This is memory. Most alcoholics report damage to short-term memory. Of course, memory gets worse for non-drinkers as they get older, but there do seem to be deficits over and above this for alcoholics. This need not be serious, as there are methods of coping, such as making lists, writing things down, practising names of people and so on. All in all, the relatives of most alcoholics can be assured that the damage that is done will probably not be of any consequence provided abstinence is maintained.

Can Alcoholism be Inherited?

There is no doubt that alcoholism runs in families. Many alcoholics have alcoholic parents and alcoholic brothers and sisters, and research into their family trees produces evidence of many more 'heavy drinkers'. It is not clear how much alcoholics learn drinking patterns from their relatives and how much they inherit their alcoholism through genetic processess. A common way of assessing the inheritance-environmental components is to look at the amount of alcoholism in persons brought up in their 'natural' homes compared with the incidence in those separated from parents early in life and brought up in foster homes. A variation of this is to compare twins reared together with those reared apart.

The results of such studies strongly suggest that there is an inherited component in addition to the environmental one. There are, however, many alcoholics where families have no known record of alcoholism, even when traced back over a few generations. The safest thing is for relatives to accept the strong possibility of an inherited element and to act accordingly. Children of alcoholics should be informed of this possibility. At Montclair, children are advised that they should consider the likelihood of their being alcoholic and not to start drinking at all. If they do elect to drink, they should watch their drinking habits closely for any sign of going beyond pleasant social drinking.

What Is Antabuse?

This drug produces a violent reaction if alcohol is drunk while there is Antabuse in the system. The use of these tablets is strongly recommended for some alcoholics during the period while the non-drinking habits are growing in strength. The reactions to alcohol when taken by those on a course of Antabuse include flushing of the face and neck, heart palpitations, dizziness, a terrible headache and vomiting. Most people who drink while on Antabuse report that they wished themselves dead.

It is recommended that someone close to the alcoholic person discuss the procedure to be followed in taking the tablets. If acceptable to both, the Antabuse tablet should be given each morning to the alcoholic by the partner, by crushing the tablet and stirring it in a glass of water. It has to be accepted by both that this has nothing to do with a lack of trust, but it does ensure that the dose is not forgotten and will relieve relatives of a certain amount of natural apprehension. The effects of Antabuse last up to seventy-two hours after the last tablet is taken. Antabuse is designed to stop impulse drinking if something goes wrong, and gives the recovering alcoholic time to think of a better way of coping. Even a small amount of alcohol can cause devastating effects while a person is on Antabuse.

One of the signs of an impending break by those on such a course is finding excuses to stop taking Antabuse. Antabuse does not interact with other medications, or with alcohol in the very small dose found in food and some drinks, so these excuses are invalid. Recovery from alcoholism is a team effort, involving AA, stress management, control of the emotions and so on. Anything that will help the alcoholic to get on top of and stay on top of this disease should be tried. Antabuse is simply an adjunct to sobriety, especially in the first two years of recovery, but it can be taken under medical supervision for longer periods.

Summary

While there is no doubt that alcoholism is a pervasive and recurrent disease with a high rate of relapse, alcoholics can and do recover once they stop drinking and remain abstinent. Those who are emotionally close to recovering alcoholics can help them best by working on the following:

1. Try to provide a calm, relaxed atmosphere.
2. Accept the fact of the alcoholism and the problems it caused in the past, but try to forgive and forget.
3. Accept the fact that alcoholism is a disease with a common set of symptoms. This disease can be stopped but never cured.

4. Avoid suspicion about whether he or she is drinking and accusations of drinking without clear evidence.
5. Develop calm, frank, open and honest communication.
6. Do not advertise the fact of the alcoholism except for a good reason.
7. Make use of the help available. For example, use counselling services freely to fix your marriage, or, where necessary, to finish it.
8. Accept that feelings of guilt or shame are not in the interests of the alcoholic or the interest of the family of the alcoholic. Don't make him or her feel guilty or allow her or him to wallow in these feelings.
9. Encourage emotional independence. Dependency underlies much alcoholic drinking.
10. Encourage assertive behaviour and do not reward submissive or aggressive behaviour.
11. Discuss keeping alcohol in the house. Usually it is not a good idea early in sobriety.
12. Watch for the symptoms of 'dry drunkenness'. If they are present, seek help.
13. Accept that an alcoholic cannot drink socially. One drink is dynamite for an alcoholic.
14. Encourage participation in AA.
15. Discourage use of mind- or mood-altering drugs unless prescribed by a personal doctor who knows about alcoholism.
16. Recognise that there is stigma attached to being an alcoholic. It occurs because most people do not understand the disease and think it is caused by lack of moral fibre and lack of will-power. This is rubbish.
17. Remember that the alcoholic will be apprehensive about resuming life without alcohol. Provide calm, relaxed support and keep communication open.
18. Do not try to protect the alcoholic. Discuss things instead.
19. Recognise that full mental and physical functioning may take many months to get back to normal.
20. Discuss the use of Antabuse.

Above all, relatives, children and all those emotionally close to an alcoholic have to try to trust and respect the recovering alcoholic. Treat him or her as a normal human being. She or he needs love and affection like the rest of us. Forget the past and concentrate on getting the present and future right. Relatives and those who want to help an alcoholic during recovery may find use for the prayer already quoted, which concludes all AA meetings.

God grant me the serenity to accept the things I cannot change,
Courage to change the things I can, and Wisdom to know the difference.

Bibliography

AA World Services Inc. (1952) *Twelve Steps and Twelve Traditions*, New York, AA Grapevine Inc.

Alford, G. S. (1980) 'Alcoholics Anonymous: an empirical outcome study', *Addictive Behaviors* 5:359-70.

Armstrong, R. G., and Hoyt, D. B. (1963) 'Personality structure of male alcoholics as reflected in the IES test', *Quarterly Journal of Studies on Alcohol* 24: 239-48.

Beckman, L. J. (1977) 'Psychosocial aspects of alcoholism in women', *Alcoholism: clinical and experimental research* 1:177.

Beckman, L. J. (1978) 'Self-esteem of women alcoholics', *Journal of Studies on Alcohol* 39:491-8.

Beckman, L. J. (1979) 'Reported effects of alcohol on the sexual feelings and behavior of women alcoholics and nonalcoholics', *Journal of Studies on Alcohol* 40: 272-82.

Beckman, L. J. (1980) 'Perceived antecedents and effects of alcohol consumption in women', *Journal of Studies on Alcohol* 41: 518-30.

Beckman, L. J., and Bardsley, P. E. (1981) 'The perceived determinants and consequences of alcohol consumption among young women heavy drinkers', *International Journal of the Addictions* 16: 75-88.

Beckman, L. J., Day, T., Bardsley, P., and Seeman, A. Z. (1980) 'The personality characteristics and family backgrounds of women alcoholics', *International Journal of the Addictions* 15: 147-54.

Bem, S. L. (1974) 'The measurement of psychological androgony', *Journal of Consulting and Clinical Psychology* 42:155-62.

Berg, N. L. (1971) 'Effects of alcohol intoxication on self-concept: studies of alcoholics and controls in laboratory conditions', *Quarterly Journal of Studies on Alcohol* 32:442-53.

Blane, H. T. (1968) *The Personality of the Alcoholic: guises of dependency*, New York, Harper and Row.

Brisset, D., Launerg, J. H., Kammeir, M. L., and Biele, M. (1980) 'Drinkers and non drinkers at three and a half years — attitudes and growth', *Journal of Studies on Alcohol* 41:945-52.

Browne-Mayers, H. N., Seelye, E. E., and Sillman, L. (1976) 'Psychosocial studies of hospitalised middle-class alcoholic women', *Annals of the New York Academy of Sciences* 273:593-604.

Clarke, S. K. (1974) 'Self-esteem in men and women alcoholics', *Quarterly Journal of Studies in Alcoholism* 35:1380-1.

Corrigan, E. M. (1980) *Alcoholic Women in Treatment*, New York, Oxford University Press.

Curlee, J. (1968) 'Women Alcholics', *Federal Probation* 32:16-20.

Curlee, J. (1971) 'Sex differences in patient attitudes toward alcoholism treatment', *Quarterly Journal of Studies on Alcohol* 32:643-50.

Dyer, W. W. (1977) *Your Erroneous Zones*, London, Sphere Books.

Finney, J. W., and Moos, R. H. (1981) 'Characteristics and prognoses of alcoholics who become moderate drinkers and abstainers after treatment', *Journal of Studies on Alcohol* 42:94-105.

Flintoff, W. (1975), in Glatt, M. M., *Alcoholism: a social disease,* London, Teach Yourself Books.

Fraser, J. (1973) 'The female alcoholic', *Addictions* 20:64-80.

Freedberg, E. J., and Johnston, W. E. (1981) 'The relationship between alcoholism treatment outcome in terms of drinking and various patient characteristics', *Journal of Occupational Medicine* 23:30-4.

Glatt, M. M. (1961) 'Treatment results in an English mental hospital treatment unit', *Acta Psychiat. Scand.* 37:143-68.

Gordon, T. (1955) *Group-centred Leadership*, Boston, Houghton-Mifflin.

Heilbrun, A. B., and Schwartz, H. L. (1981) 'Self-esteem and self-reinforcement in men alcoholics', *Journal of Studies on Alcohol* 41:1134-42.

Homiller, J. D. (1980) 'Alcoholism among women', *Chemical Dependencies: behavioral and biomedical issues* 4:1-31.

Jakubowski, P., and Lange, A. J. (1978) *The Assertive Option: your rights and responsibilities,* Champaign, Illinois, Research Press Co.

Johnson, V. E. (1980) *I'll Quit Tomorrow*, San Francisco, Harper and Row.

Johnson, S., and Garzon, S. R. (1978) 'Alcoholism and women', *American Journal of Drug and Alcohol Abuse* 5:107-22.

Kinsey, B. A. (1966) *The Female Alcoholic: a social psychological study*, Springfield, Illinois, Thomas.

Kurtz, E. (1979) *Not God: a history of Alcoholics Anonymous*, Center City, Minnesota, Hazeldean Educational Services.

Kurtz, E. (1982) 'Why AA works: the intellectual significance of Alcoholics Anonymous', *Journal of Studies on Alcohol* 43:38-80.

Mulford, H. A. (1977) 'Women and men problem drinkers' *Journal of Studies on Alcohol*, 38:1624-39.

Myers, R. D. (1978) 'Tetrahydroisoquinolines in the brain. The basis of an animal model of alcoholism', *Alcoholism: chemical and experimental research* 2:146-64.

Naylor, F. D. (1972) *Personality and Educational Achievement*, Sydney, John Wiley & Sons.

Ohlms, D. L. (1983) *The Disease Concept of Alcoholism*, Belleville, Illinois, Gary Whiteaker.

Polich, J. M., Armor, D. J., and Braiker H. B. (1980a) *The Course of Alcoholism; four years after treatment*. Prepared for the U.S. National Institute on Alcohol Abuse and Alcoholism, Santa Monica, Rand, Corp.

Polich, J. M., Armor, D. J., and Braiker, H. B. (1980b) 'Patterns of alcoholism over four years', *Journal of Studies on Alcohol* 41:397-416.

Rogers, C. R. (1969) *Freedom to Learn*, Columbus, C. E. Merril.

Schultz, A. P. (1975) 'Radical feminism: a treatment modality for addicted women', in Senay, E., Shorty, V., and Alkane, H. (eds) *Developments in the Field of Drug Abuse,* Cambridge, Mass., Schenkman.

Selby, R. B. (1981) 'Effects of self-concept in two different alcoholism treatment programmes', *American Journal of Drug and Alcohol Abuse* 8:95-105.

Sokolow, L., Welte, J., and Lyons, J. (1981) 'Alcoholics' post-treatment attitudes towards social drinking as a predictor of abstinence', *Alcoholism: clinical and experimental research* 5: 168.

Tamerin, J. S., Tolor, A., and Harrington, B. (1974) 'Sex differences in alcoholics. A comparison of self and spouse perceptions'. Paper presented at Alcohol and Drug Association Conference.

Travers, D., and Hendtlass J. (1978) 'Survey of alcoholism treatment services in Victoria'. Paper presented at the Autumn School of Studies on Alcohol and Drugs, St Vincent's Hospital, Melbourne.

Vaillant, G. E. (1983) *The Natural History of Alcoholism: causes, patterns and paths to recovery*, Cambridge, Mass., Harvard University Press.

Vanderpool, J. A. (1969) 'Alcoholism and the self-concept', *Quarterly Journal of Studies on Alcohol* 30:59-77.

Volpe, J. (1979) 'Links to sobriety', *Alcohol Health and Research World* 39-44.

Wilsnack, S. C. (1973) 'The impact of sex roles on women's alcohol use and abuse', pp. 37-63 in Greenblatt, M., and Schuckit, M. A. (eds) *Alcoholism Problems in Women and Children*, New York, Grune & Stratton.

Wood, H. P., and Duffey, E. L. (1966) 'Psychological factors in alcoholic women', *American Journal of Psychiatry* 123:341-5.

Subject Index